Lecture Notes in Artificial Intelli

Subseries of Lecture Notes in Computer Scienc

Edited by J. G. Carbonell and J. Siekmann

Lecture Notes in Computer Science

Edited by G. Goos, J. Hartmanis and J. van Leeuwen

Springer
*Berlin
Heidelberg
New York
Barcelona
Budapest
Hong Kong
London
Milan
Paris
Santa Clara
Singapore
Tokyo*

John W. Perram   Jean-Pierre Müller (Eds.)

Distributed Software Agents and Applications

6th European Workshop
on Modelling Autonomous Agents
in a Multi-Agent World, MAAMAW '94
Odense, Denmark, August 3-5, 1994
Proceedings

 Springer

Series Editors
Jaime G. Carbonell, Carnegie Mellon University, Pittsburgh, PA, USA
Jörg Siekmann, University of Saarland, Saarbrücken, Germany

Volume Editors

John W. Perram
Lindo Center for Applied Mathematics, Odense University
Forskerparken 10, 5230 Odense M, Denmark

Jean-Pierre Müller
Institute of Computer Science and Artificial Intelligence, Neuchâtel University
Rue Emile Argand 11, CH-2007 Neuchâtel, Switzerland

Cataloging-in-Publication Data applied for

Die Deutsche Bibliothek - CIP-Einheitsaufnahme

Distributed software agents and applications : proceedings /
6th European Workshop on Modelling Autonomous Agents in a
Multi-Agent World, MAAMAW '94, Odense, Denmark, August
3 - 5, 1994. John W. Perram ; Jean-Pierre Müller (ed.). - Berlin
; Heidelberg ; New York ; Barcelona ; Budapest ; Hong Kong ;
London ; Milan ; Paris ; Santa Clara ; Singapore ; Tokyo :
Springer, 1996
  (Lecture notes in computer science ; Vol. 1069 : Lecture notes in
  artificial intelligence)
  ISBN 3-540-61157-6
NE: Perram, John W. [Hrsg.]; European Workshop on Modelling
  Autonomous Agents in a Multi-Agent World <6, 1994, Odense>; GT

CR Subject Classification (1991): I.2, D.2, C.2.4

ISBN 3-540-61157-6 Springer-Verlag Berlin Heidelberg New York

© Springer-Verlag Berlin Heidelberg 1996
Printed in Germany

Typesetting: Camera ready by author
SPIN 10512855   06/3142 – 5 4 3 2 1 0   Printed on acid-free paper

Introduction

John Perram,
Lindø Center for Applied Mathematics, Department of Information Technology,
Odense University, Forskerparken 10, Odense, Denmark

Jean-Pierre Müller,
Institute of Computer Science and Artificial Intelligence
Neuchâtel University Neuchâtel, Switzerland

The Proceedings of the 6th European Workshop on Modelling Autonomous Agents in a Multi-Agent World, (MAAMAW'94) differs from its predecessors in that we have included manuscripts from two of the invited speakers.

It was originally planned that this MAAMAW should focus on applications of MAS. Indeed many of the papers are concerned with applications. However, we were overtaken by external events, mainly the rapid emergence of World Wide Web as a multi-agent application in its own right. This has qualitatively changed the way we think about agents and in many ways, clarified the relation of agents systems to other areas of software technology. We began to see the emergence of this development during the actual workshop. For this reason, we have decided to call this volume "Distributed Software Agents and Applications".

This fact was stressed by Mario Tokoro in his invited talk "Agents: Towards a Society in Which Humans and Computers Cohabitate", reproduced here. WWW is regarded as a massive distributed system of agents (users and their computers) trying to extract some added value from the chaotic mass of information available to them. This immediately tells us that both the Multi-Agent and Distributed Computing communities have much to learn from each other.

The other invited manuscript, "ARCHON and its environment" presented at the workshop by Francois Arlabosse, is a textbook example of how Multi-Agent thinking and tools can solve the very complex real world problems of distributed control in industrial systems. For such systems, it is utopian to believe that standard engineering ideas of optimal control will get us anywhere. The system is so complex and unpredictable as to defy modelling in the traditional sense.

The third invited talk by Bernado Huberman, stressed the connection between multi-agent systems and physics. The idea that a large collection of simple, interacting agents can exhibit interesting global behaviour has long been the cornerstone of statistical physics.

Odense, December 1995

Acknowledgements

Many people contribute to the production of a successful MAAMAW. First of all, there are the participants and contributors, who ensure that the high standards MAAMAW sets itself are maintained.

Secondly, there are the the local people who ensure that everything practical works. Special thanks are due to Maja Stokholm, the LCAM secretary who ensured that the right papers finished in the right places as well as administering the rather complex finances. Thanks are also due to Pernille Garcia de la Vega, who handled registrations and all the problems faced by busy participants who really don't have time to be at the workshop

One of the hallmarks of MAAMAW is the attention payed to culinary matters. Thanks are due to Grethe Hansen, the cook at the Odense Science Park for ensuring that the lunches lived up to MAAMAW's standards.

No workshop like MAAMAW could possibly be successful if not for its sponsors. The chairs would like particularly to thank Odense Steel Shipyard for arranging a tour of the yard followed by a banquet. Odense Steel Shipyard is one of the most modern yards in the world where information technology of all kinds is used in the automated production of ships. Thanks are also due to the Danish pharmaceutical company Novo Nordisk for financial support. Finally, we would like to thank Dean Jens Oddershede of the Faculty of Natural Sciences at Odense University for a variety of practical and economic assistance.

Finally, no conference of any quality can succeed without the participation of a conscientious and critical program committee. Only papers living up to the highest standards are accepted for these proceedings and this year's contributions are no exception. The members of the program committee were:-

Magnus Boman	Stockholm
John Campbell	London
Cristiano Castelfranchi	Rome
Helder Coelho	Lisbon
Yves Demazeau	Grenoble
Mauro Di Manzo	Genova
Jean Erceau	Chatillon
Jacques Ferber	Paris
Francisco Garijo	Madrid
Hans Haugenader	Munich
George Kiss	Milton Keynes
Brian Mayoh	Aarhus
Eugenio Oliveria	Porto
Jeffrey Rosenschein	Jerusalem
Walter van der Velde	Brussels
Peter Wavish	Redhill (UK)
Wouter Joosen	Leuven

Table of Contents

Agents: Towards a Society in Which Humans and Computers Cohabitate*
(Extended Abstract)

Mario Tokoro**

Faculty of Science and Technology, Keio University.
3-14-1 Hiyoshi, Kohoku-ku, Yokohama 223 Japan

Abstract. Multi-Agent Systems research is a new field. Therefore, no consensus exists on its definition or its purpose, nor does there exist any generally-agreed way of doing research in this field. In this paper I first look back at the streams of Multi-Agent Systems research, comparing them to Distributed Problem Solving, Distributed Artificial Intelligence, Parallel Artificial Intelligence, Distributed Algorithms, Open Systems, and so forth, and I try to show what Multi-Agent Systems really are. Based on this analysis, I then suggest some aims and future directions for research in this field.

1 Introduction

Multi-Agent Systems (MAS) are, as the name suggests, systems that comprise multiple agents. The word "Agent" from the Latin "agāns" to act, is defined as the producer of an effect, an active substance, a person or thing that performs an action, a representative, and so forth. Among these meanings, a representative, or a thing that performs an action, seems to describe best the word as used in MAS research. That is, it means "an individual that performs an action", so that in its broadest sense, a MAS is "a system composed of multiple individuals which perform actions".

The essential motivation of MAS research was to answer the question: "Can a higher level task be achieved by cooperation between multiple subsystems, each of which has a lower ability?" This motivation originated principally in two research fields. The first is called Distributed Problem Solving(DPS), a field that investigates the coordination of multiple subsystems as the way to obtain a higher ability. When it is conducted as research related to intelligence, it is called Distributed Artificial Intelligence (DAI). The second is called Agent-Oriented Programming, a field that investigates the methodology used to construct software, especially for Open Systems.

Two related notions, that of a Network Agent — an entity that moves around in the Internet, and the notion of an Interface Agent — an entity that handles

---

* An earlier version of this paper was written in Japanese and included in JSSST Computer Software Vol.12, No. 1, January 1995.

** *mario@mt.cs.keio.ac.jp*. Also affiliated with Sony Computer Science Laboratory, Inc.

the interface between human and computer, are important in connection with the above-mentioned two fields because they provide examples of agents that conform to, or use the ideas originating in those fields.

In the following sections, I will review these four research streams, and I will try to suggest some aims and future directions for research in MAS.

2 Distributed Problem Solving and Distributed Artificial Intelligence

Distributed Problem Solving originated with the naive question: "How should a task be divided into subtasks so that they can be processed concurrently in an efficient way?" It is a field that is application oriented and attempts to deal with real practical problems [9][6]. We also call this area Distributed Artificial Intelligence (DAI), because many of its research results have been presented at conferences related to Artificial Intelligence. It is hard to classify the papers from their contents.

In the case where necessary information about other subsystems can be obtained with negligible delay, the field is called Parallel Problem Solving (or Parallel Artificial Intelligence) and corresponds to the research on Concurrent/Parallel Algorithms. In the case where there is a time delay in retrieving information from other subsystems, or in the case where delays on subsystems and communication paths must be considered, they are genuinely in the field of "Distributed" Problem Solving (or "Distributed" Artificial Intelligence). Those studies that assume that subsystems have only incomplete (partial or containing errors) knowledge in the problem domain can be categorized within the above, and are close to the field of Distributed Algorithms.

In DPS or DAI, as each subsystem begins to have the notion of "self," they begin to exhibit different characteristics: subsystems begin to pursue different goals for their own benefit instead of the common goal. This leads DPS and DAI to Multi-Agent Systems [3]. A key distinction in such systems is that an agent which gives information to other agents may not always necessarily benefit itself. That is, in Multi-Agent Systems, agents always have to maximize their own benefit according to incomplete information about other agents. This behavior of agents is called "rational."

Generally, in MAS research, there exists the notion that agents pursue the benefits of the entire system, i.e. altruism. However, my position is that the agent should primarily concern itself with its own benefit. It is not however, always the case that 'short-termism' is a prerequisit for altruism. Interestingly, ignoring its own short-term benefit may to some extent benefit the entire system which in turn may lead to its own long-term gain and stability. This is the essence of cooperation.

A fundamental proposition of MAS research can be expressed as follows. "Can each agent obtain higher benefit by cooperating with multiple agents mutually than when it doesn't cooperate?" Here, the framework and strategy for negotiation become the objects of research. The above-mentioned proposition can, in broader terms, be rewritten as; "Can each agent obtain higher benefit by working as a group rather than working in isolation?"

An implicit understanding in MAS is that that agent interaction is not 'one off', rather each agent continuously exists in the environment and it continually interacting with others [1][16]. An agent has to make its next behavioral decision by consuming bounded resources, such as time and computational power. This very characteristic, which is particular to MAS, is called "bounded rationality". As a result, MAS exhibit a complex behavior that cannot be easily ascribed to the behavior of each agent: it begins to exhibit the characteristics of a "society". The theoretical basis of MAS in this stream can be obtainable from Game Theory [17].

3 Multi-Agent Systems as a Methodology for Software Construction

The development of pervasive networks in recent years leads to the possibility of collaborative tasks among computers: a task is processed by the most suitable computer(s). Furthermore, computer technology is developing rapidly, so that old computers are continually replaced by newer ones. The speed and the topology of networks is continuously changing. New software is developed and provides better services. New information is provided, so that we can work more effectively. In a widely distributed environment, it is impossible to know these changes completely beforehand. Such an environment is called an Open System [7][24].

In such systems, the purpose and the functionality of the entire system cannot be defined when it is designed, in contrast to the case of closed systems where those are given. Many existing software construction methodologies have been based on the premise of closed systems, or have a restricted ability to handle changes in the system architecture. As I mentioned above, widely distributed, continuously growing, networked computer systems cannot be envisaged as closed systems any more: they behave as open systems. Thus, software has to be designed without the premise that they can be fully defined.

One possible way to construct an Open System is to start by defining and implementing subsystems instead of starting from the whole. That is, the bottom-up approach without specifying the (fixed) goal instead of the top-down, decompositional approach. Each subsystem should be of a reasonable size, and should try to respond to the requests of users (humans or other agents) as much as possible. Subsystems cooperate and sometimes conflict with other subsystems for shared resources, trying to be better than other subsystems. This model of computation is very close to that of biological evolution. Ultimately, MAS, like other biological life forms come together to form a society. Therefore, the notion of an agent as a unit of individual software (or a software individual) is an indispensable factor in Open Systems.

Further, in evolving open systems it is better to dynamically select suitable co-operants to work with, rather than to work with a fixed team, since the environment changes all the time. Therefore, it is important for each software module to find suitable co-operants to maximize its rewards and to minimize the potential costs. For example, an agent could be subjected to errors and trouble caused by other harmful software modules in addition to computer and communication faults. In essence, in an evolving potentially harmfull environment, an agent should try to survive. Thus, it becomes much clearer that software modules need to exist as individuals, and the whole system becomes a Multi-Agent System forming a society of agents.

Object-Oriented Programming and Concurrent Object-Oriented Programming [34] are now effective as modern software construction methodologies. According to my understanding, the difference between an object and agent is as follows: Agent is the concept that corresponds to a living individual, while object is the concept that corresponds to a part. I think it natural that an agent is composed of objects hierarchically, just like a living individual is composed of organs, tissues and cells. Both play a complementary role as the methodology of software construction for Open Systems [32].

In order for a software module to be an individual, we think that each software module should have the following characteristics:

(1) a unit that doesn't share its components with others,
(2) a unit that receives utility of payoff,
(3) a unit of protection, and
(4) a unit of reliability or maintaining performance.

Item (1) is the most basic characteristic that the individual has. Item (2) corresponds to ingesting and using energy for action, item (3) to the immune system of our body, and item (4) to homeostasis. These characteristics must NOT be provided by the whole (or underlying) system, but each individual must possess them as part of its basic functionality.

Moreover, in order for a software module to be an element of an Open System, it should also have the following characteristics.

(5) it makes an effort to maximize benefit to itself, and to minimize its losses.

This characteristic is the very condition for an individual to survive. Indeed, it resembles the essential proposition mentioned in Section 2, but here, I put an emphasis on "survival". We think that this will lead to a service that is more beneficial and safer to users, and robust against trouble or changes.

As we can see in OMG/CORBA [23], common platforms that provide mutual services among Object-Oriented application programs in a distributed environment are under standardization in recent years. However, since there is no notion of individual, I am somewhat suspicious about the reliability and robustness of the resulting systems. As a first step in creating such a software module, i.e. an agent, we have developed a language and verification system that introduce a real-time property (more specifically, time-out on the client side) as the last resort for survival [29][26].

The five characteristics introduced above are the keys to MAS. It should be noted that MAS is a technology to cope with openness, not a technology to enhance efficiency or speed. Actually MAS may be very inefficient since each agent must consume energy for making decisions in a dynamic environment by continuously sensing it and acting for its own benefit. However, without such energy consumption, an agent cannot survive. In a sense, it may be time to change our expectation of computers from efficiency to robustness, to intimacy, or to user reliability. These will become the most important features in distributed systems, robot systems, and interactive systems.

4 Network Agents

An "agent" can be used as a unit of software that processes multiple tasks for users, moving around the Internet. Here, we call it a Network Agent. Network Agents and Interface Agents, which will be described below, are species of Software Agents.

The ingenuity of the Network Agent is that it actively moves around networks in the course of its work. The reason for having software move in networks has been, so far, that it balances loads, or it resolves communication bottlenecks [31]. However, in this case, where software moves among distributed systems as an agent, i.e. an individual trying to maximise its own goals, this is surely proposing a new paradigm. Until now, it has been hard to say that the previously proposed Network Agents satisfy the five characteristics that Software Agents should provide. Therefore, it is questionable to use them under the present circumstances. However, it is a very interesting research topic.

As Open Systems begin to be composed of agents, the behavior of whole systems becomes of interest. Agents with higher performance may flourish. Agents with ability to negotiate might be more advantageous. A group of agents that can maintain good relationships for a long time may obtain higher benefits from that stability. I think it is necessary to do research on the behavior of a society of agents and its controls [8][5] together with the methodology of software construction.

5 Interface Agents

An Interface Agent is a software module that deals with users as a representative of services that a computer system provides, or that provides a personified entity that mediates with user requests for services that the system provides.

Humans demand computer adaptability or ease of use. They expect the computer not only to understand their request precisely, but sometimes to correct their errors. Further they would like it to ask them when it cannot understand their request, and ideally, to understand everything, even if only given an incomplete request in a few words. For this, a computer needs to know more about us humans, and needs to understand human emotion as well as rational behavior. Intimate Computer is a research project in this stream [30][20]. An Interface Agent can be implemented as a Software Agent, or a set of Software Agents.

6 Future Research Directions

The four research streams mentioned in the previous sections are now beginning to join, and to flow towards a new goal. The goal is the establishment of a methodology for software to construct Open Systems viewed from an engineering perspective, and a quest for understanding what the individual is when viewed from a more scientific standpoint. Sound basic theories are important if the goal of a society in which humans and computers cohabitate is to be pursued from a solid foundation.

6.1 Aiming at Open Systems

Our engineering methodology so far has been to look for parameters that maximize a value obtained from evaluation functions, provided the boundary of the problem and the functions of the system are clear. However, this approach is not sufficient for todays software development where computer systems are distributed and open.

As a first step, software construction methods in a framework where software corresponds to individuals as mentioned in Section 3 have begun to appear. Against this background, it is an urgent necessity for us to study future software architectures for Open Systems. To do so, we must consider not only agent architecture, but also techniques and tools for the development and maintenance of open systems. Related areas such as operating systems, languages, networks, databases, and almost all fields of software are implicated

A software individual, or an Agent, acts on its own decisions. Thus it is autonomous. So far, we have thought it necessary to "program" the activities of an autonomous agent. Giving a software module real-time properties and functions to maximize utility in repetitive encounters will create agents along this line. However, an Agent might turn out to be more selfish [2] and more spontaneous, so that they might begin to reproduce themselves, and evolve through mutation and natural selection. Research in this direction has already begun under the name of Genetic Programming [13]. Furthermore, it is interesting to view Agents as Artificial Life [14], since such an agent can evolve in the given environment by itself. The mobility that Network Agents have obtained could play a major role in evolutionary software in conjunction with Genetic Programming and Artificial Life. We may need to study all these streams in creating a methodology for constructing software for Open Systems.

6.2 Understanding What an Individual Is

A complementary research project is to investigate what an individual is. The five characteristics that software should have for being an individual (see Section 3) correspond to characteristics that the living individual possesses to some level. However, even in biology, there seems to be no established theory so far for what an individual is, what self-consciousness is. The notion of autopoiehsis [33] might provide a hint. Investigation into what an individual is leads to interest in the origin and the evolution of living things [12], and to evolution and learning [11][27]. Observation of the basic behavior of living individuals and the behavior of a group of individuals is also being done in the fields of ethology [15], which is very interesting for understanding the relation between the individual and a society that is composed of individuals. Furthermore, it might be interesting to investigate the relationships between neural networks or robots, and autonomy or voluntarity [22][28].

In investigating what an individual is, it is necessary to look at us human beings, the most evolved of all living things, and to understand how we think and act. This is an important step in creating Interface Agents that make computers intimate with humans. It is said that we use the left side of our brain when thinking logically, and use the right side when thinking graphically. Operations in computers primarily resemble the processes of the left brain, and the neural net, fuzzy logic and parallel algorithms for pattern matching are developed to make processing like our right brain available and to expand the fields of computer applications. However, computers are still far from being human. The left and right brain processes are done in a relatively new part of the brain, called the neocortex. The inner brain, called the limbic system or mesencephalon, processes our emotions and more basic process for biological phenomena. These parts are more essential for living individuals, and understanding them might lead to an understanding of what an individual is, and to making computers that act more like human beings. This will also contribute to the knowledge of what basic functionality an Agent should provide.

6.3 Basic Theories

In order to achieve concrete results in MAS research, theoretical support is necessary. For this, we have mentioned already Game Theory, Molecular Biology, Ethology, Cerebrum Physiology, and so on. Here, we want to focus on Complex Systems theory [25][4] that might provide a common mathematical framework. This is a primary order theory which expresses the irreversible behavior of systems into which energy is constantly injected; dissipative systems, usually represented by nonlinear equations. It is a new scientific methodology, showing how the repetition of simple behaviors or the mixture of simple behaviors make the behavior of whole systems extremely complex, or in contrast, quite organized. This corresponds to analyzing the behaviors of individuals and the behavior of the entire system [21]. It is expected to be accepted as the basic theory for the explanation of biological phenomena and their evolution [10]. And, in general, it is hoped that it can form a basic theory for Open Systems.

6.4 A Society in Which Humans and Computers Cohabitate

Ultimately, MAS research can be seen to be producing computers that are more human. However, there are many concerns and false starts on the way. Some people worry that such computers will be able to talk about love, produce offspring, and dominate human beings some day. This can't be simply denied. However, it is a fact that we cannot feel satisfied with current computer systems. Therefore whether it is good, or not, we cannot stop computers becoming more human. In this respect, it might be better to give agents only limited functionalities [19]. Irrespective of the degree of autonomy, it is clear that the time has come to consider seriously the cohabitation of computers and humans in the real world. I strongly believe that the notion of Agents is the key to building a society in which humans and computers cohabitate.

7 Conclusion

Almost fifty years has passed since the digital computer came into existence. Some early research problems seem well-understood. For example, architecture, operating system and programming languages have been studied and developed, and are used by many users everyday. In these fields, we cannot expect much more innovative devlopment and can expect only evolutionary development. Also, in the fields that are presently in the spotlight, such as high-speed networking, user interfaces and multimedia, research is inclined to be directed more toward development for commercial reasons rather than for research which reveals fundamental properties. We think that this is good but that the time has come for computer science to expand in new directions.

Because of the pressing need to cope with Open Systems and because MAS exist at the bounderies of such fields as biology, cerebrum physiology, evolution theory and complex systems theory, we believe that MAS are a field in which we can expect great new developments. Research into MAS has just started. We think that the time has come to step out confidently into new directions.

Acknowledgment

I would like to thank the researchers at Sony Computer Science Laboratory, and graduate students at the Department of Computer Science, Keio University, for the countless active discussions I had with them. I would like to express my thanks to Eric Manning and Rodger Lea for their valuable comments and to Kei Matsubayashi, Ichiro Satoh, and Munehiro Nakazato for their help in preparing this manuscript.

References

1. Axelrod, R., *The Evolution of Co-operation*, Basic Books, Inc., 1984.
2. Dawkins, R., *The Selfish Gene (2nd Edition)*, Oxford University Press, 1989.
3. Demazeau, Y., Muller, J.-P., and/or Werner, E, *Decentralized A.I. 1, 2, and 3*, North-Holland, 1990, 1991, and 1992.
4. Devaney, R.L., *An Introduction to Chaotic Dynamical Systems (2nd Edition)* Addison-Wesley, 1989.
5. Forrest, S. (ed.), *Emergent computation*, MIT Press, 1991.

6. Gasser, L. and Huhns, M. (eds.), *Distributed Artificial Intelligence Vol.2*, Pittman, London, 1989.

7. Hewitt, C.E., The Challenge of Open Systems, Byte, April-1985, p223-242, 1985.

8. Huberman, B.A. (ed), *The Ecology of Computation*, North-Holland, 1988.

9. Huhns, M.N. (ed), *Distributed Artificial Intelligence, Vol. 1*, Pitman, London, 1987.

10. Kaneko, K. Chaos as a Source of Complexity and Diversity in Evolution, *Artificial Life*, Vol.1, No.1/2, MIT Press, Fall 1993, Winter 1994.

11. Kitano, H., Designing neural networks with genetic algorithms using graph generation system, *Complex System*, Vol.4 No.4, 1990.

12. Kitano, H., Evolution of metabolism for morphogenesis, *Proceedings of Alife-IV*, MIT Press, 1994.

13. Koza, J.R., *Genetic Programming: On the Programming of Computers by means of Natural Selection*, MIT Press, 1993.

14. Langton, C.G. (ed). *Artificial Life*, Vol.1, No.1, 2, and 3, Fall 1993, Winter 1994, Spring 1994.

15. Lorenz, K., *Das Sogenannte Böse* Dr. G. Borotha-Schoeler Verlag, 1963.

16. Matsubayashi, K and Tokoro, M. A Collaboration Strategy for Repetitive Encounters, *Proceedings of MAAMAW'94* August, 1994.

17. Maynard-Smith, J., *Evolution and the Theory of Games*, Cambridge University Press, 1982.

18. Minsky, M., *The Society of Mind*, Simon and Schuster, New York, 1987.

19. Minsky, M. and Riecken, D., A Conversation with Marvin Minsky about Agents, Comm. ACM Special Issue on Intelligent Agents, Vol.37, No.7, 1994.

20. Nagao, K. and Takeuchi, A., Social Interaction: Multimodal Conversation with Social Agents, *Proceedings of AAAI'94*, August 1994.

21. Numaoka, C. and Takeuchi, A., Collective Choice of Strategic Type, *Proceedings of International Conference on Simulation of Adaptive Behavior (SAB92)*, December 1992.

22. Ohira, T. and Cowan, J.D., Feynman Diagrams for Stochastic Neurodynamics, *Proceedings of Australian Conference of Neural Networks*, January 1994.

23. Object Management Group, The Common Object Request Broker: Architecture and Specification 1.2, *OMG*, TC Doc 93-12-43, 1993.

24. Popper, K.R. and Lorenz, K., *Die Zukunft ist Offen* R. Piper GmbH & Co., 1985.

25. Prigogine, I. and Stengers, I., *Order out of Chaos*, Bantam Books, 1984.

26. Satoh, I. and Tokoro, M., A Formalism for Real-Time Concurrent Object-Oriented Computing, *Proceedings of OOPSLA '92*, p315-326, 1992.

27. Steels, L. and Tokoro, M., Artificial Life and Real-World Computing, *Lecture Notes in Computer Science*, Vol. 1000, 1995.

28. Tani, J. and Fukumura, N., Learning Goal-directed Sensory-based Navigation of a Mobile Robot. *Neural Networks*, 1994.

29. Takashio, K. and Tokoro, M., DROL: An Object-Oriented Programming Language for Distributed Real-time Systems, *Proceedings of ACM OOPSLA'92*, p276-294, October, 1992.

30. Takeuchi, A. and Nagao, K., Communicative Facial Displays as a New Conversational Modality, *Proceedings of ACM/IFIP INTERCHI*, April 1993

31. Tokoro, M., Computational Field Model: Toward a New Computing Model/Methodology for Open Distributed Environment, *Proceedings 2nd IEEE Workshop on Future Trends in Distributed Computing Systems*, September, 1990.

32. Tokoro, M., The Society of Objects, An Invited Speech presented at OOPSLA'93 Conference, September 1993. Edited transcript is included in *OOPS Messenger*, Vol. 5, No. 2, April 1994.
33. Varela, F.J., *Principles of Biological Autonomy*, North-Holland, 1979.
34. Yonezawa, A. and Tokoro, M., eds. *Object-Oriented Concurrent Programming*, MIT Press, 1987.

ARCHON and Its Environment*

F. ARLABOSSE†

FRAMENTEC-COGNITECH †
Tour Framatome cedex 16
92084 Paris la Défense
farlabos@framentec.fr

Abstract. The ARCHON **AR**chitecture *for* **C**ooperative **H**eterogeneous **ON**-*line systems* project [9] is aiming to provide a distributed control system over existing industrial applications like Demand Management, Alarm Analysis, System Restoration Planning over huge networks i.e. the electricity distribution network. Those applications face the problem of distributed control since the control is spread all over the networks.

The paper explains the goals of ARCHON and describes in its first part the ARCHON platform by giving its architecture and implementation, while it is focused on two elements: the monitoring and the information management. In the second part the programming and debugging environment of the ARCHON platform is described through its four components : the agent instantiation tool, the Meta-data instantiation tool, the on-line tools and the data-browsing debug tools.

1 Introduction

1.1 Needs for a distributed approach

Some systems, like electrical or telecommunication networks are by definition distributed. Their control has as such been implemented in a distributed fashion, which allows to master their complexity. This means essentially a separation of control and execution. However, distributed system does not always mean distributed control, often the control is centralized, but is then facing the problem of controlling very large and complex systems and creating communication overhead in the networks. In such cases, it pays off to split the control over the network and support the decentralized control. Namely, to break the system complexity and restrict the communications, which in turn allow to lower the communication bandwidth.

The decentralized control brings both: the *scalability* of systems to cope with growing complexity of the application, and its *robustness* to failure since the control does not rely on a single site but is shared amongst many network elements. An additional advantage is gained through the *openness* of the system, new control structures may be added to upgrade and adapt systems during their lifetime.

1.2 The goals

ARCHON system aims to provide a cooperation framework for industrial distributed process control applications in general. Some key characteristics of these applications are: to deal with full blown real-size industrial applications; some of them are pre-existing systems (i.e. expert systems, simulators). These systems are working on-line and require short response-time from ARCHON (i.e. 1 second for average message transmission time between agents).

---
* The work described has been carried out in the frame of the ESPRIT II project P2256 (ARCHON) whose partners are: Atlas Elektronik, JRC Ispra, Framentec-Cognitech, Labein, IRIDIA, Iberdrola, EA Technology, Amber, Tech. Univ. of Athens, Univ. of Amsterdam, CERN, Queen Mary and Westfield College, Univ. of Porto., and CAP-Volmac

An *Agent* is mainly constituted of a software layer providing communication and cooperation facilities to an existing *Intelligent System (IS)*. ISs may be written in different languages, running on different operating systems and machines.

This paper focuses on and describes three advanced developments in ARCHON:

Monitoring facilities Efforts in ARCHON are spent on the design of robust software including error recovery in case of errors sent back by the underlying IS of agents, their breakdown, communication errors, etc.

Federated Information Management ARCHON has been designed to support the modularity of the agents. The Data handled by agents within the ARCHON are integrated through specific import and export schemas for each agent locally. In order to support this, a Federated Object-Oriented information management system AIM[1] is developed in ARCHON[2]. As such, if the data produced by one agent's IS is modified, the changes to be performed to adapt the agent community remains local to the agents, conversely to the common distributed databases with one shared global schema.

Development Environment ARCHON provides an environment allowing to enter the agents definition, to enter the structure of data (also called meta-data or schema) stored in agents, to run the ARCHON-platform, to debug, and to tune the application using the database browser.

1.3 The applications

Two demonstration applications of ARCHON project were carried out in the field of electricity distribution: Electricity generation and transmission control[2] and Management of electricity distribution.

Three other test-beds have been chosen in different fields: Particle accelerator diagnosis[3], Cement plant control and Robotics[8, 12]

2 ARCHON's architecture

The Figure 1 shows the ARCHON platform which is an instance of the software developed in the ARCHON project [9] to embed the Intelligent Systems. The figure focuses more precisely on the structure of an ARCHON agent: it is constituted by an IS and its related *ARCHON Layer*.

The *Intelligent Systems (ISs)* are the systems controlled by ARCHON, they are pre-existing or built on purpose. Typically the Intelligent systems are expert systems working on a given area, or relational or object oriented DBMSs. By extension, the *Is-Task* are the tasks which can be carried out by an IS. We call *ARCHON Layer (AL)* the concept instantiated in the platform, it provides the mean for encapsulating applicative intelligent systems into a cooperative framework. The *AL* encompasses four modules: HLCM, PCM, Monitor, and AIM.

HLCM High Level Communication Module: All message passing between agents is done through the HLCM which uses the *Session Layer SL* for the low level communications services.

PCM Planning and Coordination Module: The PCM is providing global situation assessment, planning and supervision of all cooperating behaviour the ARCHON community of agents has: conflict resolution between agents, cooperation protocols[6]...

Two models are used to describe the agents: the *Agent Acquaintance Model (AAM)* represents the minimum knowledge about the other community members with which the local agent may have to interact whereas the *Self Model (SM)* stores knowledge about *skills* and local capabilities of an agent.

The PCM delegate the execution of the local *behaviours* to the Monitor.

Monitor The Monitor is the control instance of each agent. It bridges the gap between the ARCHON layer and the heterogeneous Intelligent Systems (IS). The Monitor provides high level control facilities, allows control synchronization and parallel execution of IS Tasks clusters and finally reports the results of their execution via the *behaviours* to the PCM. The Monitor follows Goergeff's concepts[4, 5, 7] on procedural expert systems.

---

[2] The design and development of AIM is completely based on the PEER federated object management system developed at the Computer Systems Group of the University of Amsterdam[11]

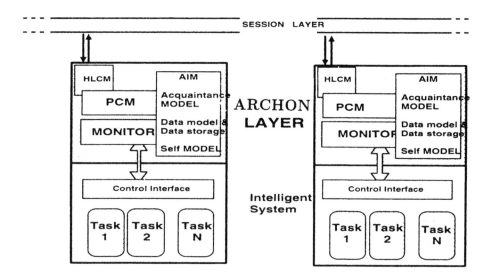

Fig. 1. Architecture of ARCHON

AIM Agent Information Management Module: AIM provides an object oriented information management model, a query and update language to define and manipulate the information. and a distributed (federated) information access mechanism to support the remote access and sharing of information among agents. AIM is used to store both the application data and the agent models[10][11].

2.1 The Monitor

Structure The Monitor uses the following data-structures: The *behaviours* encode the nominal as well as the alternative actions to fulfill a task given by the PCM. As such, *behaviours* make the link between the Monitor and the PCM. the PCM passes orders to the Monitor and the Monitor reports both: on status of the execution and final results. Each behaviour points towards a plan. A *plan* is a locus of definition of conditional sequential activities which contains the sequence of actions to be carried out by a behaviour. The plan looks like a *Petri-graph*, its nodes are actions to be carried out which are expressed under form of *Monitoring Units (MUs)* activations. The latter are processes which Monitor and control the execution of a single IS-task. The Figure 2 gives a view of the Monitor components.

When executing a behaviour, the Monitor begins to run the nominal behaviour, by executing its related plan. The plans are executed as Petri-nets, as soon as the constraints are verified, the next MU is launched. The MU produce results which allow to evaluate the next constraint. Would an MU not provide results. or constraints not be satisfied, then the plan fails. In such a case. the behaviour fails and the Monitor chooses a contingency behaviour. When there are no contingency behaviours remaining, the overall behaviour failed and the Monitor reports is inability to handle the request to the PCM.

Controlling ISs As ISs remain largely unmodified their integration into the ARCHON architecture requires various control mechanisms to integrate ISs written in different languages. running on different operating systems and machines. We describe in the following the default mechanisms

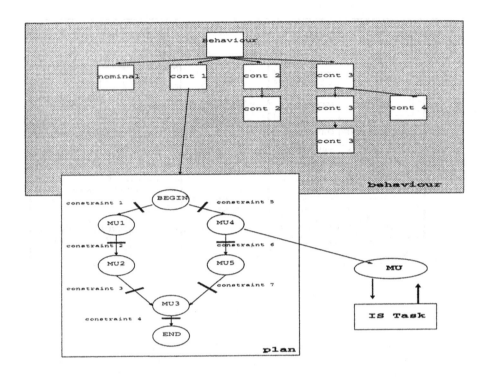

Fig. 2. Structure of the Monitor

provided by ARCHON as well as the special mechanisms which can be called when defining the agent structure. Those special mechanisms are provided under form of constraints in plans. They are marked by a †in the following.

Handling asynchronous tasks All the monitor mechanisms are working in a reactive manner, and allow to handle asynchronous tasks.

Handling of parallel executions Several asynchronous tasks may be launched at the same moment, the monitor level supports the execution of parallel tasks.

Resource allocation† The classic *LOCK* and *RELEASE* primitives allow the user to control the resource allocation among processes, thus mutual exclusion and synchronization by data are available.

Local timing facilities† A *WAIT* function permits to set a timer in the plans.

Need for additional information At any moment, an IS may ask the ARCHON layer to provide additional information. This request is immediately processed in the monitor, and if the information is not available locally, the request is forwarded to the agent community.

Asynchronous production of results† If the IS produces intermediate results in an asynchronous matter, they are kept local to the plan. If the user wants to forward those results as soon as they are produced, to the whole agent community, the *INTERMEDIATE-RESULT* constraint has to be set in the plan.

Exception handling As ARCHON works in an industrial environment, it has to be robust and provide exception handling facilities to tackle problems popping up from ISs.

IS error handling If a monitoring unit fails to produce a result, the monitor mechanisms allow to control the situation with the MU mechanism and with alternative plans and behaviours, to handle the situation in the best for the degenerated cases.

Communication errors If the ISs are hanging, down or the communications are broken between the ARCHON layer and the ISs, an automatic reconnection process is launched.

Non-nominal results† The monitor allows also to filter each result sent back from the ISs via constraints. They permit to check the type and validity, the presence of certain patterns in the IS data.

2.2 The AIM

Need for distributed information management Sharing and cooperation in complex distributed application domains requires both loose and tight coupling among agents information to support different kinds of agents interdependencies. Agents are typically both autonomous and heterogeneous. An agent is autonomous in its decision to have private information (under development work) and information to share (release information). Agents are heterogeneous due to their independent developments, pre-existence, evolution and purposes. Different local mechanisms are used to represent agents' knowledge. The structures and semantics associated to the represented information are distinct in different agents. Each agent locally can have independent focus and view defined on the remote data. A typical distributed application also needs support for modelling, fast access, and update of complex objects, for which both the meta-data (data definition) and the data is spread among several agents.

The AIM Federated Object Management System AIM is a federated, object-oriented database management system designed and implemented at the University of Amsterdam. It is primarily designed to support the application environments that are distributed, data-intensive, computation-intensive, and whose structure of data (meta-data or schema) is complex. AIM provides a coherent environment for information sharing and exchange among cooperative agents, in which all agents are essentially equal in their powers. Each agent can obtain access to information in other agents ('import schemas'), and make its own information ('local schema'), or even information received from other agents, accessible to other authorized users ('export schemas'). The schema integration and schema derivation facilities of AIM enable different agents to have distinct views on the same data, which is in particular advantageous to control the proliferation of changes through the community of agents. Since each agent defines its own 'integrated' schema, several views on the entire application can easily coexist, and there is no need for a single global schema to be agreed upon and administered centrally. This feature supports the loose-integration (coupling) among agents. However, if an application requires tight integration among all agents through a single schema, AIM can simply support it; in that case the integrated schema will be used by all agents. The distributed schema management mechanism of AIM preserves the autonomy of agents through their independent representation and interpretation of both private and shared information. The distributed query processing mechanism of AIM supports the retrieval and update of complex information (complex objects) while hiding the real physical distribution of information stored in agents. The linearization mechanism defined in AIM offers a common representation for complex object exchange, by which a complex object is converted into a linear representation which can be sent in messages among agents, and converted into a specific data-structure to be used by applications.

3 ARCHON's environment

When building an application, one needs to go through several steps:

1. Entering the agents (SM, AAM, behaviour, plan, MU, trigger),
2. Entering the application dependent data,
3. Running the ARCHON-platform
4. Debugging and tuning

These operations would be tedious if the end-user was not helped in his work by user-friendly tools. The Figure 3 shows the tools and their relation to the ARCHON-platform.

The first step is to design the agents. This is to enter the definition of the agents, the triggering conditions, the behaviours, the plans the Monitoring Units, the skills, the SMs, the AAMs,

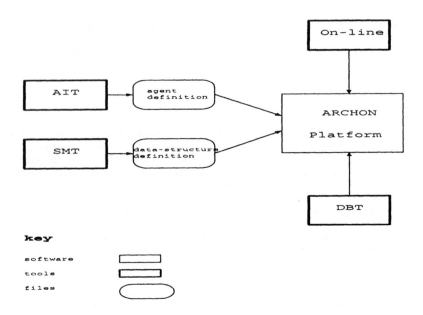

Fig. 3. Architecture of ARCHON's environment

the data, etc. Once all those elements have been defined, they need to be related so to describe in detail the agents, their skills and their cooperation scenarios. These definitions of the agents are provided by the Agent Instantiation Tool (AIT) which generates an input file for ARCHON-platform.

As the entities and concepts (data) are defined during step one, the goal of the second step is to define precisely the structures defining the data (meta-data or schema). These structures may be quite complex involving objects, hierarchies and interdependencies. They are defined by the AIM schema manipulator (SMT) which generates a file which is an input to ARCHON-platform.

In the third step, the platform is run. The ARCHON-platform offers tools to follow the progress of the application. These tools are necessary to control the application and to detect problems which may as well arise in the ARCHON software as in the application handled by ARCHON. As such, these tools allow to trace the messages flowing between the agents and to detect dead-locks. These tools are called the on-line tools.

The fourth step is dedicated to debug purposes. The AIM Database browser (DBT) permits to observe evolutions of the data in real-time, to notice their changes and to keep on the information up-to-date. Any evolution of the data may be traced, as such each of the actions taken by ARCHON may be explained in regard to the current context.

Let us give now an outline of each of the tools

3.1 The Agent Instantiation Tools (AIT)

The AIT allows to enter the Agent instantiations through a user-friendly interface. The user is guided in the creation of objects, for each of them the slots to be entered are presented with the choices available. For example, when defining a plan, the user has to specify the MU used, the AIT presents the choice of the already defined MUs and the user may select one of them or create a new one. The AIT provides error checking, so to avoid double definitions of elements, or irrelevant definitions leading to either incompleteness and un-usefulness in the agent definition.

3.2 The Meta-Data Instantiation Tools (SMT)

The AIM Schema Manipulator Tool (SMT) supports the definition, derivation and update of the schema information, namely the meta-data describing an AIM database. In specific, it supports the definition and update of types and maps (mappings) in all defined schemas, the derivation of types and maps for all derived schemas, checking the syntax, completeness, and consistency of the defined schemas and notifying the user in case of any errors.

The AIM Schema Manipulator helps the developer of an agent to define his / her schemas necessary for the distributed AIM, in a simple and systematic way. The Schema Manipulator simplifies the definition of defined schemas (local and imports) and derived schemas (exports and the integrated schema) in one agent, and supports the derivation among derived and defined schemas. The schema created with the Schema Manipulator Tool uses the Schema Definition and Derivation Language (SDDL)[1].

3.3 The ARCHON-platform on-line tools

When running the ARCHON-platform some on-line tools ease the work of the end-user by providing modular development environment and on-line test facilities. Among them, the application development environment allows to simulate an agent and permits to develop incrementally the applications by testing individually each of the modules to be integrated into ARCHON.

The trace facility shows the message flows in the platform and traces events. It allows to follow the course of actions performed in applications. This trace facility outputs messages in user-interfaces.

The dead-lock mechanism detects if the platform stops for internal reasons, if it is hanging or is a dead-lock occurred during the run. This mechanism tackles one of the most difficult problems when building an application because it differentiates problems arising in the ARCHON platform from the ones due to the application design.

3.4 The Data browsing debug tools (DBT)

The Database Browser Tool (DBT) supports the information browsing through the data and meta-data stored in AIM databases. The user can select objects and can browse through any and all objects related to that object. The DBT is aimed at helping developers and end-users to browse through the information in the AIM databases of the agents in ARCHON community. The DBT will allow retrieval of information in a relatively unstructured, but very easy to use manner.

Three kinds of browsing operations are supported by the Database Browser:

Schema Browsing The schema browser enables the user to browse through the type definitions in any schema of an agent and investigate the subtype/super-type relationships among types in the schemas.

Type Browsing The type browser displays the definition of a particular type with the mappings (attributes) defined on that type. The user can constrain the number of instances of a type displayed by specifying conditions on certain mappings and user can control the display of the values for the mappings on those objects.

Navigational Browsing The navigational browser supports the navigation of one selected object with all objects that are related to it. However in one step of the navigation, it enables the user to focus on and display other objects that are directly related to the displayed object. Therefore, on one hand any and all objects directly related to an original object can be navigated, and on the other hand, there is no loop in this navigation, even in the case of a recursive definition for an object.

The Database Browser Tool enables the user to easily switch between schema browsing, type browsing, and navigational browsing.

4 Conclusion

The ARCHON platform and its environment offers a unique set of tools and attached methodology for building large distributed heterogeneous cooperating systems. It provides all the infrastructure for an open knowledge base system giving the practical means to solve knowledge interchange and knowledge manipulation. The problem of common shared ontology is captured in the different applications, by a federated information management system. It solves concretely the problem of building interfaces between systems that have inherent differences and the ARCHON platform is a complete framework in which heterogeneous knowledge based systems and data based systems can share knowledge and cooperate to solve large, and highly demanding industrial problems. However it is sufficiently flexible to be tuned to a great variety of situations, and as the experience will cumulate building systems using ARCHON results, we are confident that norms will emerge. ARCHON will also trigger research results allowing to experiment on the integration of handling uncertainty formalisms in Distributed Artificial Intelligence.

References

1. H. Afsarmanesh, F. Tuijnman, M. Wiedijk, and L.O. Hertzberger. Distributed schema management in a cooperative network of autonomous agents. In *IEEE Intl. Conf. on Database and Expert Systems Applications*, September 1993.
2. D. Cockburn. Two model-based systems for fault diagnosis in electricity distribution systems. In *IEE colloquium: Intelligent Fault Diagnosis*, 1992. 1992/048.
3. J. Fuchs, P. Skarek, L. Varga, and E. Wildner-Malandain. Distributed cooperative architecture for accelerator operation. In *2nd Intl. Worksp on AI and ES for High Energy and Nuclear Physics*, 1992.
4. M. P. Georgeff. The representation of events in multiagent domains. In Weber, editor, *Readings in Distributed Artificial Intelligence*, page 210, Morgan Kaufmann, 1988.
5. Michael P. Georgeff and François F. Ingrand. *Research on procedural reasonning systems*. Technical Report 2851, SRI International, AI Center, 1990.
6. N.R. Jennings. Towards a cooperation knowledge level for collaborative problem solving. In B. Neumann, editor, *ECAI'92, 10th European Conference on Artificial Intelligence*, John Wiley and Sons Ltd, 1992.
7. G.R. Meijer, T.L. Mai, E. Gaussens, L.O. Hertzberger, and F. Arlabosse. Robot control with procedural expert system. In T. Jordanides and B. Torby, editors, *NATO ASI Series : Expert Systems and Robotics*, Springer Verlag, 1991.
8. E. Oliveira, F. Mouta, and A.P. Rocha. Negotiation and conflict resolution within a community of cooperative agents. In *Intl Symp. on Autonomous Decentralized Systems*, Kawasaki (JP), April 1993.
9. Archon Project. *ARCHON: an architecture for multi-agents systems*. Ellis Horwood, 1992.
10. F. Tuijnman and H. Afsarmanesh. Distributed objects in a federation of autonomous cooperating agents. In *IEEE/AAAI Intl. Conf. on Intelligent and Cooperative Information Systems*, May 1993.
11. F. Tuijnman and H. Afsarmanesh. Sharing complex objects in a distributed peer environment. In *IEEE Intl. Conf. on Distributed Computing Systems*, May 1993.
12. A. Visser, M. Wiedijk, F. Tuijnman, and H. Afsarmanesh. *Application Study: Robot Arm Control, the outcome of using distributed AIM*. Technical Report Archon UvA/TN014/11-93, Dept. of Computer Systems, University of Amsterdam, November 1993.

What Ants Cannot Do

Eric Werner *

DnaSoft
Madison, Wisconsin

Abstract. What is the relation between the complexity of agents and the complexity of the goals that they can achieve? It is argued on the basis of a fundamental conservation of complexity principle that complex goals can only be achieved if either the agents or their environment has a complexity of matching stature. This has consequences for research programs in distributed artificial intelligence, robotics and connectionism. After presenting a qualitative theory of complexity of agent systems, we also critically investigate the claims and the realities behind reactive agents, the subsumption architecture (Brooks), and the view of plans as resources (Agre, Chapman, Suchman). Finally, the implications of the complexity conservation principle for the foundations of cosmology and complexity of the universe are discussed. Puzzles appear whose possible solution relates the uncertainty principle of quantum mechanics with the second law of thermodynamics.

1 Introduction

Ant colonies are an example of a large society with apparently coordinated and cooperative behavior that results in rather complex space-time events, namely the building and maintenance of an an ant hill. That such simple creatures should be capable of such sophisticated cooperative events has long been a fascination for scientists. When the bright lights of artificial intelligence (AI) began to dim, not a few scientist looked to insects as a new metaphor for what the study of intelligence was all about. If we cannot model human intelligence, perhaps we can model the behavior of our simpler and ubiquitous neighbors, the insects. Like birds who have found a new source of food, they began to scream. They began to make grand claims as to what their insects would be capable of, not unlike the claims they had previously made for AI. Indeed, they claimed all that had gone before was not worth doing and only their latest efforts were worth any notice. Everything worthwhile can be done by insects and aren't they cute.

This essay takes a hard look at a related cluster of ideas that have come out of the philosophy that simple, reactive agents can solve all our problems, if we just throw enough of them together. A principle about complexity will be used to show the limits of cooperative action to achieve space-time events. This principle is universal and has interesting consequences for other areas of science. We will also spend time speculating about its consequences for our view of our universe.

1.1 Ants on Mars

Luc Steels [Demazeau & Mueller 90] gives an example of ant like robots on Mars that communicate by dropping and picking up pebbles. The structure and complexity of the communication, in this case the pattern of pebbles, determines the interactive behavior of the ants. The complexity necessary for complex cooperation is then projected outward onto the environment of pebble patterns. Complex pebble patterns together with simple ant response algorithms are to produce complex cooperation. The distributed agents are then controlled globally by the pattern of pebbles. Locally an ant may affect the global pebble pattern and thereby affect the global control state.

Situated agents are supposed to be simple agents that achieve complex cooperative behavior by their situated actions. Situated actions are just actions in response to situations. The more complex the environment is the more complex the action. An ant in a complex terrain, so the metaphor goes, will look as if it is controlled by a complex program while in fact the program may be very simple. Similar to the way proponents of connectionism reason that complex behavior (mental or physical) can be reduced to complex interconnections of simple neurons, the advocates of simple agents assume that complex action can be reduced to a complex environment. Actually, they claim more. They claim that complex behavior emerges out of the interactions of simple agents when put in the context of an environment.

1.2 Simple Robots Building a Space Station

So we might imagine simple robots whose purpose is to build a space station. We put them in space together with the space station parts and magically their individually simple situated action algorithms result in the space station being constructed as an emergent event out of the agents' interactions. If one really tried to realize such a scenario, we would have to include the emergent space station complexity somewhere. We assume that the complexity of the agents' programs (agent complexity) plus the complexity of the spatial distribution of agents and space station parts (environment complexity) must be at least as great as the complexity of the resulting space station construction event (goal complexity). The goal is a distributed social event that results in construction of an object. And, the latter event is more complex than the resulting static space station as object (object complexity). Since the agents are simple (of limited complexity) their algorithms will be simple, and so their protocols that determine their agent-agent interactions will be simple. Hence, the interactions will be locally simple.

Where is the global complexity of the goal to come from if not from the communication, interaction protocols?

If all the agents have the same structure, then they all have same protocols. If the agents could be distinct, then the complexity of the goal could be accounted for by the sum complexity of the set of agents. This would be the case, for example, if each agent had a very special role. The harmonizing of the various roles could then result in a very complex emergent distributed interaction event. The greater the number of agents with distinct roles, the greater the possible complexity of the emergent distributed event and the greater the complexity of the resulting constructed object.

2   The Complexity Conservation Principle

Imagine a single agent acting by himself in a very simple environment with some objects with a redundant structure and a random distribution. Let us say the agent is a robot that is to construct a space station out of tinker-toy like parts that are all alike and that join together at various points when pressed appropriately. Assume the robot has the basic skills to join such parts together. Assume further that the arrangement of parts is random and gives no hint as to how the space station is to be constructed or what it is to look like. Let us say we observe the robot construct a particular, very sophisticated structure, a space station, whenever we place him in such an environment. Assume further that the robot is guided by a plan state S that reacts to the information states I that are generated by his sensors. This plan state might be a program, it might be in the form of digital circuitry, or it might it might be in the form of a threshold distribution in a neural net. Whatever the form of the plan state S that controls the robot's actions, assume that we have a device that can read the plan states (intentional states) of such robots.

What would you say if the scientists in charge discovered that the robot had a plan state with no structure or content? We would say the scientists must have made a mistake. The complex activity of the robot must come from somewhere. Perhaps it is not in the plan state? But, recall we assumed that by definition all the robot's actions are generated by the plan state. But then you say I am contradicting myself for if the plan state has no content it cannot generate any structure.

What if we discovered the robot had a very simple plan state that indicated "do action a whatever happens", yet we observed the robot do many different actions beyond the action a? Again we would say something is wrong. Similarly, if we discovered that the robots program was very simple and yet the result was very complex, again we would say then the result is not really complex or there is something wrong. Behind these examples is a principle that is guiding our reasoning. It is much like the principle that you don't get something from nothing. I will now try to formulate this principle which I call the *complexity conservation principle, CCP*:

Principle 1 (Complexity Conservation Principle (Informal)) *The complexity of an event generated by a set of agents cannot be greater than the complexity of the agents plus the complexity of the influencing environment.*

If we have a set of agents $A_1, \ldots, A_n$ acting in an environment Ω, the environment may influence the agents in two ways: First, the environment Ω determines the action possibilities and their outcomes. Second, the agent may perceive parts of the environment Ω. The environment Ω affects the agent A by operating on the agent's information state I_A by perceptual operators θ. We assume that the agent's actions are determined by his strategic, plan state S_A. However, this strategic state can be changed by pragmatically interpreted directives $\alpha!$, i.e., communication from other agents (see [Werner 89, 95]. The contribution of the environment can be represented as an environment agent Ω with strategic state S_Ω. The environmental strategy gives the influencing environment's response to each possible action of the agents.

The complexity of the resulting interaction event e of n agents $A_1, \ldots, A_n$ with the environment Ω cannot be greater than the complexity of $A_1, \ldots, A_n, \Omega$.

Principle 2 (Complexity Conservation Principle CCP)

$$K(e) \leq K(A_1, \ldots, A_n, \Omega) = K(A_1) \oplus \ldots \oplus K(A_n) \oplus \Omega$$

where e is the space-time event-structure generated by the interaction of the agents $A_1, \ldots, A_n$ with each other and with the environment Ω. The relation $\oplus$ is an unspecified function that combines complexity values.

We assume the environment's interactions with the agent are restricted to certain degrees of freedom. This is normally the case and allows us to circumscribe the complexity of the environment to its 'strategy' of interaction S_Ω with the agent. If we would consider the entire agent or the entire local environment, we would get potentially infinite but irrelevant complexities coming into play (from the fine structure of the agents and the environment). This is based on a much deeper point, namely, that:

Principle 3 (Independence of Complexity in Levels of Ontology) *The complexity at one level of ontology need not be the same as the complexity of a more fine grained level of ontology.*

For example, the state of the gas in a balloon may be almost random, yet the balloons themselves may be very organized and highly redundant in their inter-relationships to other balloons. So, at the level of ontology of balloons and their relationships we might have very little complexity and at the level of molecules the complexity may be immense.

3 Kolmogorov/Chaitin Complexity

The complexity conservation principle was inspired by the work of the great mathematician, Kolmogorov. Toward the end of his life, Kolmogorov, who had developed the axiomatic foundations of probability theory, constructed a novel definition of complexity in order to define the concept of a random string. Intuitively, if a string is random then the information required to generate that string should be at least as great as the string itself. For, Kolmogorov reasoned, if a shorter string could be used to generate the random string, then the random string is characterizable by a string containing less information, and is, in this sense, not truly random. A random string on this view consists of irreducible information; it contains no redundancies or symmetries or organization that can be utilized to come up with a shorter more compact description of that string.

Let U be a universal Turing machine. We assume all programs, inputs and outputs of U are binary strings s of the form 1100101100..10. Each such string is, thus, a binary number. The input strings p of U are called *programs*. Let p be any program for U. $|p|$ represents the length of the program p. The *complexity K* of a string s is defined by Kolmogorov to be the length of smallest input string p that generates s on the universal computer U. More formally:

Definition 1 (Kolmogorov/Chaitin Complexity)

$$K(s) = min\{|p| : U(p) = s\}$$

The complexity of s relative to computer U is just the length of shortest program that generates s. If p is a smallest string that generates s on computer U, then if the length of s is the same as p then s is defined to *random*.

Definition 2 (Kolmogorov/Chaitin Randomness) *A string s is* random *if*

$$K(s) = |s|$$

A random string is defined to be a string that requires a program that has the length of the string itself. Simplicity and redundancy appear to be very similar concepts. So too complexity and non redundancy are also similar. For Kolmogorov a random structure is a totally non redundant structure.

If a shorter string p were able to generate s we could just substitute p for s and generate s when we needed it. Pseudo random number generators do just this. A very short program or formula generates a very long sequence of apparently random numbers. Instead of storing the pseudo random string in the computer, we just store the formula (as a subprogram) and generate pseudo random numbers as required. Of course, such a generated sequence is not random. There is a very short program that will generate the sequence.

Behind Kolmogorov's definition is an even more basic principle. In fact it has as a consequence the following:

Theorem 1 *Given a string the complexity of the string it generates cannot be greater than the string itself, up to a constant.*

(For a proof see *Theorem 1.* in the appendix.)

This theorem means that minimal programs are maximally compact. They are random in the sense that they cannot be reduced further. They contain a maximum amount of information for their size and cannot be compressed further. The complexity of a string is a measure of the minimum amount of information needed to generate the string. Hence, the difference between the actual length of a string and its complexity of a string reflects how bloated or redundant the string is.

3.1 Information Density

The *complexity ratio* is the complexity divided by the actual length of the string. It is a measure of the information density of the string.

Definition 3 (Information Density) *The* information density *of a string s is defined as:*

$$\Delta(s) = \frac{K(s)}{|s|}$$

A string has maximal information density if the complexity ratio is 1. A 0.5 ratio indicates a string that is half bloated or redundant. Such a ratio is an intrinsic measure of complexity in terms of density or compression.

3.2 A Restricted Complexity Principle

We can state the complexity conservation principle as restricted to universal Turing machines generating binary strings from binary programs. Thus, the principle is restricted to the case where the agent is a Turing machine that has a program that generates a string.

Principle 4 (Restricted Complexity Principle)

$$K(s) \leq K(p) + K(U)$$

The external program is part of the input environment and the universal Turing machine is the agent/agent strategy that interacts with the input string environment to produce an action output string. For the program p is external to the agent U.

3.3 The Relativity of Complexity

This shows that the complexity of the agent/agent strategy is important here. For a very complex computer (agent) can produce very complex strings from minimally complex input. Relative to that particular agent-computer the output string is then by definition not complex, however, relative to other non-complex agents or computers it is complex.

3.4 Complexity of Sets

Note, we must distinguish generating a set of strings from generating a particular string. Any simple counting program can generate all the binary numbers, in sequence. At each step it simple adds one to the previously generated number. In this way the space of all possible binary strings is generated. Clearly this set of all possible strings contains every random string. Thus a very simple program can generate every random string. Yet we cannot identify the complexity of these strings with the length of this counting program. The reason is that the counting program generates the *set* of all strings and not any individual string. The complexity comes in when one tries to generate a particular string and no other string.

4 Kolmogorov and the Complexity Conservation Principle

What we have done is to generalize Kolmogorov's definition to arbitrary agents interacting with an environment. We have assumed some *a priori* notion of complexity and postulated a complexity conservation principle. It is postulated that complexity satisfies the conservation principle. Kolmogorov complexity measure satisfies our principle. Indeed, it presupposes the principle. The more complex the generated string the more complex the program must be. Complex structures can only be generated by more complex structures. In the case of a random structure it can only be generated by program plus computer that contains a random representation (program or data) at least as complex as the generated random structure.

4.1 Generalizing Kolmogorov Randomness

While the complexity principle gives the limits of what can be done given information of limited complexity, this does not mean that *any* information of the required complexity will allow the agents to achieve their task. Rather, this information must be specific and complete enough for the generation of the event.

Let us generalize Kolmogorov's definition of randomness to event-structures including sequences of events. Any event is *random* if the complexity required to generate that event is equal to the size of the event itself. Here "size" might be formalized in terms of the event's space-time volume.

To avoid confusion, perhaps a better term for random event-structure is *maximally complex* event-structure. Randomness suggests an individual event whose occurrence cannot be foretold in advance. The two concepts of randomness are related in that the tokens in a random sequence (in Kolmogorov's sense) cannot be foretold without enough information that is equal in size to the sequence that we are trying to predict. Thus, without prior information of like complexity we cannot predict the sequence since we cannot generate it. As we gain information we may be able to constrain the possible sequences. Therefore, partial generation of an event-structure by partial, incomplete information may be possible. Complexity incompleteness, inherent in partial information, results, via the complexity principle, in a set of possible partial event-structures or sequences. A random (maximally complex) sequence cannot be completely specified without information equivalent in size to the sequence.

As stated, a random event cannot be generated by just any information of sufficient complexity. The significance of the complexity principle becomes clearer. It is a principle that gives the limits of what events are possible; given information (agent and environment) of some complexity K the event structure generated cannot have a complexity greater that K. This principle says nothing about the content of the information. The principle thus lends itself to proofs of general impossibility. This has been exploited by Kolmogorov and, in particular, Chaitin for various incompleteness and impossibility results (see [Chaitin 66]).

What we have done is to abstract the Kolmogorov/Chaitin definition to a general principle that has far wider application than previously recognized.

We now will look at some more examples illustrating the formation of complex structure. After that we look critically at some schools of thought. Finally, we will reflect on the complexity of the universe.

5   Complexity, Cells and DNA

Imagine a living single cell that outputs proteins by producing those proteins from its DNA. Further imagine that the cell is not influenced by any interaction with its environment but simply acts independently and produces a protein structure as output from a store of materials it has available internally, much like an oocyte. Then, the complexity of the proteins output by the cell cannot be greater than the complexity of its DNA combined with the complexity of the cell. If it were to produce output more complex than itself, we would seek an explanation based on some environmental influence, because the complexity conservation principle would be guiding our reasoning.

Now imagine that the cell receives input in the form of a virus that encapsulates a new strand of DNA and splices it to the cell's internal DNA. With its virally modified DNA, the cell can now produce more complex output. It is much like a Kolmogorov string generating computer where the input string is now transmitted by a virus.

Now if the cell is a true oocyte and starts dividing to eventually produce an organism. By the complexity conservation principle it follows that the complexity of the space-time event of generating the mature organism cannot be greater than the complexity of the influencing environmental factors and the complexity of the original single cell oocyte. Which means that most of the complexity of the organism is contained in its DNA. External maternal factors (proteins and other chemical signals that emanate from the mother) may be quite complex and are part of the influencing environmental factors. Furthermore, the materials that make up the new cells that are forming are also part of the influencing environment. What is so counter-intuitive about this is that the original cell is so small and thereby, apparently simple. However, as we now know not only is the cell not simple, but is very complex even without considering its DNA. When we include the DNA in the complexity we get an enormous complexity.

6   Complexity and Building a Space Station

If the complexity is not in the agent or in the set of agents, then the only other source of the complexity of the interaction event is the environment.

6.1   Spatial Distribution

The complexity might be in the structure of the environment itself. Thus, in our example, the complexity might be in the spatial distribution of the parts of the space station. The spatial distribution would have to contain the information (complexity) of the resulting distributed event. The parts might be so arranged that a simple distributed algorithm would suffice to connect the parts together to form the space station. This does not mean, although it could be the case that, the parts are so arranged to visually look like the three dimensional space station. A simple transformation might suffice to bring about such a conforming visual projection.

6.2 Distributed Information

If, however, the parts are simply dumped and scattered randomly in a region of space, then their spatial arrangement would provide no information about the construction event. The only alternative is some other information source in the environment that gives the necessary state and control information so that the robots are able to construct the space station. This information might be associated with each part. Each part has its own instructions for its construction to its neighbor part. Each part may have a unique identifier or at least type identifier. In effect, the complexity of the instruction set is distributed over the parts. The robots react to the instructions with their simple action interpreting programs. The more complex the instructions the more complex the resulting distributed event may be. Program complexity has now been moved externally to the non robot environment.

6.3 Distributed External Subinstruction Sets

Another way of achieving the same end is to have a master external instruction set with each agent having either unique subinstruction sets or where each dynamically checks off what he is about to do. Here the complexity is again external. The communication is by the checking off of executed instructions much like a blackboard architecture.

Each agent might be given his own particular instructions which it then executes. This is similar to each robot having his own role, as above, except that the role-program is now external to the agent.

6.4 Distributed External Instruction Set

A final alternative is that each agent has an entire external instruction set for the construction of the space station. Much like the case where there is one external plan that all agents share, in this case the plan is redundantly copied for each agent. This is analogous to each agent being individually complex with an internal instruction set except that, again, the complexity is transferred to the environment. The complexity of the group is in this case about the same as that of the individual since each agent instantiates the same role. If subinstruction sets are not somehow indicated for each agent then communication is required to coordinate who does what in the common plan. This may require additional complexity in terms of communication protocols, interaction protocols, and even dominance hierarchies for conflict resolution.

6.5 Internal Complexity

Of course, each agent may have an internal set of instructions for building its part of the space station. That just moves the complexity from outside the agent to inside the agent. The resulting space-time event of building the space station is still limited by the combined complexity of the agents and the complexity of the environment consisting in this case of the parts and their arrangement in space. And, finally, we could have a mixture of internal and external instructions. Again new complexity is not generated.

7 The Limits of Cooperative Action

Like all agents, ants are bounded, first, by the space of possible future actions that are available to them at all. Let us call this space Ω_{Ants}. In addition, like all agents, they are limited by what they *can* do at any given time t because of the limited *information* I they have about the state H_t of the system Ω_{Ants}. Information creates abilities by more creating possible strategies for the agent (For the theory of abilities see [Werner 90,91] and for utilitarian and probabilistic ability see [Werner 95]). However, even with perfect information, which makes all informationally possible strategies, at least in principle, available to the agent, the agent may still not have a *representation* of the strategy and in that sense cannot use it even if it is in his logical space of possible strategies. To generate complex behavior the ant or group of ants must have sufficiently complex strategies not just logically available but actually accessible as representations either explicitly or implicitly in their neural-biochemical system. Note, 'representation' does not necessarily mean a symbolic representation, but can be any physical system organized to represent information. Structurally complex systems can give birth to structurally complex objects and events. It is known that in fact ants are highly complex creatures. Some ants even make use of visual maps of their environment for navigation.

The overall point here is that complex distributed events can only be achieved if either the set of agents and/or their environment is sufficiently complex. If the agents are simple then only a complex environment, including explicit or implicit, complex programs, will make the achievement of complex goals possible. The environment is the program. If, however, the environment is simple and the set of agents is simple then complex goals are impossible to achieve. Complex social events require complex agents or a complex environment.

8 Reactive Agents

A school of thought has emerged in recent years as a reaction to the symbolic programming paradigm of 'classical AI'. This diverse collection of researchers has made grand claims that sound much like the original exaggerations that were made when classical artificial intelligence first showed some promise. Two kinds of arguments seem to dominate the rhetoric of this group. One claim, which I and almost any rational person would agree with, is that agents must react to their environment. Robots cannot just sit there and plan what to do when environmental circumstances demand action. Any real time system must be able to react quickly to changing, unpredictable circumstances. A traditional planning approach will not work because planning takes time. There are different responses as to how to deal with such situations.

The problem is the over reaction to the simple fact that robots, agents and real-time systems must be reactive. The claim is that symbolic reasoning or, more extremely, any sort of higher level reasoning is not needed. We only need reactive simple agents who in concert will solve all our problems. Somehow the solution will emerge magically out of their interactions. We don't need programming. Like all magic there is a sleight of hand going on, and the complexity conservation principle helps to expose the fallacy of this line of reasoning; it tells us that you don't get something for nothing. In fact, closer examination of the way these simple reactive agents, robots and multi-agent systems are constructed reveals the solution is placed quite carefully in the agents' programs in either hardware or software, or in a contrived environment.

The most radical would have us give up planning altogether and only have precompiled reactive strategies that react to any given circumstance. There are severe problems with this approach. First, there is the complexity problem. The complexity of the resulting reaction is limited by the complexity of the agent's strategy and the complexity of the environment. Now, it is argued if we observe an ant in a complex environment the ant's behavior looks complicated even though it is generated by very simple reactive strategies. The problem is that the ant has very few alternatives and the environment influences the ant more than the other way around. Therefore, the possible states that the ant can achieve are greatly limited. It's complexity merely mirrors the complexity of the environment. The ant does not generate any significant complexity on its own.

The point is that the possibilities for a simple reactive agent or a collection of such is limited by their lack of complexity. Many sequences of states are just not achievable. This is in line with our intuitions that ants don't play chess. And they don't construct complex objects on Mars unless there is sufficient information programmed or hard-wired into them.

9   Problems with the Subsumption Architecture

Let us consider one important proposal for the architecture of reactive agents in greater detail. Brooks [Brooks 86] realized classical planning approaches to robotic activity would not result in real-time systems that reacted flexibly to their environment.

Classically, vision and planning proceeded in steps. First, low level processing of visual input was done, then higher level processing to come up with an interpreted image or model. Finally, planing of action could be done by projecting possible outcomes of actions relative to the model of the environment obtained through visual analysis. On this approach decisions were not made until all the low level steps were completed. This led to slow and rigid reactions on the part of the robot. Some excellent work using this classical approach was done by Brooks himself [Brooks 82].

Brooks rightly criticized this approach and came up with a very interesting solution. Why not let all these processes act in parallel? Do the low level processing in parallel with the high level planning. Furthermore, let each level be able to make choices. Then, so the reasoning went, the robot could react on the basis of local information, e.g., a wall being too close, without having to wait for the result of a high level planner that may be thinking about how to circumvent the obstacle ten meters away rather than the wall next to it.

I am very sympathetic to this approach, but since only the lower levels of the subsumption architecture were implemented, I was skeptical of its workability. Furthermore, the implicit and explicit claims of the sufficiency of the reactive layers, were problematic in view of the complexity conservation principle. To test these ideas I organized a seminar to build a Brooksian robot. We designed a subsumption architecture for a four legged robot. We simulated the architecture on computer both internally in the relations of the processors and the control messages they exchanged, as well as, externally in a graphic display of the four-legged robot. Furthermore, we actually constructed the robot. In the process of design some severe limitation with this architecture became apparent to me. I would like to share these with the computer science community since they have more general implications about the nature of planning and control.

9.1 The Subsumption Architecture

The subsumption architecture consists of layers of control implementing levels of competence. These layers are to function semi-autonomously and in parallel. Its purpose is to control the actions of a reactive robot.

Levels of competence "A level of competence is an informal specification of a desired class of behaviors for a robot over all environments it will encounter. A higher level of competence implies a more specific desired class of behaviors...each level of competence includes as a subset each earlier level of competence. Since each level of competence defines a class of valid behaviors it can be seen that higher levels of competence provide additional constraints on that class." [Brooks 86].

Layers of Control Corresponding to each level of competence is a control system (layer of control) where a control layer n is able to examine data from layer n-1 and to inject data into level n-1 suppressing the normal data flow. The layer n-1 is unaware of the layer above it which sometimes interferes with its data path. Layer n consists of it plus the layers below it. Layer n achieves level n competence.

9.2   A Critical Analysis

Each level of competence can be interpreted as a class of strategies that the robot follows. The level 0 is supposed to constrain the behavior the least and, therefore, corresponds to the largest strategy class. Each new level of competence constrains the class of strategies allowed at lower levels. Behaviors are just simple strategies.

However, there is a problem here. A partial strategy corresponding to a class of strategies and does generally not pick out a unique response for a given situation. Instead, it allows several possible actions. The higher level of competence then constrains these possible actions further. In terms of control layers, this partial constraint on behavior leaves choices open for the higher control layer. It then is further reduces the choice set. On this view higher levels of competence constrain the class of behaviors allowed by levels below, and still higher layers of control further constrain the choices of the lower control layers.

The actual control layer is supposed to be an independently functioning unit in the absence of the higher layers. But, that means the layer 0 of control is a complete (pure) strategy that determines a unique choice for any given situation. That means that the corresponding level of competence picks out a unique behavior for any given situation. But then further levels of competence do not constrain lower levels, and higher layers of control do not constrain the set of choices.

This indicates that there is a contradiction between Brooks concept of levels of competence as levels of increasing constraints on behavior and his concept of layer of control if that means a fully specified strategy. Indeed, he allows individual layers to work concurrently on different goals. "The suppression mechanism then mediates the actions that are taken."[Brooks 86, p.17]

It may be that his notion of layer of control is contradictory. On the one hand a layer of control only partially specifies a choice and on the other hand it gives a unique choice with possible suppression by a higher layer. The higher level then gives the result if there is a contradiction between layers.

An alternative view is that higher levels don't constrain lower levels rather lower levels are more specific than higher levels. This inverse view would make lower levels give unique choices while higher levels give only partial goals. This inverse view corresponds to the view that higher level plans only partially constrain the behaviors of the agent. Lower level reactive strategies actually determine the behavior in particular circumstances.

In fact, it appears to be a mixture of the two. With higher and lower layers of mutually constraining each other with the behavior emerging out of all the levels of competence and layers of control.

There are competing views of control:

1. As constraints
   (a) Higher level further constrains lower level
   (b) Lower level further constrains higher level
   (c) Mutual constraints of higher and lower levels

2. As conflicting specific alternatives with some method for resolving conflicts (suppression, which in effect gives priority to the higher layer of control)

On Brooks' account the higher level does not just suppress the lower level input or output but actually replaces it. Thus, the conflict is resolved by the higher strategy winning out. However, if this were the only method of resolving plan conflicts then low level strategies would always be dominated. A complete higher level strategy would then rigidly determine the next move no matter what the local circumstances might be. This would go against the whole idea that low level strategies are to react to local changes, e.g., obstacles as when getting past a crowd on the way to the train station. In such a case the local strategy must dominate the higher strategy temporarily. Thus control cannot just pass from higher to lower layers.

Indeed, in Brooks' actual example architecture there is a level 1 module with both an input from a higher level 2 and an input from a lower level 0 layer of control. This module must integrate both inputs and, in effect, gives a compromise plan from the two choices of the higher and lower level plans. While the architecture of the example works and solves the problem of strategic conflict, it is *not* an example of the subsumption architecture. For we have explicit modules or layers that resolve plan conflicts of two distinct layers. This middle *compromise layer* does not easily fit into the hierarchical subsumption architecture. It is not a level of competence or behavior at all. It is doing meta control of the robot by fusing different strategic control layers.

Note, we have left out the temporal dimension. Thus, it may be that lower control layers give specific answers as to what to do in any given circumstance, but higher layers such as planning constrain the overall direction over time. However, this is inconsistent. For if the lower level provides a pure local strategy then that will generate a global pure strategy that will in general contradict the higher layer global strategy.

The issue is that a robot must act. If each layer of control really is independent, then each layer generates a pure strategy of action for the robot. Otherwise, the layer would offer no decision or a random decision in any specific situation. As soon as each layer of control makes specific decisions about actions (about the same control variables), we have each layer in conflict with every other layer all the time. If the higher layer always wins, then we may as well get rid of the lower layers. Similarly, if the lower level always wins we don't need the higher level.

A way out would be to say that the higher layers control independent control variables (degrees of freedom). But certainly we still have the conflicts for mutually controlled degrees of freedom.

Furthermore, sometimes low layers of control need to dominate higher levels. Thus, in collision avoidance the low level layer of control may need to have priority over the high level planner that has not considered the upcoming obstacle.

These are all real problems that real robotic systems must solve. There are actually more severe problems that the designer of a system of robots must face. How are the robots going to coordinate their activity when the tasks are more complex and this complex information is *not* given by the environment? Then, by the complexity conservation principle, the complex event will never emerge through the interactions of simple homogeneous agents. Neither will the complexity emerge magically by communication. Only if the communication protocols are complex enough or suitably connected to complex information and intentional states can non environmentally induced complexity emerge (see [Werner 89] for a theory of communication and cooperation for multi-agent systems.)

10   Plans as Resources (Agre, Chapman, Suchman)

The view of plans as resources corresponds to the view of lower levels of control being more specific and higher levels less specific. Plans as linguistic requests fits in with this view of plans as constraints. By 'constraint' we mean a condition that indicates a more specific subset of behaviors from a larger set of possible particular actions.

There is a tension in this work that appears to result from a systematic confusion of plan states as intentional states that guide a given agent and plans as recipes analogous to linguistic directives. Plan states need not be linguistic at all. They may and should partially constrain the agent's actions. This is a quite different notion than a plan as medium of communication that one agent passes to another or one agent communicates to himself and so directs himself. Let us call plan states or intentional states that partially control an agent $plans_1$ and plans as (partially) ordered sequence of language like directives $plans_2$.

In my theory of communication I explicitly distinguish between these two concepts of plans. One the one hand, there are plan states S_A (intentional states, $Plans_1$) that partially guide the agent A. These may be supplemented by lower level reactive tactics (much like in the Brooksian paradigm). On the other hand, there are linguistic ways of communicating control information from one agent to another or internally from the agent to himself (self-directives). The latter $plans_2$ have the form $\alpha_1, \ldots, \alpha_n$ where each α_i is directive in the plan language.

This second view of plans really presupposes the first concept. For the 'plan language' that is used to communicate directives must be pragmatically interpreted by the agent. On my theory this process of interpretation of the directives that make up $plans_2$ results in operators that act on plan states ($plans_1$).

Thus, for example, a $plan_2$ of directives $\alpha_1, \ldots, \alpha_n$ is interpreted pragmatically by $Prag$ such that $Prag(\alpha_i)$ is an operator that if accepted transforms the $plan_1$ state S of the agent to conform to the directive α. The total $plan_2$ then transforms the $plan_1$ state S_A of the agent A as follows:

$$Prag(\alpha_n), \ldots, Prag(\alpha_1)(S_A) = S'_A$$

where the new intentional plan state S'_A reflects the newly added $plan_2$ information. The resulting plan state may only partially control the actions of the agent A. Thereby, one can see, on my view, speech acts such as directives (commands, requests) used in the process of communicative interaction can structure, form and create complex intentions in another agent. The agent is not rigidly determined by the resulting intentional state.

If Agre, et al., hypothesize that the internal structure of $plan_1$ states consists of $plan_2$ like directives then severe problems arise. For high level language like $plan_2$ states must be interpreted. It is not at all apparent that such an interpretive process normally goes on. In fact, in this case I would side more with the reactive school that would have $plan_1$ states be low level non linguistic, non-symbolic structures that direct the agent. Whatever their nature, they do not seem to consist of language in the sense of natural language. They may simply be complex neural control states. Indeed planning itself as a process of constructing $plan_1$ states can be, but need not be, a linguistic process. The animal world is replete with examples of planned action and yet they do not possess anything like a natural language. Furthermore, planning as visualization of alternative actions by an agent need not be a linguistic or symbolic process. It may simply involve simulation of a complex domain with the agent performing simulated actions in that domain.

11 Connectionism

The complexity conservation principle also has implications for connectionism. A parallel argument holds for the limitations of connectionism. It is assumed that complex behavior will somehow emerge as result of putting neuron like agents together by connecting them. This naive argument is simply wrong given a redundant structure of connections, i.e., simple connection structure. For then the behavior produced will be no more complex than that of the neuron network plus the environment. If the neuron network structure is highly redundant, then we have a situation analogous to a computer with an empty memory or only a simple program. The only possible complexity arising will be from input from the environment.

If the neural net model is enriched by adding thresholds of varying weights, then a new complexity dimension has been added. However, the basic argument is the same. Complex output from a neural network is only possible if the neural network state is complex and/or the environment is complex.

Can complexity emerge? Yes, local complexity can emerge in a neural network if we allow interactions with a complex environment. Learning and perception allow the gradual buildup of complex neural states. The visual scene interacts with the robot's neural network to create a complex visual state. The complexity is transferred from the environment to the neural state.

12 Evolution and Complexity

If we consider two systems A and B interacting by some interaction $\otimes$ to give a result $A \otimes B$ leading to a new state in both A and B, the only source of complexity are the states and laws of A and B together with the laws of interaction $\otimes$. If this interaction does not lead to an increase in ontology, the complexity of both A and B will be affected. While the individual complexity of A and B may change dynamically with the interaction, the total complexity of the system $< A, B, \otimes >$ cannot increase according to the complexity conservation principle unless the interactions specified by the laws are indeterministic. In the case of life, the environment is much more complex than life itself. This imbalance of complexity makes possible a continual flow of complexity, through adaption, selection and evolution, from the environment to the organism and condensed in its DNA. Some like Langton (see [Waldrop 92]) have argued that complexity is only interesting in some middle range between highly constant systems and totally random systems. However, what is random and what is not random also depends on the complexity of the observer-agent who interprets and makes use of that complexity.

The evolution and increasing complexity of life forms does not contradict the complexity conservation principle. Instead, it is in accordance with the principle. Genetic algorithms [Holland 75] are a way of transferring complexity form the world to the organisms that interact with that world.

13   Organization and Other Puzzles

If a simple agent attempts to generate a structure larger than itself, we get redundancies, repetitions or patterns in the resulting structure which some would consider organization. One might speculate with Langton [Waldrop 92] that organization occupies a middle ground between total simplicity and randomness.

Organization is not random. To be organized means not to be disorderly. Disorder is associated with chaos and randomness. So a random structure is not an organized structure. So organization implies there is some simplicity, non complexity, or redundancy. We do speak of complex organizations. We can think of a modular system with a simple high level structure consisting of lower level modules of increasing complexity. We organize the work on a complex process by dividing it up into simpler tasks that can be performed by simpler systems.

How does organization occur? Certainly a complex program can generate a structure simpler than itself. If a program is to generate an organized structure out of simpler elements, is the organized structure simpler than the set of non organized elements of the structure?

Another theme is that agents need organization to achieve complex tasks. Or is organization needed to achieve organized tasks?

Can a random program, i.e., very complex program, be used to generate an organized structure, a redundant less complex structure? It seems that the program contains the structure it generates. This is what we call information.

14   On the Complexity of the Universe

The complexity of the universe and how it arose is a serious problem for cosmologists. Cosmology is the branch of physics concerned with the origin and evolution of the universe. Physicists and cosmologists regard it as a fundamental problem of how the present complexity of the universe could have arisen if the state of the early universe, following the big bang, was a simple state. They were relieved to find evidence of anisotropy of the cosmic microwave background radiation [Smoot 92]. For such anisotropy may be evidence of complexity in the early universe. The reasoning utilized by physicists makes implicit use of the complexity conservation principle. For without the principle one would not have to worry about increasing complexity at all. Indeed, the complexity conservation principle presents some serious problems and puzzles for the foundations of physics and cosmology.

14.1 Entropy and Complexity

The second law of thermodynamics states that the entropy of the total system is always increasing or a least never decreasing. Yet entropy is a measure of randomness or disorder. In this sense, entropy is also a measure of complexity. Here we must distinguish *epistemological entropy* which is a measure of uncertainty. If I is an information set of whose states have various probabilities, then the entropy of I is the log of the weighted average of those possibilities. The greater the epistemological entropy the greater the uncertainty or lack of information given by the information set. The entropy that increases as a result of the second law of thermodynamics is *phenomenological entropy* or *real entropy*. This is an actual physical property of a system and not just an epistemological state of an observer. This latter entropy is a measure of disorder and cannot be reduced by gaining more information about the system. When real entropy increases the complexity of the system increases as well. It takes more information to describe the state of a system that has more entropy. Thus, the second law of thermodynamics implies that the complexity of the universe is increasing.

How can the complexity of the universe be increasing when the complexity conservation principle appears to hold for all generating structures? We can view the universe as consisting of a state and the laws generate the next state. In a deterministic universe the present state of the universe completely determines the next state of the universe. If there are indeterministic laws, then the laws generate a *set* of next possible states. But, in either case, if the generating laws satisfy the principle of the conservation of complexity, then the generated state or states can be no more complex than the previous state plus complexity of the laws of the universe.

14.2 A Laplacian Universe

If, however, we apply the complexity conservation principle then the complexity of the early universe must be at least as great as the complexity of the present universe. In a Laplacian universe, a deterministic universe, the increase in complexity presents a serious conceptual problem. In such a universe the complexity conservation principle appears to be in direct conflict with the second law of thermodynamics.

14.3   Complexity and Quantum Mechanics

In a nondeterministic universe the next state is not completely determined by the present state. There we may find the universe meandering toward increasing complexity. Assume that the second law of thermodynamics is correct. Then the complexity of the universe is increasing. By the complexity conservation principle this complexity must come from some source. The complexity cannot increase in a deterministic universe. If the only source of indeterminism in the universe is quantum mechanics by way of the Heisenberg uncertainty principle, then the second law of thermodynamics should be derivable from the complexity conservation principle and the uncertainty principle and quantum mechanics.

Conjecture 1 *Given the complexity conservation principle, there is a derivation of the second law of thermodynamics from quantum mechanics and the uncertainty principle.*

In other words, the increasing entropy of the universe as a part of the increasing complexity of the universe, should be explainable by the ultimate source of indeterminism, quantum mechanics. If it is not so explainable then by the complexity conservation principle there must be yet an additional source of complexity.

14.4   Freedom and Complexity

If man is truly free, he is outside the laws of the universe and can choose which of the multiple future universes to enter. This free act of the will, then can increase the complexity of the universe. In such a case the soul is the source of complexity. The soul would be the interacting system outside of the universe whose input increases the complexity of the universe. Free acts from the perspective of the physical universe would appear to be unpredictable, random events. If we allow that there is a God and that God interacts with the universe, then God may be a source of complexity for the universe much like the environment is a source of complexity for an agent. Analogous to a virtual reality game, where the player's actions cannot be predicted by the computer, the virtual universe responds to the user action like another player. The actions of the player can increase the complexity of the virtual universe because the player is independent of that virtual universe. So too might the soul be player in our universe, the body like a glove to be worn for a lifetime and then discarded.

15   Conclusion

Fundamental to information and uncertainty is that information reduces possibilities and increases abilities of agents [Werner 90-91]. Information reduces epistemological entropy, and at the same time, increases structure, in the sense of adding to the representation the agent has of the world. The representation the agent has of the world thus increases in complexity with increasing information. This increase in complexity allows the agent to generate more complex output. This is consistent with the complexity conservation principle in that it constrains an agent to generating no greater complexity than he already has. The generation of structure or information requires a like amount of structural complexity. We have seen that this poses limits on not only on any agent (human, virtual, or robotic) or group, but also on the complexity of the state and dynamic formation of the universe itself. The concept of complexity may be so difficult to grasp and formalize because it is such an inseparable part of existence and its patterns.

16   Appendix I: Kolmogorov/Chaitin Complexity

Let U be a universal Turing machine. Let p be any program for U. If s is any string then $|s|$ represents the length of the string s.

Definition 1 (Kolmogorov/Chaitin Complexity)

$$K(s) = min\{|p| : U(p) = s\}$$

Theorem 1. *Given a string p the complexity of the string s it generates cannot be greater than the string itself, up to a constant.*

$$K(s) < K(p) + c$$

Proof. Let p be a minimal string that generates string s on computer U. Then $K(s) = |p|$, the length of p. If $K(p)$ is less than $K(s)$ then by definition there is a program x that generates p and the length of x is less than the length of p, $|x| < |p|$. This implies we could construct a program y that takes x generates p and then generates s. The length of y will be the length of x plus some constant c (for the extra subprogram to generate p from the intermediate output x), i.e, $|y| = |x| + c$. If the length of y is less than the length of p, i.e., $|y| < |p|$ we have a contradiction. For then we have a minimal program y that generates s but whose length is less than p. But, by assumption p was a minimal program for s. Hence, a string p cannot generate a string of complexity greater than itself up to some constant c.

References

[Agre 91] Agre, P., "What are plans for?", *AI Magazine*, 1991.

[Brooks 82] Brooks, R.A., "Symbolic Error Analysis and Robot Planning," INTERNATIONAL *Journal of Robotics Research*,1, No. 4, pp. 29 - 68, 1982.

[Brooks 86] Brooks, R., "A Robust Layered Control System for a Mobile Robot," *IEEE Journal of Robotics and Automation*, vol. RA-2, No. 1, March 1986

[Chaitin 66] Chaitin, G.J., "On the length of programs for computing finite binary sequences," *J. ACM*, vol. 13, pp. 547-569, October 1966.

[Demazeau & Mueller 90] Y. Demazeau & J-P. Mueller (eds.), *Decentralized AI, Vol. I*, Elsevier Science Publishers (North Holland), 1990.

[Demazeau & Mueller 92] Y. Demazeau & J-P. Mueller (eds.), *Decentralized AI, Vol. II*, Elsevier Science Publishers (North Holland), 1992.

[Holland 75] Holland, J. H., *Adaption in Natural and Artificial Systems*, Ann Arbor, University of Michigan Press, 1975.

[Khinchin 49] Khinchin, A.I., *Mathematical Foundations of Statistical Mechanics*, Dover Publ., New York, 1949.

[Kolmogorov 65] Kolmogorov, A.N., "Three Approaches to the definition of the concept 'quantity of information'," *Probl. Peredachi Inform.*, vol. 1, pp. 3-11, 1965.

[Kolmogorov 68] Kolmogorov, A.N., "Logical basis for information theory and probability theory", *IEEE Trans. Information Theory*, vol. IT-14, pp. 662-664, September 1968.

[Shannon 48] Shannon, C.E., "The Mathematical Theory of Communication", Bell Syst, Techn. Journ., vol. 27, 379-423; 623-656, 1948.

[Smoot 92] Smoot, G.F., et al., *Astrophysical Journal*, vol. 396, L1-L5, 1992.

[Waldrop 92] Waldrop, M.M., *Complexity, The Emerging Science at the Edge of Order and Chaos*, Simon & Schuster, New York, 1992.

[Werner 88] Werner, E., "The Modal Logic of Games", WISBER Report B48, University of Hamburg, Hamburg, Germany 1988.

[Werner 89a] Werner, E., "Tensed Modal Logic", WISBER Report B49, University of Hamburg, Hamburg, Germany, 1989a.

[Werner 89b] Werner, E., "Cooperating Agents: A Unified Theory of Communication and Social Structure", *Distributed Artificial Intelligence, Vol. 2*, M. Huhns & L. Gasser (eds.), Morgan Kaufmann and Pitman Publishers, London, pp. 3-36, 1989b.

[Werner 90] Werner, E., "What Can Agents Do Together? A Semantics of Cooperative Ability", *ECAI-90, Proceedings of the 9th European Conference on Artificial Intelligence*, Stockholm, Sweden, Pitman Publishers, pp. 694-701, 1990.

[Werner 91] Werner, E., "A Unified View of Information, Intention, and Ability", *Decentralized AI, Vol. II*, Y. Demazeau & J-P. Muller (eds.), Elsevier Science Publishers (North Holland), 1992.

[Werner 95] Werner, E., "Logical Foundations of Distributed Artificial Intelligence", *Foundations of Distributed Artificial Intelligence*, G. Ohare & N. Jennings (eds.), John Wiley, forthcoming, 1995.

Towards a Theory of Cooperative Problem Solving

Michael Wooldridge

Dept. of Computing
Manchester Metropolitan University
Chester Street, Manchester M1 5GD
United Kingdom

`M.Wooldridge@doc.mmu.ac.uk`

Nicholas R. Jennings

Dept. of Electronic Engineering
Queen Mary & Westfield College
Mile End Road, London E1 4NS
United Kingdom

`N.R.Jennings@qmw.ac.uk`

Abstract. One objective of distributed artificial intelligence research is to build systems that are capable of cooperative problem solving. To this end, a number of implementation-oriented models of cooperative problem solving have been developed. However, *mathematical* models of social activity have focussed only on limited aspects of the cooperative problem solving process: no mathematical model of the entire process has yet been described. In this paper, we rectify this omission. We present a preliminary model that describes the cooperative problem solving process from recognition of the potential for cooperation through to team action. The model is formalised by representing it as a theory in a quantified multi-modal logic. A key feature of the model is its reliance on the twin notions of *commitments* and *conventions*; conventions (protocols for monitoring commitments) are formalised for the first time in this paper. We comment on the generality of the model, outline its deficiencies, and suggest some possible refinements and other future areas of research.

1 Introduction

Distributed Artificial Intelligence (DAI) is concerned with all forms of social activity in systems composed of multiple computational agents [1]. An important form of interaction in such systems is *cooperative problem solving* (CPS), which occurs when a group of logically decentralised agents choose to work together to achieve a common goal. Relevant examples include a group of agents moving a heavy object, playing a symphony, building a house, and writing a joint paper. As these examples indicate, CPS is a common and important process in human societies, and there is increasing evidence to support the claim that it will be similarly important in future computer systems. A number of models of the CPS process have been devised by DAI researchers. Some of these models represent frameworks for implementing CPS systems, and for managing cooperative activities in such systems at run-time (e.g., [15, 5]). Other, more formal models have been developed in an attempt to characterise various aspects of CPS (e.g., [10, 8, 17]).

As is the case in mainstream AI, the differing motivations and approaches of formalists and system builders has meant that there has been little cross-fertilisation between the two areas. The former camp has concentrated on isolated aspects of the CPS process, whereas work in the latter camp has concentrated on devising protocols for the entire CPS process. However, the key assumptions and design decisions of implementation-oriented CPS models tend to be buried deep inside the associated software; this can make it difficult to extract general principles or results from implementations.

This paper goes some way to bridging the gap between theory and practice in DAI. We develop a four-stage model of CPS, which we make precise by expressing it as a theory in a quantified multi-modal logic. The development of this model was driven by an analysis of CPS in both natural and artificial systems; the result is a theory that is accessible to both formalists and system builders. For formalists, the model represents a first attempt to capture the properties of CPS in a mathematical framework, with the corollary that properties of the model may be established via formal proof. For system builders, the model can serve as an abstract, top-level specification of a CPS system, which can inform the development of future DAI applications. The model deals with a number of issues that have hitherto been neglected by DAI theorists; for example, it considers the process by which an agent recognises the potential for cooperation, and begins to solicit assistance. Note that although we have attempted to develop a model that deals with CPS from beginning to end, we do not claim that our model is the final word on the subject; it would not be possible to present, in such a short paper, a theory that dealt with all conceivable aspects of a process as complex as CPS (see §5).

The remainder of this paper is structured as follows. The following section presents an overview of the formal framework used to represent the model. In §3, the notions of commitments and conventions, which play a key role in our model, are discussed and subsequently formalised; the model of CPS is then developed in §4. Some conclusions are presented in §5.

2   A Formal Framework

This section gives an overview of the formal framework in which the model of CPS will be expressed. This framework is a quantified multi-modal logic, which both draws upon and extends the work described in [3, 13]. Unfortunately, space restrictions prevent us from defining the language in full here; a complete formal definition of the language's syntax and semantics may be found in [17].

Informally, the operators of the language have the following meanings. The operator true is a logical constant for truth. (Bel i φ) and (Goal i φ) mean that agent i has a belief, or goal of φ respectively. The = operator is usual first-order equality. The $\in$ operator allows us to relate agents to groups of agents; it has the expected set-theoretic interpretation, so ($i \in g$) means that the agent denoted by i is a member of the group denoted by g. The (Agts α g) operator means that the group denoted by g are precisely the agents required to perform the actions in the action sequence denoted by α. The A operator is a *path quantifier*: Aφ means that φ is a *path formula* that is satisfied in all the futures that could arise from the current state[1]. The operators $\neg$ (not) and $\vee$ (or)

---

[1] There is a distinction made in the language between *path* and *state* formulae: state formulae are evaluated with respect to the 'current state' of the world, whereas path formulae are evaluated with respect to a course of events. The well-formed formulae of the language are identified with the set of state formulae [6].

have classical semantics, as does the universal quantifier $\forall$; the remaining classical connectives and existential quantifier are assumed to be introduced as abbreviations, in the obvious way. (Happens α) is a path formula that means that the action α happens next; α; α' means the action α is immediately followed by α'; $\alpha|\alpha'$ means either α or α' happen next; φ? is a test action, which occurs if φ is 'true' in the current state; $\alpha*$ means the action α iterated.

Some derived operators. A number of derived operators will now be introduced. First, the usual connectives of linear temporal logic: $\varphi\,\mathcal{U}\,\psi$ means φ is satisfied *until* ψ becomes satisfied; $\Diamond\varphi$ means φ is *eventually* satisfied; $\Box\varphi$ means φ is *always* satisfied. These connectives are used to build path formulae. The path quantifier E is the dual of A; thus Eφ means φ is a path formulae satisfied on *at least one* possible future.

$$\varphi\,\mathcal{U}\,\psi \stackrel{\text{def}}{=} (\text{Happens }(\neg\psi?; \varphi?)^*; \psi?) \qquad \Box\varphi \stackrel{\text{def}}{=} \neg\Diamond\neg\varphi$$
$$\Diamond\varphi \stackrel{\text{def}}{=} \text{true}\,\mathcal{U}\,\varphi \qquad\qquad \text{E}\varphi \stackrel{\text{def}}{=} \neg\text{A}\neg\varphi$$

(Singleton g i) means g is a singleton group with i as the only member. (Agt α i) means i is the only agent of action α.

$$(\text{Singleton } g\ i) \stackrel{\text{def}}{=} \forall j \cdot (j \in g) \Rightarrow (j = i)$$
$$(\text{Agt } \alpha\ i) \stackrel{\text{def}}{=} \forall g \cdot (\text{Agts } \alpha\ g) \Rightarrow (\text{Singleton } g\ i)$$

To represent an action α *achieving* a goal φ, we introduce a derived operator Achieves.

$$(\text{Achieves } \alpha\ \varphi) \stackrel{\text{def}}{=} \text{A}((\text{Happens }\alpha) \Rightarrow (\text{Happens }\alpha; \varphi?))$$

We will have a number of occasions to write A(Happens α), (action α occurs next in all alternative futures), and A$\neg$(Happens α) (action α does not occur next in any alternative future), and so we introduce abbreviations for these.

$$(\text{Does } \alpha) \stackrel{\text{def}}{=} \text{A}(\text{Happens } \alpha) \qquad (\text{Doesn't } \alpha) \stackrel{\text{def}}{=} \text{A}\neg(\text{Happens } \alpha)$$

We find it convenient to define knowledge as true belief, rather than by introducing it as yet another primitive modality.

$$(\text{Know } i\ \varphi) \stackrel{\text{def}}{=} \varphi \wedge (\text{Bel } i\ \varphi)$$

We also find it convenient to use the notions of *mutual* mental states. Although we recognise that such states are idealised, in that they are not realisable in systems which admit the possibility of failed communication, they are nevertheless valuable abstraction tools for understanding multi-agent systems. The mutual belief of φ in a group of agents g is written (M-Bel g φ); the mutual goal of φ in g is written (M-Goal g φ), and the mutual knowledge of φ is written (M-Know g φ). We define mutual mental states as *fixed points.*

$$(\text{M-Bel } g\ \varphi) \stackrel{\text{def}}{=} \forall i \cdot (i \in g) \Rightarrow (\text{Bel } i\ \varphi \wedge (\text{M-Bel } g\ \varphi))$$
$$(\text{M-Goal } g\ \varphi) \stackrel{\text{def}}{=} \forall i \cdot (i \in g) \Rightarrow (\text{M-Bel } g\ (\text{Goal } i\ \varphi))$$
$$(\text{M-Know } g\ \varphi) \stackrel{\text{def}}{=} \varphi \wedge (\text{M-Bel } g\ (\text{M-Know } g\ \varphi))$$

3 Commitments, Conventions, and Intentions

The key mental states that control agent behaviour are intentions and joint intentions — the former define local asocial behaviour, the latter control social behaviour [2]. Intentions are important as they provide both the stability and predictability (through the notion of commitment) that is needed for social interactions, and the flexibility and reactivity (through the mechanisms by which commitments are monitored) that are required to deal with a changing environment. Previous attempts to formalise (joint) intentions have made no distinction between a commitment and its underlying convention; we clearly distinguish the two concepts: a *commitment* is a pledge or a promise; a *convention* is a means of monitoring a commitment — it specifies both the conditions under which a commitment might be abandoned, and how an agent should behave, should such a circumstance arise [8].

Commitments have a number of important properties (see [8] and [3, pp217–219] for a discussion), but the most important is that *commitments persist*: having adopted a commitment, we do not expect an agent to drop it until, for some reason, it becomes redundant. The conditions under which a commitment can become redundant are specified in the associated convention — examples include the motivation for the goal no longer being present, the goal being achieved, and the realisation that the goal will never be achieved [3].

When a group of agents are engaged in a cooperative activity, they have a joint commitment to the overall aim, as well as individual commitments to the specific tasks that they have been assigned. This joint commitment is parameterised by a social convention, which identifies the conditions under which the joint commitment can be dropped, and also describes how the agent should behave towards fellow team members. For example, if an agent drops its joint commitment because it believes that the goal will never be attained, then it is part of the notion of 'cooperativeness' inherent in joint action that it informs fellow team members of its change of state. In this context, social conventions provide general guidelines, and a common frame of reference in which agents can work. By adopting a convention, every agent knows what is expected both of it, and of every other agent, as part of the collective working towards the goal, and knows that every other agent has a similar set of expectations.

Formally, we define a convention as a set of rules, each rule consisting of a re-evaluation condition ρ and a goal γ: if ever an agent believes ρ to be true, then it must adopt γ as a goal, and keep this goal until the commitment becomes redundant.

Definition 1. *A convention, c, is an indexed set of pairs: $c = \{(\rho_k, \gamma_k) \mid k \in \{1, \ldots, l\}\}$, where ρ_k is a re-evaluation condition, and γ_k is a goal, $\forall k \in \{1, \ldots, l\}$.*

Joint commitments have a number of parameters. First, a joint commitment is held by a group g of agents. Second, joint commitments are held with respect to some goal φ; this is the state of affairs that the group is committed to bringing about. Third, joint commitments are held relative to a *motivation*, which characterises the justification for the commitment. They also have a *pre-condition*, which describes what must initially be true of the world in order for the commitment to be held. For example, in most types of joint commitment, we do not expect participating agents to initially believe that the object of the commitment, φ, is true. Finally, a joint commitment is parameterised by a convention c. Joint commitment is then informally defined as follows.

> **Definition: (Joint commitments)** A group g is jointly committed to goal φ with respect to motivation ψ, pre-condition *pre*, and convention c iff: (i) pre-condition *pre* is initially satisfied; and (ii) until the termination condition is satisfied, every agent in g either (a) has a goal of φ; or (b) believes that the re-evaluation condition of some rule in c is satisfied, and has the goal corresponding to that re-evaluation condition; where the termination condition is that the goal part of some convention rule is satisfied.

More formally:

Definition 2. *If* $c = \{(\rho_k, \gamma_k) \mid k \in \{1, \dots, l\}\}$ *is a convention, then:*

$$(\text{J-Commit } g \ \varphi \ \psi \ pre \ c) \stackrel{\text{def}}{=} \forall i \cdot (i \in g) \Rightarrow pre \wedge \text{A}((p \vee q)\,\mathcal{U}\,r)$$

where

$$p \stackrel{\text{def}}{=} (\text{Goal } i \ \varphi) \qquad q \stackrel{\text{def}}{=} \bigvee_{l=1}^{k}(\text{Bel } i \ \rho_l) \wedge \text{A}[(\text{Goal } i \ \gamma_l)\,\mathcal{U}\,r] \qquad r \stackrel{\text{def}}{=} \bigvee_{m=1}^{k} \gamma_m.$$

This general model can be used to capture the properties of many different types of joint commitment. For example, we will now specify a social convention that is similar to the Levesque-Cohen model of joint persistent goals (JPGs) [10]. Let

$$pre_{JPG} \stackrel{\text{def}}{=} \neg(\text{Bel } i \ \varphi) \wedge (\text{Bel } i \ \text{E}\Diamond\varphi)$$

$$c_{JPG} \stackrel{\text{def}}{=} \left\{ \begin{array}{l} ((\text{Bel } i \ \varphi), (\text{M-Bel } g \ \varphi)), \\ ((\text{Bel } i \ \text{A}\Box\neg\varphi), (\text{M-Bel } g \ \text{A}\Box\neg\varphi)), \\ ((\text{Bel } i \ \neg\psi), (\text{M-Bel } g \ \neg\psi)) \end{array} \right\}.$$

A group with a joint commitment parameterised by a pre-condition pre_{JPG}, and convention c_{JPG} will have a shared mental state identical in all important respects to that implied by the JPGs of Levesque-Cohen. We use joint commitments to define joint intentions, which are held by a group g with respect to an action α and motivation ψ. In general, it is possible to make conventions a parameter of joint intentions. However, this would complicate our subsequent formalism, and we therefore leave this refinement to future work. For the purposes of this paper, we simply assume that joint intentions are defined over the JPG-like convention c_{JPG}; this gives us a model of joint intentions similar to that in [10, p98].

$$(\text{J-Intend } g \ \alpha \ \psi) \stackrel{\text{def}}{=} (\text{M-Bel } g \ (\text{Agts } \alpha \ g)) \ \wedge$$
$$(\text{J-Commit } g \ \text{A}\Diamond(\text{Happens } (\text{M-Bel } g \ (\text{Does } \alpha))?; \alpha) \ \psi \ pre_{JPG} \ c_{JPG})$$

Thus a joint intention in g to do α means having a joint commitment that eventually g will believe α will happen next, and then α happens next. An individual intention by agent i to do α with motivation ψ is a special case of joint intention.

$$(\text{Intend } i \ \alpha \ \psi) \stackrel{\text{def}}{=} \forall g \cdot (\text{Singleton } g \ i) \Rightarrow (\text{J-Intend } g \ \alpha \ \psi)$$

4 The Cooperative Problem Solving Process

In this section, we present a four-stage model of CPS, which we formalise by expressing it in the logic described in §2. The four stages of the model are:

1. Recognition: The CPS process begins when some agent recognises the potential for cooperative action; this recognition may come about because an agent has a goal that it is unable to achieve in isolation, or, more generally, because the agent prefers assistance.
2. Team formation: During this stage, the agent that recognised the potential for cooperative action at stage (1) solicits assistance. If this stage is successful, then it will end with a group having a joint commitment to collective action.
3. Plan formation: During this stage, the agents attempt to negotiate a joint plan that they believe will achieve the desired goal.
4. Team action: During this stage, the newly agreed plan of joint action is executed by the agents, which maintain a close-knit relationship throughout; this relationship is defined by an agreed social convention, which every agent follows.

Although we believe that most instances of CPS exhibit these stages in some form, we stress that the model is *idealised*. We recognise that there are cases which the model cannot account for, and we highlight these wherever appropriate. Our aim has been to construct a framework that describes CPS from beginning to end, but is *abstract* (in that details which might obscure more significant points have been omitted). (We once again stress that although space restrictions mean that we cannot completely define the logic used to represent the model here, a complete definition *is* presented in [17].)

4.1 Recognition

CPS begins when some agent in a multi-agent community has a goal, and recognises the potential for cooperative action with respect to that goal. Recognition may occur for several reasons:

- The paradigm case is that in which the agent is unable to achieve its goal in isolation, due to a lack of resources, but believes that cooperative action can achieve it. For example, an agent may have a goal that, to achieve, requires information only accessible to another agent; without the cooperation of this other agent, the goal cannot be achieved.
- Alternatively, an agent may have the resources to achieve the goal, but does not want to use them. There may be several reasons for this: it may believe that in working alone on this particular problem, it will clobber one of its other goals, or it may believe that a cooperative solution will in some way be better (e.g., derived faster, more accurate).

In order to more precisely define the conditions that characterise the potential for cooperative action, it is necessary to introduce a number of subsidiary definitions. First, we require definitions of single- and multi-agent *ability*: what it means to be able to bring about some state of the world. Several attempts to define multi-agent ability have appeared in the literature (e.g., [14]). However, there is currently no consensus on the appropriateness of these definitions. For this reason, we adapt the well-known model of ability proposed by Moore [12].

> **Definition: (Single-agent ability)** Agent i can achieve φ iff there is some possibly complex action α of which i is the sole agent, such that either: (i) i knows that after it performed α, φ would be satisfied; or (ii) i knows that after it performed α, it could achieve φ.

Clause (i) is the base case, where an agent knows the identity of an action that will achieve the goal φ directly. Clause (ii) allows for the possibility of an agent performing an action in order to find out how to achieve φ. This recursive definition is easily generalised to the multi-agent case.

> **Definition: (Multi-agent ability)** Group g can achieve φ iff there is some possibly complex action α and some group g', such that it is mutually known in g that $g' \subseteq g$, and g' are the agents of α, and it is mutually known in g that either (i) after α was performed, φ would be satisfied; or (ii) after α was performed, g would have the multi-agent ability to achieve φ.

Once again, clause (i) represents the base case, where the group is mutually aware of the identity of some action that could be performed by some subset of the group (whose identity must also be known), such that performing the action would achieve the goal directly. Clause (ii) is the recursive case, where the group is required to know the identity of some action and subset of agents such that performing the action would bring them closer to the goal.

A more precise definition of potential for cooperation can now be given.

> **Definition: (Potential for cooperation)** With respect to agent i's goal φ, there is potential for cooperation iff: (i) there is some group g such that i believes that g can jointly achieve φ; and either (ii) i can't achieve φ in isolation; or (iii) i believes that for every action α that it could perform which achieves φ, it has a goal of not performing α.

Note that in clause (i), an agent needs to know the identity of a group that it believes can cooperate to achieve its goal. This is an overstrong assumption. It precludes an agent attempting to find out the identity of a group that can achieve the goal, and it does not allow an agent to simply broadcast its goal in the hope of attracting help (as in the CNET [15]). However, catering for these cases would complicate the formalisation a good deal, and obscure some more important points. We therefore leave such refinements to future work.

The ideas introduced above are readily expressed using the language we described in §2. First, we write (Can i φ) iff i can achieve φ in isolation.

$$(\text{Can } i \ \varphi) \stackrel{\text{def}}{=} \exists \alpha \cdot (\text{Know } i \ (\text{Agt } \alpha \ i) \wedge (\text{Achieves } \alpha \ \varphi)) \quad \vee$$
$$\exists \alpha \cdot (\text{Know } i \ (\text{Agt } \alpha \ i) \wedge (\text{Achieves } \alpha \ (\text{Can } i \ \varphi)))$$

Multi-agent ability is a generalisation of single-agent ability.

$$(\text{J-Can } g \ \varphi) \stackrel{\text{def}}{=} \exists \alpha \cdot \exists g' \cdot (\text{M-Know } g \ (g' \subseteq g) \land (\text{Agts } \alpha \ g') \land (\text{Achieves } \alpha \ \varphi)) \quad \lor$$
$$\exists \alpha \cdot \exists g' \cdot (\text{M-Know } g \ (g' \subseteq g) \land (\text{Agts } \alpha \ g') \land (\text{Achieves } \alpha \ (\text{J-Can } g \ \varphi)))$$

We can now formally state the conditions that characterise the potential for cooperation.

$$(\text{PfC } i \ \varphi) \stackrel{\text{def}}{=} (\text{Goal } i \ \varphi) \land \exists g \cdot (\text{Bel } i \ (\text{J-Can } g \ \varphi)) \land$$
$$\left[\begin{array}{l} \neg(\text{Can } i \ \varphi) \ \lor \\ (\text{Bel } i \ \forall \alpha \cdot (\text{Agt } \alpha \ i) \land (\text{Achieves } \alpha \ \varphi) \Rightarrow (\text{Goal } i \ (\text{Doesn't } \alpha))) \end{array} \right]$$

4.2   Team Formation

Having identified the potential for cooperative action with respect to one of its goals, a rational agent will solicit assistance from some group of agents that it believes can achieve the goal. If the agent is successful, then at the conclusion of this *team formation* stage, the agent will have brought about a mental state wherein the group has a joint commitment to collective action. (There will not yet be a joint intention to act; this comes later.) An agent cannot guarantee that it will be successful in forming a team; it can only *attempt* it. We adapt the model of attempts developed by Cohen-Levesque [4, p240].

> **Definition: (Attempts)** An attempt by agent i to bring about a state φ is an action α performed by i with the goal that after α is performed, φ is satisfied, or at least ψ is satisfied.

The ultimate goal of the attempt — the thing that i hopes to bring about — is represented by φ, whereas ψ represents 'what it takes to make an honest effort' [4, p240]. If i is successful, then bringing about ψ will be sufficient to cause φ.

The team formation stage can then be characterised as an assumption made about rational agents: namely, that an agent which recognises the potential for cooperative action will solicit assistance.

> **Assumption: (Team formation)** An agent i, who believes that there is potential for cooperative action with respect to its goal φ, will eventually attempt to bring about in some group g, (that it believes can jointly achieve φ), a state wherein: (i) it is mutually believed in g that g can jointly achieve φ, and g are jointly committed to team action with respect to i's goal φ; or, failing that, to at least cause in g (ii) the mutual belief that i has a goal of φ and the mutual belief that i believes g can jointly achieve φ.

Part (i) represents the commitment that the group has towards i's goal φ if i is successful in its attempt to solicit assistance; we discuss what team action means in §4.4. Note that an agent might have its own reasons for agreeing to participate in a cooperative action, that are unconnected with the request by the agent that recognises the potential for cooperation. However, we have not attempted to deal with such cases here.

The team formation assumption implicitly states that agents are veracious with respect to their goals, i.e., that they will try to influence the group by revealing their true goal. We do not consider cases where agents are mendacious (i.e., they lie about their goals), or when agents do not reveal their goals. (We refer the interested reader to [7, pp159–165] for a discussion and formalisation of these considerations.)

We write {Attempt i α φ ψ} for an attempt by i to achieve φ by performing α, at least achieving ψ. Following Cohen-Levesque, we use curly brackets to indicate that attempts are complex actions, not predicates [4, p240].

$$\{\text{Attempt } i\ \alpha\ \varphi\ \psi\} \overset{\text{def}}{=} \begin{bmatrix} (\text{Bel } i\ \neg\varphi) \wedge (\text{Agt } \alpha\ i) \wedge \\ (\text{Goal } i\ (\text{Achieves } \alpha\ \varphi)) \wedge \\ (\text{Intend } i\ (\text{Does } \alpha;\ \psi?)) \end{bmatrix} ?;\ \alpha$$

We introduce an abbreviation to simplify subsequent formalisation: (Pre-Team g φ i) means that (i) g mutually believe that they can jointly achieve φ; and (ii) g are jointly committed to becoming a team with respect to i's goal φ.

$$(\text{Pre-Team } g\ \varphi\ i) \overset{\text{def}}{=} (\text{M-Bel } g\ (\text{J-Can } g\ \varphi)) \wedge$$
$$(\text{J-Commit } g\ (\text{Team } g\ \varphi\ i)\ (\text{Goal } i\ \varphi)\ pre_{JPG}\ c_{JPG})$$

(Team is defined in §4.4.) The main assumption concerning team formation can now be stated.

Assumption 1 $\models \forall i \cdot (\text{Bel } i\ (\text{PfC } i\ \varphi)) \Rightarrow \text{A}\Diamond\exists g \cdot \exists \alpha \cdot (\text{Happens } \{\text{Attempt } i\ \alpha\ p\ q\})$
where

$$p \overset{\text{def}}{=} (\text{Pre-Team } g\ \varphi\ i)$$
$$q \overset{\text{def}}{=} (\text{M-Bel } g\ (\text{Goal } i\ \varphi) \wedge (\text{Bel } i\ (\text{J-Can } g\ \varphi))).$$

If team formation is successful then for the first time there will be a social mental state relating to i's goal, which contrasts with i's individual perspective that has guided the process until this stage.

4.3 Plan Formation

If an agent is successful in its attempt to solicit assistance, then there will be a group of agents with a joint commitment to collective action. But collective action cannot begin until the group agree on what they will actually do. Hence the next stage in the CPS process: plan formation.

We saw above that a group will not form a collective unless they believe they can actually achieve the desired goal. This, in turn, implies that there is at least one action that is known to the group that will take them 'closer' to the goal (see the definition of J-Can, above). However, it is possible that there are many agents that know of actions the group can perform in order to take the collective closer to, or even achieve the goal. Moreover, some members of the collective may have objections to one or more of these actions. For example, an agent may believe that a particular action has hitherto unforeseen and damaging consequences. It is therefore necessary for the collective to come to some agreement about exactly which course of action they will follow. *Negotiation* is the mechanism via which such agreement is reached.

Negotiation usually involves agents making reasoned arguments for and against courses of action; making proposals and counter proposals; suggesting modifications or amendments to plans; and continuing in this way until all the negotiators have reached agreement[2]. Negotiation has long been recognised as a process of some importance for DAI (see, e.g., [16]). Unfortunately, analyses of negotiation demonstrate that it is also extremely complex — a rigorous attempt at formalisation is quite beyond the scope of this paper[3]. Instead, we simply offer some observations about the weakest conditions under which negotiation can be said to have occurred.

What can we say about negotiating a plan? First, we note that negotiation may *fail*: the collective may simply be unable to reach agreement, due to some irreconcilable differences. In this case, the minimum condition required for us to be able to say that negotiation occurred at all is that *at least one* agent proposed a course of action that it believed would take the collective closer to the goal. However, negotiation may also succeed. In this case, we expect a team action stage to follow — we shall say no more about team action here, as this is the subject of the next section.

We can make a number of other tentative assumptions about the behaviour of agents during negotiation. Most importantly, we might assume that they will *attempt to bring about their preferences*. For example, if an agent has an objection to some plan, then it will attempt to prevent this plan being carried out. Similarly, if it has a preference for some plan, then it will attempt to bring this plan about.

We shall now make the above discussion more precise. First, we define *joint attempts*: what it means for a group of agents to collectively attempt something. As might be expected, joint attempts are a generalisation of single-agent attempts.

> **Definition: (Joint attempts)** An attempt by a group of agents g to bring about a state φ is an action α, of which g are the agents, performed with the mutual goal that after α is performed, φ is satisfied, or at least ψ is satisfied (where ψ represents what it takes to make a reasonable effort).

Next, we state the minimum conditions required for negotiation to have occurred.

> **Assumption: (Negotiation)** If group g are a pre-team with respect to agent i's goal φ, then g will eventually jointly attempt to bring about a state where it is mutually known in g that g are a team with respect to i's goal φ, or, failing that, to at least bring about a state where some agent $j \in g$ has made g mutually aware of its belief that some action α can be performed by g in order to achieve φ.

In other words, the group will try to bring about a state where they have agreed on a common plan, and intend to act on it. Failing that, they will bring about a state where

---

[2] It may also involve agents lying, or being cunning and devious, though we shall not consider such cases here.

[3] But see [9] for preliminary work on logical models of argumentation.

at least one of them has proposed a plan that it believed would achieve the desired goal. The other, more tentative assumptions about agent behaviour during negotiation are as follows.

> **Assumption: (Making preferences known)** If group g are a pre-team with respect to agent i's goal φ, and there is some action α such that it is mutually believed in g that α achieves φ, and that g are the agents of α, then every agent $j \in g$ that has a preference that α does/does not occur will attempt to ensure that α does/does not occur, by at least making g mutually aware of its preference for/against α.

We are once again assuming that agents are veracious, in that they attempt to influence the team by revealing their true preferences, rather than by lying, or concealing their true preferences.

We begin by formalising joint attempts.

$$\{\text{J-Attempt } g \ \alpha \ \varphi \ \psi\} \stackrel{\text{def}}{=} \left[\begin{array}{l} (\text{M-Bel } g \ \neg\varphi) \land (\text{Agts } \alpha \ g) \land \\ (\text{M-Goal } g \ (\text{Achieves } \alpha \ \varphi)) \land \\ (\text{J-Intend } g \ (\text{Does } \alpha; \psi?)) \end{array} \right] ?; \alpha$$

The main assumption characterising negotiation can now be given. (Team is defined below.)

Assumption 2 $\models (\text{Pre-Team } g \ \varphi \ i) \Rightarrow A\Diamond\exists\alpha \cdot (\text{Happens } \{\text{J-Attempt } g \ \alpha \ p \ q\})$ *where*

$p \stackrel{\text{def}}{=} (\text{M-Know } g \ (\text{Team } g \ \varphi \ i))$

$q \stackrel{\text{def}}{=} \exists j \cdot \exists \alpha \cdot (j \in g) \land (\text{M-Bel } g \ (\text{Bel } j \ (\text{Agts } \alpha \ g) \land (\text{Achieves } \alpha \ \varphi))).$

To formalise the assumption that members make their preferences known, we need to capture the notion of an agent trying to cause and trying to prevent a group performing an action.

$(\text{Try-to-cause } i \ g \ \alpha) \stackrel{\text{def}}{=}$
$\exists\alpha' \cdot A(\text{Happens } \{\text{Attempt } i \ \alpha' \ (\text{Does } \alpha) \ (\text{M-Bel } g \ (\text{Goal } i \ (\text{Does } \alpha)))\})$

The definition of $(\text{Try-to-prevent } i \ g \ \alpha)$ is similar to Try-to-cause, and is therefore omitted.

Assumption 3 *Agents who have a preference for some action make the team mutually aware of their preference:*

$\models \forall g \cdot \forall i \cdot \forall \alpha \cdot (\text{Pre-Team } g \ \varphi \ i) \land (\text{M-Bel } g \ (\text{Agts } \alpha \ g) \land (\text{Achieves } \alpha \ \varphi)) \Rightarrow$
$[\forall j \cdot (j \in g) \land (\text{Goal } j \ (\text{Does } \alpha)) \Rightarrow (\text{Try-to-cause } j \ g \ \alpha)].$

Agents who prefer some action not to be performed make the team mutually aware of their preference:

$\models \forall g \cdot \forall i \cdot \forall \alpha \cdot (\text{Pre-Team } g \ \varphi \ i) \land (\text{M-Bel } g \ (\text{Agts } \alpha \ g) \land (\text{Achieves } \alpha \ \varphi)) \Rightarrow$
$[\forall j \cdot (j \in g) \Rightarrow (\text{Goal } j \ (\text{Doesn't } \alpha)) \Rightarrow (\text{Try-to-prevent } j \ g \ \alpha)].$

If plan formation is successful then the team will have a joint commitment to the goal, and will have agreed to the means by which they will pursue this goal. Ideally, we would like to specify that the group also negotiate a convention for monitoring team action. Unfortunately, we have no direct way of representing such behaviour: it would require quantification over formulae of the language, and such a meta-level notion cannot be represented at the object level in a normal modal language such as that used here (see §5).

4.4 Team Action

If a collective is successful in its attempt to negotiate a plan, then we expect that collective to follow up negotiation with action. This gives us the fourth, and final stage in our model: team action. For this stage, we simply require that the team jointly intend some appropriate action.

> **Definition: (Team action)** A group g are considered a team with respect to i's goal φ iff there is some action α, such that: (i) α achieves φ; and (ii) g have a joint intention of α, relative to i having a goal of φ.

The formalisation of Team is simple.

$$(\text{Team } g \ \varphi \ i) \stackrel{\text{def}}{=} \exists \alpha \cdot (\text{Achieves } \alpha \ \varphi) \wedge (\text{J-Intend } g \ \alpha \ (\text{Goal } i \ \varphi))$$

From the definition of J-Intend, we know that the group will remain committed to mutually believing they are about to perform the action, and then performing it. Moreover, if ever one of them comes to believe, for example, that i no longer has a goal of φ, then the social convention dictates that the agent will make the team aware of this, and team action will end.

5 Concluding Remarks

In this paper, we have presented an abstract formal model of cooperative problem solving, which describes all aspects of the process, from recognition of the potential for cooperation through to team action. This model considers a number of issues that have hitherto been neglected by DAI theorists. For example, it defines the conditions under which there is potential for cooperative action, and shows how an agent's individual mental state can lead it to attempt to build a social mental state in a group. The model has a number of other properties, which we shall briefly discuss in this section.

Although we have not explicitly considered communication, our model is nevertheless consistent with one of the best current theories of *speech acts*: in [4], Cohen-Levesque proposed a theory in which illocutionary acts are treated as *attempts* to bring about some mental state in a conversation participant. At a number of points, our model predicts precisely such attempts; for example, the model predicts that an agent which recognises the potential for cooperation will attempt to bring about a joint commitment to collective action in some group that it believes can achieve its goal.

Another interesting property is that the model consists of a set of *liveness* properties [11]. This is consistent with the view of agents as *intelligent reactive systems*, responding in a *reasoned* way to their goals, and events that occur in their environment.

The model also predicts that agents will attempt to initiate social interaction if they have goals that are dependent on other community members. In order to do this, the agents must have some knowledge about the abilities, skills, and interests of their acquaintances.

Finally, the model predicts that once a group of agents are formed into a collective, they will attempt to negotiate a plan that they believe will achieve the desired objective. Moreover, they will make their preferences known with respect to such plans, and are not required simply to accept another agent's proposals; they are thus autonomous, rather than benevolent.

There are a number of issues that we intend to address in future work, the most obvious of which is the need for refinement of the model, as highlighted in the main text. Additionally, there are a number of ways in which the language we have used for representing the model needs to be extended. The two most significant points are the need to quantify over complex action expressions, and the need to be able to represent meta-level notions at the object level.

References

1. A. H. Bond and L. Gasser, editors. *Readings in Distributed Artificial Intelligence*. Morgan Kaufmann Publishers: San Mateo, CA, 1988.
2. M. E. Bratman. *Intentions, Plans, and Practical Reason*. Harvard University Press: Cambridge, MA, 1987.
3. P. R. Cohen and H. J. Levesque. Intention is choice with commitment. *Artificial Intelligence*, 42:213–261, 1990.
4. P. R. Cohen and H. J. Levesque. Rational interaction as the basis for communication. In P. R. Cohen, J. Morgan, and M. E. Pollack, editors, *Intentions in Communication*, pages 221–256. The MIT Press: Cambridge, MA, 1990.
5. E. H. Durfee. *Coordination of Distributed Problem Solvers*. Kluwer Academic Publishers: Boston, MA, 1988.
6. E. A. Emerson and J. Y. Halpern. 'Sometimes' and 'not never' revisited: on branching time versus linear time temporal logic. *Journal of the ACM*, 33(1):151–178, 1986.
7. J. R. Galliers. *A Theoretical Framework for Computer Models of Cooperative Dialogue, Acknowledging Multi-Agent Conflict*. PhD thesis, Open University, UK, 1988.
8. N. R. Jennings. Commitments and conventions: The foundation of coordination in multi-agent systems. *Knowledge Engineering Review*, 8(3):223–250, 1993.
9. S. Kraus, M. Nirke, and K. Sycara. Reaching agreements through argumentation: A logical model. In *Proceedings of the Twelfth International Workshop on Distributed Artificial Intelligence (IWDAI-93)*, pages 233–247, Hidden Valley, PA, May 1993.
10. H. J. Levesque, P. R. Cohen, and J. H. T. Nunes. On acting together. In *Proceedings of the Eighth National Conference on Artificial Intelligence (AAAI-90)*, pages 94–99, Boston, MA, 1990.
11. Z. Manna and A. Pnueli. *The Temporal Logic of Reactive and Concurrent Systems*. Springer-Verlag: Heidelberg, Germany, 1992.

12. R. C. Moore. A formal theory of knowledge and action. In J. F. Allen, J. Hendler, and A. Tate, editors, *Readings in Planning*, pages 480–519. Morgan Kaufmann Publishers: San Mateo, CA, 1990.

13. A. S. Rao and M. P. Georgeff. Social plans: Preliminary report. In E. Werner and Y. Demazeau, editors, *Decentralized AI 3 — Proceedings of the Third European Workshop on Modelling Autonomous Agents and Multi-Agent Worlds (MAAMAW-91)*, pages 57–76. Elsevier Science Publishers B.V.: Amsterdam, The Netherlands, 1992.

14. M. P. Singh. Group ability and structure. In Y. Demazeau and J.-P. Müller, editors, *Decentralized AI 2 — Proceedings of the Second European Workshop on Modelling Autonomous Agents and Multi-Agent Worlds (MAAMAW-90)*, pages 127–146. Elsevier Science Publishers B.V.: Amsterdam, The Netherlands, 1991.

15. R. G. Smith. *A Framework for Distributed Problem Solving*. UMI Research Press, 1980.

16. K. P. Sycara. Multiagent compromise via negotiation. In L. Gasser and M. Huhns, editors, *Distributed Artificial Intelligence Volume II*, pages 119–138. Pitman Publishing: London and Morgan Kaufmann: San Mateo, CA, 1989.

17. M. Wooldridge. Coherent social action. In *Proceedings of the Eleventh European Conference on Artificial Intelligence (ECAI-94)*, pages 279–283, Amsterdam, The Netherlands, 1994.

A Tool for Handling Uncertain Information in Multi-Agent Systems[1]

Love Ekenberg   **Mats Danielson**   **Magnus Boman**

Department of Computer and Systems Sciences
Royal Institute of Technology and
Stockholm University
Electrum 230
S-164 40 KISTA
SWEDEN

Abstract

We focus on the strategy problem arising as a manager faces situations involving a choice between a finite set of strategies, having access to a finite set of agents reporting their opinions. The most preferred strategy is determined from the agents' individual opinions and the relative credibility of each agent. The evaluation method used is primarily based on the principle of maximising the expected utility. The evaluation results in a set of admissible strategies. These strategies can be further investigated with respect to their relative strengths and also with respect to the number of values consistent with the given domain that make them admissible.

1. Introduction

The study of implementable rational agents is pivotal to multi-agent systems [Bachman 1991]. Interdisciplinary studies in decision theory and multi-agent systems go back at least 15 years (see, e.g., [Tenney 1981]). We focus on the strategy problem arising as a manager faces situations involving a choice between a finite set of strategies, having access to a finite set of agents reporting their opinions. The manager is set on choosing the most preferred strategy given the agents' individual opinions and the relative credibility of the opinion of each agent. Our method has been developed for human managers, but the ideas and results described below may be used for other intelligent agents. It is highly applicable to simpler forms of co-operation, such as deductive co-operative multidatabase systems, as shown in [Boman 1993]. Moreover, parts of the method have been used as the core of an inductive tool for query answering in federated information systems more efficient [Boman 1994].

To overcome the difficulties associated with providing adequate information underlying deliberations, different approaches to relax the pointwise quantitative nature of estimates have been suggested. For instance, in [Choquet 1953/54], [Dempster 1967], [Good 1962], and [Smith 1961] mathematically sound bases for the integration of

---

[1] An earlier version of this paper can be found in the proceedings of the Scandinavian Research Seminar on Information and Decision Networks, April 1994, University College of Växjö, Sweden.

probability intervals with classical probability theory have been developed. They can also be used for the representation of problems of the kind treated in this paper. Of particular concern here is not only representation, but also how problems modelled with numerically imprecise information can be evaluated. In addition to using interval statements, we use inequality statements to express comparisons between different kinds of statements, a feature lacking in the above mentioned approaches.

Consequently, the method we propose does not encourage the agents to present statements with an unrealistic degree of precision, but rather sentences like "The strategy S_{13} is desirable", "The utility of strategy S_{13} is greater than 0.5", or "The utility of strategy S_{13} is within the interval from 0.6 to 0.8". It is important to realise that the agents do not have to quantify their opinions at all. It is often sufficient to merely order them to produce a conclusive result.

The treatment of credibilities is quite similar. The manager is asked to rank the credibility of the different agents by quantifying them as in the case of opinions, or by (partially) ordering them. Hence, typical sentences are "The credibility of agent A_1 is greater than the credibility of agent A_2" or "The credibility of agent A_1 is between 0.5 and 0.8". The manager may also use default values for terms such as very credible, or define a full mapping of natural language terms into numerical values. The set of opinion and credibility statements constitutes an *information base*. Formally, an information base has the form of linear systems of equations. By procedures primarily based on the principle of maximising the expected utility, the information base can then be evaluated.

In the diagrams below, one possible output from such an evaluation is shown. Two strategies, Strategy 1 and Strategy 2, represented by different diagrams, are considered. The heights of the bars associated with each of the two strategies illustrate the proportion of the information base in which each strategy is *admissible*. The intuition behind this formal concept is that no other strategy is considered to be better in a certain part of the information base. The differences on the horizontal axes show the magnitude of the differences between the strategies considered. A strategy should have as tall bars as possible. In this case, Strategy 1 is thus inferior to Strategy 2.

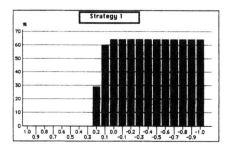 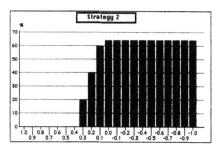

If, after the evaluation, it is still impossible to reach a conclusive result, the manager could be content with the fact that all the strategies are indistinguishable, given the information base. More likely, he would like to examine the strategies more thoroughly. It is then possible to restrict the set of admissible strategies by means of sensitivity analyses. With this kind of analysis the manager modifies the original information base in order to obtain a new one, hopefully with enough information for a definite choice.

The method is based on definitions originally proposed in [Malmnäs 1990] and [Malmnäs 1994], and further developed in [Ekenberg 1994a]. The algorithms behind the method have been implemented for different platforms [Danielson 1995].

2. Credibility Bases

A credibility base contains expressions about the credibility of each agent. To make the qualitative statements of credibility computable, we translate them into expressions of a certain form. Here, we will handle four types of possible credibility statements.

1. Agent A_i is credible, the opinion of agent A_i is worth considering, agent A_i is not credible, etc.
2. The credibility of A_i equals m, is more than m, is less than m.
3. The credibility of A_i lies between a_i and b_i.
4. The credibility of A_i is equal to the credibility of A_j, is approximately equal to the credibility of A_j, is more credible than A_j, etc.

The following interpretations are suggested for the above sentences. Each k_i below is a positive real number used for expressing the different statements above. Hence k_1 could be, e.g., 0.5, if we decide that for E to be credible, it must have a credibility of at least 0.5.

1.1 $(p_i \geq k_1, k_2 \geq p_i)$.
1.2 $(p_i \geq k_3, k_4 \geq p_i)$.
1.3 $(p_i \geq k_5, k_6 \geq p_i)$.
2.1 $p_i = m$.
2.2 $(p_i \geq m, k_7 \geq p_i)$.
2.3 $(m \geq p_i, p_i \geq k_8)$.
3.1 $(p_i \geq a_i, b_i \geq p_i)$.
4.1 $p_i = p_j$.
4.2 $p_j + k_9 \geq p_i, p_i + k_{10} \geq p_j$.
4.3 $p_i \geq p_j$.

We call the conjunction of expressions of the four types above, together with the equality $\Sigma p_j = 1$, the *credibility base* W(p). We will also refer to the expressions within parentheses as *intervals*.

3. Solution Sets and Regular Consistency

A list of numbers $[n_1,...,n_k]$ is a *solution vector* to a credibility base W(p) containing variables p_i, i = 1,...,k, if n_i can be consistently substituted for p_i in W(p). The set of solution vectors to a credibility base constitutes a *solution set*. This solution set is a convex polytope, i.e., an intersection of a finite number of closed half spaces. It seems a reasonable requirement that this polytope is not empty; it must be possible to consistently substitute numbers for the credibility variables. If a manager has generated a credibility base with an empty solution set, it seems very hard to understand the meaning of what he has actually expressed. (A number n satisfies an interval

($p_i \geq a_i$, $b_i \geq p_i$) iff n, substituted for p_i, simultaneously satisfies $p_i \geq a_i$ and $b_i \geq p_i$.)

Moreover, since the manager works with numerically imprecise information, it might be misleading only to check whether the credibility base is consistent. For example, when a manager has stated that the different credibilities are within quite large intervals, implying great ignorance, he would probably be dissatisfied if, in effect, his credibility base were only to be consistent with one solution vector. Therefore, the method also supports the possibility of checking if the base is consistent within certain regions, and not only for isolated solutions. Thus, the manager can require that there exists a minimal interval I_i for each interval in the credibility base with the following property: Let Y be the solution set to a credibility base W(p), let p_i be a credibility variable in W(p), let the ith position in the solution vectors correspond to this variable, and let J_i denote the interval expressed by the interval containing p_i. For every number $n_i \in I_i \subseteq J_i$, there must exist numbers $n_1,\ldots,n_{i-1},n_{i+1},\ldots,n_k$, such that $[n_1,\ldots,n_{i-1},n_i,n_{i+1},\ldots,n_k] \in Y$.

When a credibility base satisfies this condition for all p_i in W(p), it is said to be *regularly consistent*. If the manager is content with only satisfiability, he may relax this stronger requirement. The description of regular consistency can easily be implemented by a sequence of definitions.

Def: With each interval ($p_i \geq a_i$, $b_i \geq p_i$) in a credibility base W(p), a number in the interval [0,1] is associated. The list of these numbers is denoted by $[r_i]^{W(p)}$.

Def: Given a credibility base W(p) containing the intervals
($p_1 \geq a_1$, $b_1 \geq p_1$),..., ($p_n \geq a_n$, $b_n \geq p_n$), $\Delta(W(p))$ is the list $[s_1,\ldots,s_n]$, where $s_i = b_i - a_i$.

Def: Given a credibility base W(p) containing the intervals
($p_1 \geq a_1$, $b_1 \geq p_1$),..., ($p_n \geq a_n$, $b_n \geq p_n$), $\Delta(W(p)) \geq [r_i]^{W(p)}$
means that for each s_i in $\Delta(W(p))$ and r_i in $[r_i]^{W(p)}$, $s_i \geq r_i$.

In the definition below, we use the set union operation to denote list concatenation, and the set difference operation to denote deletion of elements in a list.

Def: Given a credibility base X, containing a list Z of all intervals
$[(p_1 \geq a_1$, $b_1 \geq p_1$),..., ($p_n \geq a_n$, $b_n \geq p_n$)] in X, $\Omega(X)$ is generated by the following procedure.

    a. Let $X_0 = X$, and $Z_0 = Z$.

    b. For all intervals ($p_i \geq a_i$, $b_i \geq p_i$) in the list Z of intervals in X: Substitute the interval ($p_i \geq \inf(\{n_i : n_i$ is at the ith position in a solution vector to $X_{i-1}\})$, $\sup(\{n_i: n_i$ is at the ith position in a solution vector to $X_{i-1}\}) \geq p_i$) for the interval ($p_i \geq a_i$, $b_i \geq p_i$) in the list Z_{i-1}, and call the result Z_i. Let $X_i = (X_{i-1} - Z_{i-1}) \cup Z_i$.

    c. Let $\Omega(X) = X_n$.

Informally, $\Omega(X)$ is like X, but contains the (in some sense) maximal intervals, where each value in the intervals is a solution relative to X. This definition has a computational meaning, since the intervals are determined when supremum and infimum are determined. That it is sufficient to compute supremum and infimum follows from two standard convexity observations:

(i) If Γ is a convex set, and $f(x)$ is a convex function on Γ, then the set
$\{x \in \Gamma : f(x) \geq c\}$ is convex for any c;
(ii) The intersection of two convex sets is also a convex set.

Now it is easy to determine if the interval represented by $\Omega(W(p))$ is greater than the numbers in $[r_i]^{W(p)}$, and the concept of regular consistency can be defined.

Def: $W(p)$ is regularly consistent given $\{R_i\}^{W(p)}$ iff $\Delta(\Omega(W(p))) \geq \{R_i\}^{W(p)}$.

Every new expression in the credibility base can be checked for regular consistency. If an earlier regularly consistent credibility base becomes inconsistent by adding a new interval $(p_i \geq a_i, b_i \geq p_i)$, the above algorithms are easily modified to give the agent information of the adequate estimation by calculating the extremes of the maximal admissible interval of p_i for regular consistency.

4. Strategy Bases

The strategy base contains expressions about individual agents' opinions of the utilities of different strategies. Hence, it consists of a number of expressions that express various strategy estimates. To make an agent's qualitative statements of strategies tractable we, as in the case of credibility statements, translate them into quantitative expressions. We will handle five types of possible strategy statements.

1. The strategy E_i is desirable, E_i is better than the worst (possible) outcome, E_i is undesirable, etc.
2. The utility of the strategy E_i equals m, is greater than m.
3. The utility of strategy E_i lies between a_i and b_i.
4. The strategy E_i is as desirable (or undesirable) as strategy E_j, more desirable than E_j, the utility of E_i is approximately equal to the utility of E_j.
5. The difference in utility between E_i and E_j is greater than the difference in utility between E_k and E_m. (For simplicity, we assume that the utility of E_i is greater than the utility of E_j, and that the utility of E_k is greater than the utility of E_m.)

Expressions of type 1 and 4 are qualitative, and they have to be transformed into quantitative expressions.

The following interpretations are suggested for the sentences in 1 to 5:

1.1 $(s_i \geq k_1, k_2 \geq s_i)$.
1.2 $(s_i \geq k_3, k_4 \geq s_i)$.
1.3 $(s_i \geq k_5, k_6 \geq s_i)$.
2.1 $s_i = m$.
2.2 $(s_i \geq m, k_7 \geq s_i)$.
3.1 $(s_i \geq a_i, b_i \geq s_i)$.
4.1 $s_i = s_j$.
4.2 $s_i \geq s_j$.
4.3 $s_j + k_8 \geq s_i, s_i + k_9 \geq s_j$.
5.1 $s_i + s_m \geq s_j + s_k$.

The system $\Omega(G(s))$ is a linear system of equations in the strategy variables, constructed from $G(s)$ by a procedure similar to the construction of $\Omega(W(p))$. (Note that the treatment of the credibility and strategy bases are similar. However, given that the strategy S is the disjunction $s_i \lor s_j$, then $\min(s_i,s_j) \leq s \leq \max(s_i,s_j)$ is also added if $i \neq j$.)

Def: G(s) is regularly consistent given $\{R_i\}^{G(s)}$ iff $\Delta(\Omega(G(s))) \geq \{R_i\}^{G(s)}$.

5. Information Bases

We can now formalise the concept of an information base.

Def: An *information base representing k agents and m strategies* is a structure $(W(p), [r_i]^{W(p)}, G(s), [r_i]^{G(s)})$. $W(p)$ is a credibility base with expressions in credibility variables $\{p_1,...,p_k\}$, expressing the relative credibility of the different agents. $G(s)$ is a strategy base with expressions in strategy variables $\{s^1_1,...,s^1_k,...,s^m_1,...,s^m_k\}$ expressing the utility of the strategies according to the different agents. s^i_j denotes agent j's opinion of strategy i. It is assumed that the variables' respective ranges are real numbers in the interval $[0,1]$. $[r_i]^{W(p)}$ and $[r_i]^{G(s)}$ are lists of real numbers in the interval $[0,1]$.

6. Comparing Strategies

Relative to a particular information base, which strategy should be chosen? To be able to answer that question, we introduce the concept of t-admissibility. The concept of a t-admissible strategy is crucial in understanding the central parts of the evaluative phase. The following definitions are adapted to our concept of information base derived from the definitions in [Malmnäs 1994] and [Ekenberg 1994a], and make use of the utility principle for evaluating the strategies.

Def: Let the decision situation involve the credibility $p_1,...,p_t$, and let s^i_j denote agent j's opinion of strategy i, then $E(S_i) = p_1 s^i_1 +...+ p_k s^i_k$.

Def: Given a real number $t \in [-1,1]$, S_i is *at least as t-good as* S_j given $W(p) \cup G(s)$ iff $E(S_i) - E(S_j) - t \geq 0$ for all instances of the credibility and strategy variables that are solutions to $W(p) \cup G(s)$.

Def: Given a real number $t \in [-1,1]$, S_i is *t-better than* S_j given $W(p) \cup G(s)$ iff S_i is at least as t-good as S_j given $W(p) \cup G(s)$, and there exists at least one instance of the credibility and strategy variables that is a solution to $\{E(S_i) - E(S_j) - t > 0\} \cup W(p) \cup G(s)$.

Def: Given a real number $t \in [-1,1]$, S_i is a *t-admissible₁ strategy* given $W(p) \cup G(s)$ iff no other strategy is t-better given $W(p) \cup G(s)$.

The definition of a t-admissible strategy, with $t = 0$, conforms to the usual one in statistical decision theory [Lehmann 1959]. However, for computational reasons, we will state the definition of t-admissibility somewhat differently.

Def: S_i is a *t-admissible₂ strategy* given $W(p) \cup G(s)$ iff for each $j \neq i$:
  (i) there are instances of the credibility and strategy variables that constitute a solution to $\{E(S_i) - E(S_j) + t > 0\} \cup W(p) \cup G(s)$, or
  (ii) there is no instance of the credibility and strategy variables that constitutes a solution to $\{E(S_j) - E(S_i) - t > 0\} \cup W(p) \cup G(s)$.

Now we can see that S_i is a t-admissible₁ strategy given $W(p) \cup G(s)$ iff S_i is a t-admissible₂ strategy given $W(p) \cup G(s)$.

The definition of t-admissible$_2$ strategy seems reasonable, but we will make the concept of t-admissibility even stronger. As in the discussion about regular satisfiability for W(p) and G(s), we demand that in order to be t-admissible, there should not only be isolated solutions.

To simplify checks for satisfiability used in the definitions below, we use a theorem from [Malmnäs 1994]. (We assume an information base underlying the theorem and the definitions below.)

Theorem: Let $E(S_i) - E(S_j) + t > 0$ be a bilinear inequality in credibility and strategy variables in W(p) and G(s).

The system $A(p,s,t) = \{E(S_i) - E(S_j) + t > 0\} \cup W(p) \cup G(s)$ can be reduced to a disjunction of linear systems in the credibility variables, $L(i,j,t) = \{L_1,...,L_N\}$, with the following property: $A(p,s,t)$ has a solution iff $L(i,j,t)$ has a solution.

Def: The system $A(p,s,t) = \{E(S_i) - E(S_j) + t > 0\} \cup W(p) \cup G(s)$ is *regularly solvable given W(p) $\cup$ G(s)* iff $\Delta(\Omega(L_s \cup W(p))) \geq \{R_i\}^{W(p)}$ for some L_s in $\{L_1,...,L_N\}$.

Def: S_i *is a t-admissible$_3$ strategy given W(p) $\cup$ G(s)* iff for all j≠i, the systems $\{E(S_i) - E(S_j) + t > 0\} \cup W(p) \cup G(s)$ are regularly solvable given $W(p) \cup G(s)$.

Hence, we can determine if a strategy is t-admissible$_3$ by reducing $\{E(S_i) - E(S_j) + t > 0\} \cup W(p) \cup G(s)$ (i≠j) to linear systems in the credibility variables for every i, and apply ordinary linear programming algorithms.

The principle of maximising the expected utility is not always the most preferred decision rule. (Other criteria have been suggested in, e.g., [Wald 1950], [Hurwicz 1951], and [Savage 1951].) Thus, in many decision contexts, the manager may want, for example, to exclude particular strategies whose consequences are, in some way, too risky. This is the case even when the probabilities for disastrous events are extremely low. Thus, a reasonable requirement on a decision tool seems to be that it should provide the manager with the opportunity to take such criteria into account when evaluating the different strategies. This particular problem is treated in [Ekenberg 1994b].

7. The Concept of Proportion

This section shows how it can be determined which strategy is the best one when the set of t-admissible strategies contains more than one element.

Assume that the expression $E(S_i) - E(S_j) + t > 0$ is satisfied only near the boundaries of the credibility and strategy intervals. When confronting a real-life problem, the agents and the manager are encouraged to be deliberately imprecise. Thus, values close to the boundaries seem to be the least reliable ones. A problem with the definitions above is that the procedure for determining if a strategy is t-admissible$_3$ is very sensitive to the different interval boundaries in W(p) and G(s). The most immediate solution is to study in how large parts of G(s) and W(p) the expression $E(S_i) - E(S_j) + t > 0$ is satisfied. For example, a strategy could be admissible for 90 percent of the solution vectors to the strategy base, and for 80 percent of the solution vectors to the credibility base. This can be determined for example by a Monte Carlo method as suggested in [Malmnäs 1994]. However, this approach is very inefficient and regards boundary points as equally essential as points close to the middle of the different intervals.

As a complement to Monte Carlo methods, we suggest the use of the concept of *proportion*. The idea behind this concept is to investigate how much the different intervals can be decreased before the expression $E(S_i) - E(S_j) + t > 0$ ceases to be satisfied. By this procedure we can study the stability of a result by gaining a better understanding of how important the boundary points are for the result. The best way to understand the concept of proportion is to regard it as a negative measure. In many situations all strategies become t-admissible$_3$, for, e.g., t = 0.1, and it is then important to investigate when a strategy ceases to be t-admissible$_3$. The strategy that should be chosen given the information base could, for example, be the remaining one when the other strategies have ceased to be t-admissible$_3$. By integrating the concept of proportion with the procedures for handling admissibility above, a procedure that takes account of the amount of consistent instances of credibility and strategy variables where the strategies are admissible can be defined. A full account of the concept of proportion can be found in [Ekenberg 1994a].

The comparison between the strategies shows in how large a proportion the strategies are t-admissible$_3$, and we propose that a manager should choose the strategy that, for every t-value, has the largest proportion with respect to the information base under consideration, but, we should remember that the proportion is an approximation. Thus, it is natural to check how sensitive the different proportions are to changes in the information base. In many other methods, a manager performs a sensitivity analysis by varying the variables one at a time. This is unnecessarily restrictive since he can obtain more information on how the intervals affect the solution. For example, the manager can simultaneously vary one or more intervals to discover credibility or strategy variables that are especially critical.

8. Conclusion

We have described, using a series of definitions, the necessary concepts associated with the implementation of a tool for handling uncertain information in multi-agent systems. Our theoretical and empirical results show that, in spite of the high complexity of some of the sub-problems involved, such a tool can indeed be implemented and successfully used in real-life situations. The definition of a t-admissible$_3$ alternative above is strongly dependent on the principle of maximising the expected utility. This is not necessary, since the method can quite straightforwardly be adapted to other criteria as well. Moreover, the above ideas can readily be generalised to any kind of intelligent multi-agent system, since the method primarily functions as a tool for evaluation.

References

Bachman, M., and Hurley, S. (eds.): 1991, *Essays in the Foundations of Rational Decision*, Blackwells.

Boman, M.: 1993, A Logical Specification of Federated Information Systems, DSV Report 93-019-DSV, Ph.D. thesis, Department of Computer and Systems Sciences, Stockholm University.

Boman, M., and Ekenberg, L.: 1994, "Eliminating Paraconsistencies in 4-valued Cooperative Deductive Multidatabase Systems with Classical Negation", *Proceedings of Cooperating Knowledge Based Systems 1994*, Keele University Press, pp.161-176.

Choquet, G.: 1953/54, "Theory of Capacities", *Ann. Inst. Fourier* 5, pp.131-295.

Danielson, M.: 1995, Computing Best Choices Using Imprecise Information, Report 95-012-DSV, Ph.Lic. thesis, Department of Computer and Systems Sciences, Royal Institute of Technology, Stockholm.

Dempster, A.P.: 1967, "Upper and Lower Probabilities Induced by a Multivalued Mapping", *Annals of Mathematical Statistics*, XXXVIII, pp.325-339.

Ekenberg, L.: 1994a, Decision Support in Numerically Imprecise Domains, Ph.D. thesis, Report 94-003-DSV, Department of Computer and Systems Sciences, Stockholm University.

Ekenberg, L., and Malmnäs P-E.: 1994b, "Generalized Procedures for Handling Security Levels in Decision Situations", Research Report, Department of Computer and Systems Sciences, Stockholm University.

Good, I. J.: 1962, "Subjective Probability as the Measure of a Non-measurable Set", *Logic, Methodology, and the Philosophy of Science*, eds. Suppes, Nagel, Tarski, Stanford University Press, pp.319-329.

Hurwicz, L.: 1951, "Optimality Criteria for Decision Making under Ignorance", *Cowles Commission Discussion Paper* No. 370.

Lehmann, E.L.: 1959, *Testing Statistical Hypothesis,* John Wiley and Sons.

Malmnäs, P-E.: 1990, Real-Life Decisions, Expected Utility and Effective Computability, Research Report HSFR No. 677/87.

Malmnäs, P-E.: 1994, "Towards a Mechanization of Real Life Decisions", *Logic and Philosophy of Science in Uppsala,* eds. Prawitz and Westerståhl, Kluwer Academic Publishers, Dortrecht, pp.231-243.

Savage, L.: 1951, "The Theory of Statistical Decision", *Journal of the American Statistical Association* 46, pp.55-67.

Smith, C.A.B.: 1961, "Consistency in Statistical Inference and Decision", *Journal of the Royal Statistic Society*, Series B, XXIII, pp.1-25.

Tenney, R., and Sandell jr., N.: 1981, "Strategies for Distributed Decisionmaking", *IEEE Transactions on Systems, Man and Cybernetics 11* (8), pp.527-538.

Wald, A.: 1950, *Statistical Decision Functions,* John Wiley and Sons.

DA-SoC:
A Testbed for Modelling Distribution Automation Applications Using Agent-Oriented Programming

Staffan Hägg
Department of Computer Science
and Business Administration
University of Karlskrona/Ronneby
Ronneby, Sweden
Staffan.Hagg@ide.hk-r.se

Fredrik Ygge
Department for Research
and Development
ElektroSandberg/Sydkraft
Malmö, Sweden
Fredrik.Ygge@ide.hk-r.se

Rune Gustavsson
PhD, Professor
Swedish Institute of Computer Science
Kista, Sweden
Department of Computer Science
and Business Administration
University of Karlskrona/Ronneby
Ronneby, Sweden
rune@sics.se, rune@ide.hk-r.se

Hans Ottosson
Director
Distribution Systems
& Market Applications
Corporate Research & Development
Sydkraft
Malmö, Sweden

Abstract

As computing systems are being applied to ever more demanding and complex domains, the infeasibility of constructing a single, monolithic problem solver becomes more apparent. Furthermore, important applications such as different types of management control systems for power generation and distribution are inherently distributed. A promising novel research direction to overcome complexity barriers in the design and maintenance of complex distributed applications is based on the view of such systems as societies of cooperating agents.

In this paper we describe an agent oriented design for load management in an automated power distribution system and a testbed for implementations of such systems. We also present an agent with some novel and important features. The research reported here is a cooperation between the authors' affiliations mentioned above, and it is a part of the larger projects, Intelligent Distribution Automation (IDA) at Sydkraft, Sweden, and Societies of Computation (SoC) at the University of Karlskrona/Ronneby, Sweden.

1   Introduction

As computing systems are being applied to ever more demand-ing and complex domains, the infeasibility of constructing a single monolithic problem solver becomes more apparent. To combat this complexity barrier, system engineers are starting to investigate the possibility of using multiple, cooperating problem solvers in which both control and data are distributed. Each *agent* has its own problem solving competence; however, it needs to interact with others in order to solve problems which lie outside its domain of expertise, to avoid conflicts and to enhance its problem solving.

Important application domains, such as different types of man-agement control systems for telecommunication and power distribu-tion, are inherently distributed. As those systems become more and more integrated and provide new types of services, novel agent orient-ed architectures have become natural extensions of more traditional architectures for distributed systems.

In this paper we outline an agent oriented design for load man-agement in an automated power distribution system. The testbed ex-plores new technologies to meet future network operations and management requirements of Distribution Automation (DA).

1.1   The SoC Project

Societies of Computation is a research project at the University of Karlskrona/Ronneby in Sweden. The SoC provides a framework for assessments of agent-oriented architectures of tomorrow's distributed systems and the use of those systems in industrial applications. For more detail, see [Gustavsson94].

Research within the SoC framework is conducted in cooperation with the Swedish Institute of Computer Science (SICS), the Technical University of Lund, The University of Kalmar, and with the industrial partner Sydkraft. The Sydkraft Group consists of some 50 wholly or partly owned companies, most of which are active in the electricity sec-tor. The research reported in this paper is also supported by Blekinge Research Foundation, Ronneby SoftCenter, and Ronneby local govern-ment.

1.2   Outline of the Report

Chapter 2 of the report gives a background to the work at hand, and chapter 3 shows the principal architecture of the society of agents. In chapter 4 the testbed is described, and chapter 5 gives an example of how a DA application can be implemented on the testbed. The report ends with related work, conclusions, and an outline of future activi-ties. The agent language is given in the appendix.

2 Background

2.1 Distribution Automation

Power distribution grids are evolving very rapidly into multi service integrated networks. As such they are converging with public and private tele/data communication networks, both in transport mechanisms and in higher level inter-operability between networks. This will be necessary in the near future.

Power distribution is the distribution of electricity from the 50kV level to the end user (e.g. a household at 220V). DA is a very important issue for energy production and distribution companies of today. DA is commonly defined as follows: *Automation of all processes (both technical and administrative) at energy (gas, electricity, district heating) distribution companies' sites.*

There are at present a number of DA related projects world-wide. The Intelligent Distribution Automation (IDA) project at Sydkraft is one of them. IDA's main aim is to develop DA services, using distributed computers and data communication. Among the most interesting services in (future) power distribution automation, we identify:

- Remote meter reading
- Fault detection and location
- Grid restoration
- Minimizing of losses
- Load management
- Remote or automatic control of transformers, capacitor cells, etc. in order to achieve higher quality electricity

Besides these services supporting the distribution of electricity, there are similar services for gas, district heating, water, etc. The challenge is to design and maintain networks that can deliver sustained high quality services to the customer. In a future market this could be a matter of survival.

Services in DA are often related to large and geographically dispersed distribution grids. The efficient management of such grids requires well structured computer networks and a lot of automated, distributed control. As pointed out above, the main purpose of the DA-SoC is to achieve those goals by utilizing structured societies of agents.

In this report we will concentrate on one DA service: load management in static grids. This service has a suitable level of complexity for a first generation of the DA-SoC testbed.

The main purpose for the load management service is to reduce the amplitude of power peaks, in case of a production shortage, limitations due to bottlenecks in the grid, or when the customer wants to reduce his power peaks.

2.2   Why Multi-Agent Systems?

Efficient and flexible management of power distribution high-lights several advantages of an agent-oriented system approach, compared to more standard approaches for design of open distributed systems. The following list of features characterizes important aspects of a DA system.

- Complexity: The environment of hardware, controlling software, and functionality can be very complex, which requires powerful structuring tools.
- Heterogeneity: The underlying hardware and software components as well as the basic communication methods can be very heterogeneous, which requires powerful abstraction mechanisms.
- Dynamics: The DA system must be able to handle frequent changes in the environment, such as reconfigurations, load changes and faults, while maintaining system goals.
- Levels of distribution and abstraction: Power distribution is, physically, hierarchically organized and heavily distributed. The design and functionality of the DA system must be able to reflect this organization.
- Real-time properties: The DA system is a real-time system with different real-time demands for different operations and at different levels.

The SoC Multi-Agent System (MAS) approach of realizing a DA system offers a number of interesting properties addressing the issues above:

- It is inherently modular with distributed control.
- It supports evolutionary design.
- It has reasoning and abstraction mechanisms.
- It has a model of interaction, including a high level communication protocol, handling cooperation between heterogeneous agents.

The purpose of this report is to show how these properties of a MAS can be useful for the design of a DA system, and to describe how these ideas are realized in the testbed for modelling such systems.

2.3   Threads of Theoretical Background

The DA-SoC testbed is a project in the SoC framework. In SoC we pursue R&D in three parallel strands: theoretical foundations, generic technologies, and applications.

Theoretical foundations includes, as background, work done elsewhere. There is work on belief, desire, and intention from a philosophical perspective [Bratman90]. A formalization of an agent's rational behaviour in modal logic is given by [Cohen90]. An extension of those ideas to include the interaction between agents, especially in a real-time environment is given by [Rao92]. Furthermore, the proposal of Agent-Oriented Programming (AOP) [Shoham91, Shoham93] as a programming paradigm and AGENT0 as an agent language has influenced us when defining a language for reasoning, action and communication.

Another thread of theoretical background comes from the field of Distributed Systems. This includes synchronization, scheduling, and communication issues. But rather than trying to adapt distributed algorithms to a MAS, we identify two major problems with traditional approaches for distributed systems: the lack of an ability to reason about heterogeneity and change as such, and the difficulty in finding distributed algorithms that are both efficient and fault tolerant. For a good overview see e.g. [Coulouris88] or [Tanenbaum92]. Therefore, we view MAS and AOP as new vehicles for designing DA systems with distributed control.

3   Architecture of the DA-SoC

The general architecture of the DA-SoC is as follows:

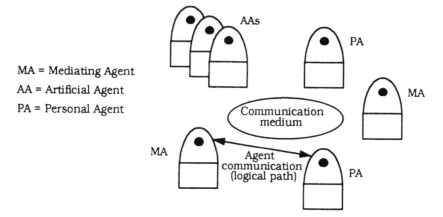

MA = Mediating Agent
AA = Artificial Agent
PA = Personal Agent

Figure 1   *A society of communicating agents*

Mediating agents maintain different services to other agents in the society, utilizing the resources on the communication medium at hand. Resources could be e.g. a database, a communication line, or an interface to a controlled industrial process. A personal agent is an intelligent user interface, and an artificial agent is the society's primary problem solver. The type of communication medium is not specified; the existence of a transport service (cf. OSI Transport Level) is assumed, upon which agent communication is built.

The agent head consists of three parts: a monitor for communication with the body and with other agents, an interpreter for the agent language, and an internal database. The database contains models of agents' object world (beliefs), a set of goals and plans to direct its actions, and a Model of Interaction (MoI).

The DA Agent Language (DAAL, see Appendix) consists of three types of constructs, control constructs, database manipulation constructs, and action constructs. Programming the agent head means first defining a MoI, which is built up of a set of Interaction Plans, expressed in DAAL. Then Agent Plans are programmed in DAAL, and finally the agent is given initial beliefs and goals. The ability in DA-SoC to actually program the MoI allows the designer to tailor agent interaction and coordination of joint activities.

The models of the body, of other agents, and the agent's mental state is declarative, using the BEL operator. BEL(ME time_t fact_f), where fact is on the form fact_id(parameter1 parameter2 ...), means that at time time_t this agent believes fact_f. If fact_f relates to the agent body, this belief is part of the body model; otherwise it is part of the mental state. If agent a holds BEL(b time_t fact_f), it means that this belief is part of a's model of b. In this case, the belief is in the database, due to a message from b, a message from another agent about b, or caused by some reasoning related to b.

Reasoning within the agent head is procedural and goal-driven. When the goal GOAL(a t fact) is set, it is entered into the goal queue, for effectuation at time t. It is then (at time t) matched with plan declarations in the plan library, and upon success, the matched plan is executed.

The ability to create models, to reason about them, and changing them, gives a tool for distributed decision-making with a minimal

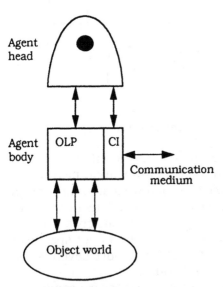

Agent head

Agent body — OLP | CI

Communication medium

Object world

Figure 2   An agent

The agent is divided into two parts (**Figure 2**), a head and a body. The agent body consists of an object level program (OLP), which can be any kind of traditional program, and a communication interface (CI).

For an MA, the OLP can be e.g. a database interface or a real-time control system. For a PA the OLP can be a graphical system, while an AA has a minimal body with only the CI. The CI is implementation dependent.

Head - body communication follows a well-defined connection oriented protocol.

dependency on communication. An agent has beliefs about the capabilities and states of other agents. These beliefs can be changed dynamically, without reconfiguration of the whole system; and at the time of a decision, it can be made without explicit communication. This is an important property, as the application is dependant on an unreliable communication network.

At this stage of the project (and the current status of the testbed), the model structure is quite simple, as described above, but it is possible to give the agents learning abilities, thereby emphasising the independency of agents. This is also one of the items for future activities in the project.

4   Testbed Description

4.1   General Concepts

The first implementation is an emulation of the agent society on a single IBM compatible PC, based on MS-DOS/Windows operating system. The Dynamic Data Exchange (DDE) communication mechanism is used for data transportation services.

When developing applications, the testbed allows the programmer to create agents, program them and enter them into the society of already executing agents. They can independently be stopped, modified and restarted.

4.2   Implementation

The testbed consists of two Windows applications:
- *Agent Manager* and
- *Agent Setup Program*

The Agent Manager is the overall controlling application, with features as listing all the agents in the society and logging all messages between agents. It is configured as a DDE-server.

Every agent has its own instance of the Agent Setup Program. With this program it is possible to set up the agents as desired. The configuration of an agent can include the following steps:
- Load a complete agent from disk or start with a new.
- Define a body for the agent.
- Add, delete or modify plans in the agent's head. Editing plans is done with standard Windows editors, allowing many to plans to be edited simultaneously, text to be cut and copied between plans etc. Plans can be saved to disk in a plan file, which is has a special file format, where several plans are saved in the same file. This allows the user to assemble related plans in some sort of libraries.
- Manually add or delete initial goals and beliefs.

- Define the maximum number of beliefs and goals, respectively, allowed in the agents head. This prevents running out of memory because of erroneous growing databases.
- Save parts of the agent to disk. When the agent is properly configured it can be started, stopped, modified and restarted, as mentioned above.

The Agent Setup Program allows the user to debug the agent by watching, manually adding or deleting the current goals and beliefs. They can also be logged in files. These features are available regardless of if the agents is stopped or running. The Agent Setup Program is configured as a DDE-client.

5   Load Management: A Sample DA Application

5.1   Problem Overview

As stated in Section 1.2 we will first address the load management problem in a static power grid.

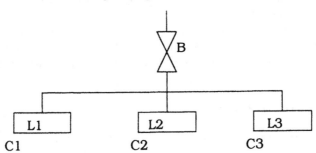

Figure 3   *A load management area*

Figure 3 illustrates a load management situation. In this particular example three customers, C1 - C3, have one controllable load each, L1 - L3, which are supplied with electricity through the bottleneck B. The loads might only be either fully connected or disconnected. There are primarily three situations when it would be desirable to disconnect one or more of the loads:

- Remote request: Shortage of power in the production or overload in the distribution grid at some level above B. The required power is larger than the power that can be delivered.
- Local control: Overload in the bottleneck B. The required power is larger than the constraint power in B.
- Customer control: The customer might want to avoid having too high a peak power.

The first one is a typical negotiation situation: the initiator of the load management operation is not prepared to disconnect loads in the load management area without considering the cost. A negotiation has to take place between the initiator and the controllers of the loads to find out which load is the most appropriate one to disconnect in the current situation, regarding the more or less complex contracts between the customers and the producer or distributor.

The second case is quite different. Here, one or more loads must be disconnected, even if it means a cost for the distributor. Otherwise, the overload might destroy the bottleneck, e.g. a transformer, which would lead to power failure for all loads. Thus, it is only a question of which load(s) to disconnect.

The third situation is similar to the first one. Here, the customer, or the agent representing him, has to decide whether to disconnect the load or pay charges to the producer or distributor.

5.2   Problem Solving Methods

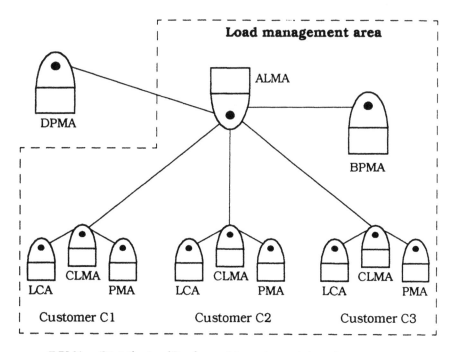

DPMA = Distributor/Producer Management Agent
ALMA = Area Load Management Agent
BPMA = Bottleneck Power Measurement Agent
CLMA = Customer Load Management Agent
LCA = Load Control Agent
PMA = Power Measurement Agent

Figure 4   *Logical relations*

A DA-SoC architecture corresponding to **Figure 3** is given in **Figure 4**. Case one above (remote request) is represented as a request from the DPMA. In the logical relations perspective, case two (local control) appears when the BPMA indicates that the power consumption in the load management area is too high. Finally, case three is represented as an indication from a PMA to its CLMA.

If the ALMA receives a request for load management, a negotiation takes place between the ALMA and the CLMAs, to find out the cost for the desired power reduction, and to conclude which load(s) to disconnect (if any). Parameters in the contract with a customer might be:

- how much is the distributor allowed to disconnect at various times
- the price for power at different times
- for how long are the loads allowed to be disconnected each day
- the longest period of disconnection

We note that each agent has its local view of the network and that the agent is organized in a hierarchical structure, reflecting among other things different real-time constraints and levels of competence.

5.3   Implementation

This section shows a small part of the implementation. The agent plan *reduce_power* in **Figure 5** belongs to the ALMA and repre-

```
AGENT PLAN $agent reduce_power($req)
                    //An agent wants to reduce power in the area
BEGIN
          ?BEL(ME $VOID more_to_reduce($to_reduce))
          // Am I currently asking customer load agents for power?
          IF SUCCESS THEN
          BEGIN // Yes, I am waiting for a reply. Redo with new values
                    ~GOAL(ME $VOID check_for_responses())
                              // Cancel the check for responses.
                    ~BEL(ME $VOID more_to_reduce($to_reduce))
                              // Retract the old belief about reduction
                    BEL(ME NOW more_to_reduce(EVAL(Add($req
                    $to_reduce)))) // Insert new belief about reduction
          END
          ELSE // There is no current request for reduction
                    BEL(ME NOW more_to_reduce($req))
                              // Insert new belief about reduction
          SACT(request($every_agent NOW ask_for_power()))
                    // Ask all agents if they have power to spare
          ?BEL(ME $VOID comm_time($c_time)) // comm_time tells
                    // how long I should wait for a response
          GOAL(ME LATER(NOW $c_time) check_for_responses())
                    // Check for responses when comm_time has expired
     END
```

Figure 5   *An agent plan of the ALMA*

sents a part of the process of detecting an overload, finding the cheapest disconnectable power, and disconnecting it. The plan handles the request for a reduction of power; it updates the ALMA's belief about how much to reduce, asks every other agent how much power they can spare and, finally, sets up a goal to handle the responses later (when they arrive).

```
INTERACTION PLAN request(ME $time $$pred)
BEGIN
        GOAL(SENDER $time $$pred)
END

INTERACTION PLAN inform(ME $time $$pred)
BEGIN
        BEL(SENDER $time $$pred)
END
```

Figure 6   *Interaction plans of the ALMA*

The interaction plans *request* and *inform* in **Figure 6** are used by other agents to add goals to the ALMA and beliefs to its database, respectively. As they are programmable, agents can be given different ways of interaction, according to their roles in the overall system.

6   Related Work

The ARCHON architecture [Wittig92] is used for DA. The DA-SoC architecture has, in comparison to ARCHON, less complex agents, but a larger expected society of agents. Therefore they can be implemented farther out in the distribution network.

The PRS system [Ingrand92] is used for applications in several real-time domains. Compared to PRS, the DA-SoC architecture has a more distinct head - body dichotomy. Thereby, part of the real-time demands are given to dedicated control systems.

TEAM-CPS [Covo92] is an agent architecture for communication network management systems, with a structure similar to DA-SoC. Again, DA-SoC is designed for less complex agents and a higher degree of distribution.

The AGENT0 language [Shoham91] allows agent interaction, but our DAAL is, in comparison, more flexible with its programmable MoI. Though, the extensive analysis of the MoI lies outside the scope of this report, and will be presented elsewhere.

7 Conclusions and Future Activities

Our design and experiments with the DA-SoC testbed for Multi-Agent Systems for realizing services such as load management in static grids have illustrated the power of the agent oriented approach for this class of applications. However, much research and development remains of course, before we can have a full fledged implemented system at Sydkraft.

The next phase of the DA-SoC project will include the following:
- extensive assessments of our powerful agent language
- development and testing of different types of addressing mechanisms embedded as interaction plans in our language
- assessments of the Echelon Local Operating Network (LON) as an implementation infrastructure for the next generation of DA-SoC
- design and implementation of additional services in Distributed Automation
- work on theoretical foundations for MAS, such as team formation of agents, and articulation work in cooperation between agents
- introduction of learning abilities within agents
- identification of suitable tests for assessments of quality of service for different cooperation models

The next version of DA-SoC is expected at the beginning of next year.

Appendix: The Agent Language

agent:	string | var | ME | SENDER
basic_condition.	SUCCESS | term relation term | (condition) | NOT basic_condition
block:	BEGIN statementlist END
boolop:	AND | OR
condition:	basic_condition boolop condition | basic_condition
criterion:	string // pre-defined or user-defined function
expression:	EVAL(function(plist))
fact:	fact_const | fact_var
fact_const:	fact_id(plist)
fact_id:	string
fact_var:	$$string
function:	string // pre-defined or user-defined
modal:	modalop(agent time predicate)
modalop:	string
plan:	AGENT PLAN agent fact_const statement | INTERACTION PLAN modal statement
plist:	pterm plist | ε
pterm:	string | var | expression

relation:	= | < | >
seconds:	// float
statement:	ACT(fact) | SACT(modal) | GOAL(agent time fact) | ~GOAL(agent time fact) | BEL(agent time fact) | ~BEL(agent time fact) | ?BEL(agent time fact) | CHOOSE(criterion(var)) | block | IF condition THEN statement ELSE statement | IF condition THEN statement | EXIT
statementlist:	statement statementlist | ε
string:	// any alpha-numeric string not beginning with $ // and without white-space or comment marks
term:	time | agent | pterm
time:	var | NOW | LATER(time time) | EARLIER(time time)
var:	$string | $VOID

DELIMITERS:	any sequence of white-space (space, tab, CR or NL)
COMMENTS:	any text starting with // to end of line (CR or NL)
CASES:	the interpreter is case sensitive

References

[Bratman90] Bratman M. E.: "What Is Intention?", in Intentions in Communication, MIT Press, ISBN 0-262-03150-7.

[Cohen90] Cohen P. R., Levesque H. J.: "Persistence, Intention, and Commitment", in Intentions in Communication, MIT Press, ISBN 0-262-03150-7.

[Coulouris88] Coulouris G. F., Dollimore J.: "Distributed Systems, Concepts and Design", Addison-Wesley, ISBN 0-201-18059-6.

[Covo92] Covo A., Gersht A., Kheradpir S., Weihmayer R.: "New Approaches to Resource Management in Integrated Service Backbone Long Haul Communication Networks", Proc. IEEE Network Operations and Management Symposium, 1992.

[Gustavsson94] Gustavsson R., Hägg S.: "Societies of Computation - A Framework for Computing & Communication," University of Karlskrona/Ronneby, Research Report 1/94, ISSN 1103-1581.

[Ingrand92] Ingrand F.F., Georgeff M.P., Rao A.S.: "An Architecture for Real-Time Reasoning and System Control", IEEE Expert, pp. 34-44, December 1992.

[Rao92] Rao A. S., Georgeff M. P.: "Distributed Real-Time Artificial Intelligence, Final Research Report, July 1990 to June 1992, available at the Australian Artificial Intelligence Institute, 1 Grattan Street, Carlton, Victoria 3053, Australia.

[Shoham91] Shoham Y.: "AGENT0: A Simple Agent Language and Its Interpreter," Proceedings of the Ninth National Conference on Artificial Intelligence, July 14-19, 1991.

[Shoham93] Shoham Y.: "Agent-oriented programming," Artificial Intelligence 60, 1993.

[Tanenbaum92] Tanenbaum A. S.: "Modern Operating Systems", Part 2, Prentice-Hall, ISBN 0-13-595752-4.

[Wittig92] Wittig T., ed.: "ARCHON, an architecture for multi-agent systems", Ellis Horwood, ISBN 0-13-044462-6.

APPEAL: A Multi-Agent Approach to Interactive Learning Environments

J. Masthoff & R. Van Hoe

Institute for Perception Research/IPO

PO Box 513, 5600 MB Eindhoven, The Netherlands

E-Mail: masthoff@prl.philips.nl, vanhoe@prl.philips.nl

Abstract

In this paper an agent-based approach to interactive learning environments (ILE) is proposed. It is argued that current interactive learning systems, especially the intelligent tutoring systems, do not satisfy the minimal requirements of an ILE. A specification is given of an agent-based approach to ILE in which situated agents are associated with different aspects of the teacher's behaviour. It is argued that the interaction between these teacher agents and the student agent results in a highly adaptive and interactive learning system that satisfies the requirements of an ILE. The most promising is perhaps that the behaviour of the teacher seems already fairly complex even with a very limited amount of simple behaviours of the agents.

1 Intelligent Tutoring Systems: Adaptive Interactive Learning Environments?

The main problem with traditional computer aided instruction (CAI) systems was that they were unable to provide adaptation or individualization. In response to this and other problems CAI faced, Self (1974) argued that an interactive learning program should contain knowledge of how to teach, knowledge of what is being taught, and knowledge of who is being taught. Carbonell (1970) also argued that the CAI problem could not be solved without the use of AI techniques. Consequently, CAI systems have evolved into what are now usually called "Intelligent Tutoring Systems" (ITS).

A central assumption of ITSs is that the cognitive diagnosis of a learner's errors is an essential step towards meaningful individualized tutoring; the student model is mandatory to the goal of cognitive diagnosis, and consequently to the goal of adaptation. More specifically it is assumed that: 1. student modelling allows feedback adequate to correct any misconceptions or missteps that result in error; and 2. beyond error correction, a dynamic representation of the developing knowledge of each student determines what to teach next and how to teach it (Snow & Swanson, 1992).

In ITSs the student is modelled in terms of the domain expert, either in terms of what knowledge units the expert has but the student does not (overlay model) or in terms of what knowledge units (i.e., buggy rules) the student has and the expert not (process model). In line with the expert system approach, it is assumed that both types of student model can be used with an inference engine.

Although the ITS approach to adaptive training has its merits, there are many problems associated with it. Since current interactive learning environments are developed according to an expert system methodology, the expert module is the central component of those systems.

A consequence of the expert system approach is that the student is modelled in terms of the representation model of the expert module. In the ITS literature (e.g., Wenger, 1987) it is often argued that the expert module should be transparent, so that each reasoning step can be inspected and interpreted by the student. However, it is not at all obvious that the representation model of the expert module corresponds to the cognitive representations of the student. There is indeed empirical evidence that expert knowledge structures do not provide the most useful models for teaching (McArthur et al., 1988; Roschelle, 1990). This implies that student modelling should be conducted in terms of the cognitive model of the student, and not in terms of the expert module.

ITS researchers are trying to develop an adaptive system based on a representation-driven approach rather than a situation-based (data-driven) approach. O'Shea (1979) has argued that one of the most important aspects of any CAI program is its response-sensitivity: an interactive learning program is more response-sensitive than another when it is more adaptive to the individual learning needs of the student than the other system. In a classical ITS system the student's performance is interpreted within the representation model of the expert. Hence the degree of response-sensitivity of the ITS is determined by the extent to which the set of all possible behaviours of the student fits within the representation framework of the ITS. As the student's performance is rarely consistent and it is in fact impossible to predict the full range of student behaviours, the response-sensitivity or adaptivity of ITSs is limited. (see, e.g. empirical research (Payne & Squibb, 1990)). In other words, classical ITSs are not robust as they cannot cope with unexpected, i.e., not predefined, behaviour of the student. Moreover, as further instruction is based on the hypothesized knowledge state of the student and not on the student's behaviour itself, problems can arise because the student's performance was misinterpreted within the expert module.

Last but not least, ITSs are very complex systems which require a lot of implementation time and consume a lot of computing resources. Consequently the performance of ITSs is very poor which makes on-line adaptive training quite difficult.

2 Minimal Requirements for Interactive Learning Environments

In this section, the minimal requirements for an ILE are discussed briefly:

- *Interactivity.* Tackling the problem of the design of an ILE means in the first place addressing the specific problems involved in the development and the use of interactive machines. The interaction in a computer-based learning environment can be considered as a dialogue between two equal and collaborative partners, i.e., the instructional system and the student, where special rules apply in order to promote learning and where the communication goes along a narrow channel, but where also the conventional behavioural repertoire can be exploited (Bouwhuis & Bunt, 1993).

- *Adaptive instruction.* One of the characteristics of the collaborative nature of an instructional system is its adaptivity. At the general level this implies that throughout the instruction session there is moment-to-moment adaptation of the instruction to the needs of the individual student.

- *Robustness.* The interactive system must cope appropriately and in a timely fashion with the always changing behaviour (i.e., learning) of the student, and unexpected behaviour or errors of the student should not lead to total collapse of the system.

- *Direct monitoring of the learning process.* The main goal of the ILE in the tutorial dialogue is to support or optimize the learning process of the student. This implies that the actions of the instructional system are based on a model of human learning.

- *Evaluation research: user-centred approach.* Empirical research is central to the design of ILEs. By analogy with Norman & Draper (1986) we could call this methodology the user-centred design of interactive learning environments. This approach implies that at *all* stages the design process of an interactive learning system should be based on (1) fundamental research on the learning process the system will support, and (2) continual user testing with the prototype.

- *Parsimony.* An ILE should have a simple, but efficient architecture.

3 The APPEAL System

APPEAL (A Pleasant Personal Environment for Adaptive Learning) is an interdisciplinary project which started in 1993 at the Institute for Perception Research (IPO). Persons with a background in computer science, computational linguistics, experimental psychology and phonetics are involved. The main goal of this project is to develop an appealing intelligent learning environment, which meets the requirements mentioned above. Interaction should be more varied and flexible, i.e. highly adaptive to the student's performance. A prototype, also called APPEAL, has been developed. This prototype will function as a research carrier.

The APPEAL system has been designed in a modular way. Its architecture is shown in figure 1. The instruction network contains the course material. Its structure provides information about the relative level of difficulty of the various lessons and exercises. The student history contains a history of the student's performance. The dialogue with the student is determined by the teaching expert. This component represents the general didactic side of teaching. We believe that it is independent of the chosen domain, and that it can be used in various applications ranging from the teaching of language to that of mathematics. The domain model contains information specific to the domain, which, in the system we have implemented, happens to be the language Dutch. The domain expert generates, on the basis of information from the teaching expert, exercises and examples, and evaluates the student's answers. This component represents the domain specific side of teaching. The interface manager provides the interface of the system to the student.

In this paper we focus on the teaching expert which we have implemented using agents. For more detailed information about the other components of the APPEAL system see (Van Hoe et al., 1995; Appelo et al., 1994).

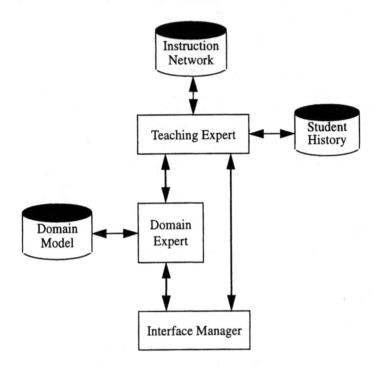

Fig. 1. Architecture of the Appeal system

4 The Situated Agent Approach

The agents in APPEAL are situated agents as in the work of Connah and Wavish (Wavish & Connah, 1990; Connah, 1993) and Chapman and Agre (Agre & Chapman, 1987; Chapman, 1991), and are inspired by the work of Brooks (1986, 1991) and Steels (1989) on autonomous robots, and the work of Suchman (1987) on situated action.

In this section we describe briefly this situated agents approach. For a more detailed overview of the relevance of the situated agent approach for cognitive science in general, and cognitive psychology in particular, we refer to the special 1993 issue of Cognitive Science on situated action.

We can take Shoham's (1993, p. 52) description of agents as a starting point for our discussion of situated agents: "an entity that functions continuously and autonomously in an environment in which other processes take place and other agents exist".

This description needs to be explained and extended as follows:

Situatedness. An agent's most important resource in determining what to do is its immediate situation, rather than internal plans of action;

Interactivity and emergent functionality. The activity pattern emerges from the dynamical interaction between an agent and its environment, rather than being explicitly designed as a property of an agent or the environment. In general, the relation between agents can either be cooperative, to solve a common goal or share a common resource, or competitive.

Autonomy and self-organization. On a micro-level, autonomy implies that the activities of the individual agents do not require constant external guidance. On a macro-level, autonomy implies self-organization, i.e., there is no central authority to control the overall interactions between the agents.

Cognitive economy. An immediate implication of the situatedness principle is the cognitive economy principle. Certain facts relevant to the explanation of the agent's behaviour are not represented by that agent, but are to be found only in the presenting external situation. Agents do not maintain a symbolic model of the world: the world is its own best representation. This implies that perception is central in the functioning of an agent, as it is the agent's only access to the concrete situation.

Parallelism. Agents function continuously, i.e., concurrently with each other, in a multi-agent environment.

Predictability. The environment in which the agents are functioning is partially unpredictable.

Behaviour-based. Agents are described in terms of their behaviour at different levels of granularity in response to other behaviour in their environment rather than in terms of their knowledge.

5 The Teacher Analysed

From an observer's point of view, a human teacher seems to be very complex. That is why we have decided to decompose teaching into smaller components which are easier to think about. Concentrating on the different aspects of a teacher's behaviour which are adapted to the student, we can distinguish the following:

- *Navigation*
  The teacher navigates through the course material, determining at any time which topic to discuss. The speed and order in which the material is taught depend on the performance and interests of the student.

- *Practice*
  Within a given subject, those exercises and examples are given that fit best to the performance of the student.

- *Instruction*

  In the case of bad performance or lack of performance, the student is instructed and helped with his task. The amount of instruction needed depends on the student.

- *Feedback*

  The teacher reacts in different ways to the student. He or she tries to distinguish between errors and slips, and is more or less enthusiastic or disappointed.

- *Presentation*

  Material can be presented in many different ways. For instance in mathematics, depending on the level of the student, additions are presented using formulas, pictures, or even real apples (say).

- *Student model*

  A lot of the adaptations we have just mentioned depend on some knowledge about the history of the student's performance. So, another aspect of the teacher's behaviour is to keep a record of this.

We have associated an agent with each of these different aspects of the teacher's behaviour.

6 Behaviours of the Agents

As a basis for the behaviours of the various agents we drew on the literature and on certain cognitive models. We will now discuss some of the behaviours of the agents and the theories they are based upon.

6.1 Navigation Agent

The behaviour of the navigation agent is based on the notion of controlled complexity as described in (Wood, Wood, & Middleton, 1978). The student should be confronted with problems that lie beyond his current level of competence but not so far beyond that he or she is unable to master the problem being presented. Problems should be neither too easy nor too difficult.

We use rules like

> *If the student's performance is not improving any more and he or she performs sufficiently well then go on to a more difficult kind of exercise or topic.*

and

> *If the student's performance is not improving and he or she does not perform sufficiently well then return to a less difficult type of exercise or topic.*

A history of the student's performance is maintained in the student history to determine whether the preconditions of these rules hold. We will come back to this in more detail when discussing the behaviour of the student model agent.

To determine which new topic or exercise to address or to which to return, information from the instruction network and student history is used. In the instruction network information can be found about which topics or kinds of exercise are considered beforehand to be the more difficult. The student history (as maintained by the student model agent) provides information about which topics and exercises a student has already encountered and his or her performance on these.

6.2 Practice Agent

The navigation agent determines which topic and kind of exercise will be addressed. In most cases however, the topic to be taught consists of a number of items of which the relative difficulty level is not necessarily known beforehand. For instance, with the conjugation of the verb 'to be' as topic, there could be an item for each person. The practice agent decides at any time which item will be presented in an exercise or example.

The most efficient way of teaching seems to be to confront a student with those items he does not know yet. The difficulty is that it is not always obvious what a student knows. As a basis for the behaviour of the practice agent we took quite trivial hypotheses. In the first place, we are convinced that performance of the student in the past predicts future performance. To be more precise, we believe that:

$$P(\ incorrect(b,n)\ |\ incorrect(b,n\text{-}1)\ ) > P(\ incorrect(b,n)\ |\ correct(b,n\text{-}1)\ )[1]$$

In natural language this comes down to: 'the chance that a student answers incorrectly to an item, is greater when he or she answered incorrectly the last time it was presented than when he or she answered correctly'. This assumption led to the idea of using two sets to represent the items to be taught, a 'good' set and a 'bad' set. The good set contains the items correctly answered the last time they were presented. The bad set contains the incorrectly answered ones. Initially all the items to be taught are in the bad set. The assumption implies that the chance that a student does not know an item is bigger when that item is in the bad set than when it is in the good set. So, an item should have a greater chance of being presented to the student when it is in the bad set than when it is in the good set. This is expressed in the following formula.

$$P(\ present(b)\ |\ b\ in\ bad\ set\ )\ = k\,P(\ present(b)\ |\ b\ in\ good\ set\ ),\quad k > 1$$

---

1. where incorrect(b,n) stands for an incorrect answer to the n-th presentation of item b

In natural language: 'the chance that an item is presented to the student is k times as great when that item is in the bad set than when it is in the good set, with k greater than one'. When k is very large, an item answered correctly (so, in the good set) is only presented to the student again when the bad set is empty (i.e. all other items have been answered correctly the last time they were presented). If a student never forgot an item that has been answered correctly once, this would be a very good strategy. We have however as a second assumption that a student tends to forget. This is expressed by the formula:

$$P (\, incorrect(b,n) \, \wedge \, \neg slip(b,n) \mid correct(b,n\text{-}1) \,) > 0$$

The chance that a student answers an item incorrectly, i.e. makes a real error not a slip, is greater than zero even when he or she answered correctly the last time it was presented. This made us choose k not too large. We have chosen k equals 10. Notice that our task sequencing strategy only has one parameter. This makes it far simpler than those existing strategies which also try to take the student's performance into account. We are currently evaluating this strategy and model and comparing it with existing ones.

6.3 Instruction Agent

The instruction agent is an important agent in the system as it not only determines the adaptivity, but also the interactivity level of the system. The behaviour of the instruction agent is determined by the rule "If the student succeeds, when next intervening offer less help. If the student fails, when next intervening take over more control." (Wood, Wood, & Middleton, 1978, p. 133). Furthermore, the instruction agent is based on a layered model of intervention varying between the "general verbal encouragement" level and the "demonstration" level, whereby each layer represents a different level of control from the side of the teacher agent. This implies that the behaviour of the instruction agent is contingent on the performance of the student (cf., situatedness principle); the most appropriate intervention is chosen on the basis of the student's success.

Currently our instruction agent uses a quite simple form of layered intervention, with only two levels. It has, among others, the following rules:

If the student does not act then try to encourage him or her by saying something like 'you must do something to proceed'.

and

If the student even after encouragement does not act then he or she should be helped by making the exercise some what easier.

For instance, in a kind of jigsaw exercise in which the student has to construct a sentence from words, a word is put in the correct place. We intend to extent this behaviour with more layers of intervention.

Essential for the behaviour of the teacher is that out of the cooperation between practice agent (i.e., controlled complexity) and instruction agent (i.e., contingency rule and layered intervention model) a tutorial dialogue emerges with a mixed, varying locus of control: as long as the student cannot master the problems he or she is confronted with, the teacher is more or less in control, once the student succeeds in solving the problem, he or she takes over more control. The layered intervention model of the instruction agent also encompasses different types of ILEs. The 'general encouragement' level corresponds with microworld systems which are user-controlled systems, whereas the 'demonstration' level corresponds with classical ITSs in which control is in the (virtual) hands of the system.

6.4 Feedback Agent

As a first rule we have that feedback should be immediate. For instance, in the before mentioned jigsaw exercise the student gets immediate feedback when he or she tries to put a word where it does not belong. The word bounces back and a sound is produced.

As described in (Norman, 1981) a distinction can be made between real errors and slips, which are errors that occur when someone does an action that is not intended. We have as hypotheses that:

$P (slip(b,n)) > 0$

$P (slip(b,n) \mid correct (b,n\text{-}1)) >> P (slip(b,n) \mid incorrect (b,n\text{-}1))$

Slips occur and most frequently after the same item has been answered correctly before.
These hypotheses led to the following rule:

> *If an incorrectly answered item belonged to the good set, there is a fair possibility that the student has made a slip. In that case the student will get the opportunity to correct his answer.*

The feedback agent also determines the degree of enthusiasm or lack of it with which the student's answer will be greeted. It uses amongst others the following rules:

> *If the student answers correctly and his or her last answer was correct then give weak positive feedback like 'okay'.*

> *If the student answers correctly and his or her last answer was incorrect then give very positive feedback like 'excellent'.*

This last rule is meant to keep the student motivated.

6.5 Presentation Agent

We have not yet implemented the presentation agent. We will briefly describe our views of the behaviour of this agent. The behaviour of the presentation agent can be compared with the task of the director of a television broadcast of a soccer game.[1] The default rule of the director is that as long as the game goes up and down the field, the television viewer gets a general overview of the whole soccer field. However, when a goal is scored the director focuses in on the goal-scorer and replays the goal-scoring in slow motion. As in the case of the broadcast director, the presentation agent tries to choose at each moment in the learning session the optimal representation for the student.

The presentation agent is based on a layered model, whereby each layer represents a different level of abstraction. The general rule determining the behaviour of the presentation agent is that information is presented at the abstract level (cf., the default rule of the director). However, when a student is having difficulties with a particular exercise or is asking for more explanation, the presentation agent can decide to focus in on the problem in another, more concrete representation format. It is obvious that efficient behaviour of the presentation agent will depend on the collaboration with the other agents, especially the student model agent (for information on the performance level of the student) and the feedback and instruction agents (those are the agents requesting a specific representation format).

6.6 Student Model Agent

All the agents mentioned so far, need some information about the history of the student's performance. The student model agent maintains this kind of information. We decided what exactly to record by looking at which information the other agents need. So, student modelling did not become a goal per se, but is only used to supply the other agents with the information they need.

In the first place, the student model agent maintains the good set and bad set needed by the practice agent. The following rules are used for this purpose:

If the student answered incorrectly to the item presented, it is added to the bad set and removed from the good set.

If the student answered correctly, the item is added to the good set and removed from the bad set.

For the navigation agent, information regarding which topics and exercises the student has encountered and his or her performance on these is maintained. This means that

---

1. This comparison is due to Mike Graham, Philips Research Laboratories, England.

not only a good set and bad set for the current exercise is kept but for all exercises the student has done so far. The expression 'the student performs sufficiently well', in the precondition of the rules of the navigation agent, has been formalised as 'at least 95% of the items is contained in the good set'. Whether the student's performance is improving is determined by comparing the size of the current good set with the size of that set before a certain number of items has been presented. For this purpose, a history of the number of items in the good set is maintained for the current exercise.

6.7 Postman Agent

An extra agent, called the postman agent, is added to transfer incoming messages from the other modules of the system into a format the other agents can understand.

6.8 Interaction

There is no control component. The behaviour of the system emerges from the interaction between the agents. To give an example of this interaction: the navigation agent, practice agent and instruction agent compete sometimes. When the student is performing badly, the practice agent tries to present more exercises of the same kind to the student. The navigation agent tries to return to an easier kind of exercise or topic, and the instruction agent tries to give extra instruction. Which agent wins eventually depends on the internal states of the agents and the history of the student's performance.

7 Concluding Remarks

The first prototype of our system was ready in december 1993. It is argued that our multi-agent architecture satisfies the minimal requirements of ILEs discussed in section 2. According to an agent-based approach, interactivity and adaptivity are emergent properties of the interaction between the student and the teacher.The persons, with various backgrounds, to which we have shown APPEAL were surprised by the variety of the system's responses and its adequate reactions to the student's behaviour.

As robustness is concerned: in the course of more than 50 demonstrations the system has never behaved in an undesirable way. The system coped even with very unexpected behaviour from the visitors.

The definition of the agents has been and will be based on user-centred research into the interactive learning process. Based on empirical research the behaviours of the agents will be fine-tuned. The system as a whole will be evaluated when the course material has been extended.

It is our experience that the use of agents (the RTA programming language in particular) results in a simple, but efficient architecture. Response times are very acceptable, and the amount of storage space needed for the agents and the student model is limited. It is quite simple to extend the behaviour of the agents, and we plan to do this. To prove the domain independence of the teaching expert, another domain, namely reading, has been implemented.

There is still a lot to be done: the behaviour of the instruction agent should be extended with more layers of intervention, the presentation agent still has to be implemented, the behaviours of the other agents have to be fine-tuned and extended. But it is promising that the behaviour of the teacher seems already fairly complex even with a very limited amount of simple behaviours of the agents. So, we are only at the beginning but we seem to be on the right track.

Acknowledgements

The implementation of the agents has been done in the RTA programming language. RTA is a concurrent and declarative programming language for developing agent-based systems. The language was developed by Wavish and Connah (1990) at Philips Research Laboratories, England.

We would like to thank David Connah for his comments on earlier versions of this paper.

References

Agre, P.E., & Chapman, D. (1987). *Pengi: An implementation of a theory of activity.* Proceedings of the AAAI Conference (pp. 268-272). Seattle, Washington.

Van Hoe, R., Masthoff, J., Appelo, L., Harkema, H., De Pijper, J.R., & Rous, J. (1995). APPEAL: a multimedia environment for adaptive learning. In: *IPO annual progress report 29.*

Appelo, L., Leermakers, M., & Rous, J. (1994). *Language exercise generation in an interactive learning environment.* IPO Manuscript 1012.

Bouwhuis, D., & Bunt, H. (in press). Interactive instructional systems as dialogue systems. In L. Verhoeven (Ed.), *Training for literacy.* Dordrecht: Foris.

Brooks, R. (1986). A robust layered control system for a mobile robot. *IEEE Journal on Robotics and Automation, 2,* 14-23.

Brooks, R. (1991). Intelligence without representation. *Artificial Intelligence, 47,* 139-159.

Carbonell, J.R. (1970). *Mixed initiative man-computer instructional dialogues.* Doctoral dissertation, MIT, Cambridge, Massachusetts.

Chapman, D. (1991). *Vision, instruction, and action.* Cambridge, MA: The MIT Press.

Connah, D.M. (1993). The design of interacting agents for use in interfaces. In M.D. Brouwer-Janse & T.L. Harrington (Eds.), *Human-machine communication for educational systems design* (pp. 197-206). Berlin: Springer-Verlag.

Green, J.G., Chi, M.T.H., Clancey, W.J., & Elman, J. (Eds.) (1993). Situated Agents [Special issue]. *Cognitive Science, 17.*

McArthur, D., Statz, C., Hotta, J., Peter, O., & Burdorf, C. (1988). Skill-oriented task-sequencing in an intelligent tutor for basic algebra. *Instructional Science, 17,* 281-307.

Norman, D.A. (1981). Categorization of Action Slips. *Psychological Review, 88*, 1-15.

Norman, D.A., & Draper, S.W. (Eds.) (1986). *User centered system design.* Hillsdale, NJ: Lawrence Erlbaum.

Payne, S., & Squibb, H. (1990). Algebra mal-rules and cognitive accounts of error. *Cognitive Science, 14*, 445-481.

Roschelle, J. (1990). *Designing for conversations.* Paper presented at the Annual Meeting of the American Education Research Association, Boston.

Self, J.A. (1974). Student models in computer-aided instruction. *International Journal of Man-Machine studies, 6*, 261-276.

O'Shea, T. (1979). A self-improving quadratic tutor. *International Journal of Man-Machine studies, 11*, 97-124.

Shoham, Y. (1993). Agent-oriented programming. *Artificial Intelligence, 60*, 51-92.

Snow, R.E., & Swanson, J. (1992). Instructional psychology. *Annual Review of Psychology, 43*, 583-626.

Suchman, L.A. (1987). *Plans and situated actions: The problem of human-machine communication.* Cambridge: Cambridge University Press.

Steels, L. (1989). Cooperation between distributed agents through self-organisation. *Journal on Robotics and Autonomous systems.*

Wavish, P.R., & Connah, D.M. (1990). *Representing multi-agent worlds in ABLE.* Technical Note, Philips Research Laboratories.

Wood, D., Wood, H., & Middleton, D. (1978). An experimental evaluation of four face-to-face teaching strategies. *International Journal of behavioral Development, 1*, 131-147.

Wenger, E. (1987). *Artificial Intelligence and Tutoring Systems.* Los Altos, California: Morgan Kaufmann

Language Constructs for Coordination in an Agent Space

Stijn Bijnens, Wouter Joosen and Pierre Verbaeten

Department of Computer Science
KULeuven
Belgium
e-mail: Stijn.Bijnens@cs.kuleuven.ac.be

Abstract. This paper describes an open language framework based on concurrent object-oriented programming. In this computational model, autonomous active objects are used to specify interacting agents. Many researchers have indicated the suitability of concurrent object-oriented programming as a base for multi-agent languages [Pog94][Sho93], but we claim that powerful coordination constructs are needed to achieve better expressive power in the language. Our language framework supports two kinds of semantics for coordination in the agent space :

- Sender-initiated coordination by means of pattern-based group communication.
- Receiver-initiated coordination by means of multi-object synchronisation constraints.

Both facilities are integrated in the type-system of the language. A type serves as a partial specification of an agent's behaviour. Type-based coordination combined with a meta-level enables an efficient simulation of the agent space on a distributed memory machine.

1 Introduction

An agent space is a system composed of a set of intelligent agents which can cooperate, compete or coexist. Agents interact by sending messages to each other. Message are pieces of information exchanged among agents and are treated as stimuli by the receiving agent. Different types of messages can be exchanged [ST90] (, e.g. action messages, observation messages, ...).

Concurrent object-oriented programming is a powerful paradigm to model autonomous agents that interact with each other. Agent-oriented programming [Sho93] specializes the object-oriented notions by fixing the state (now called mental state) of the objects (now called agents) to consist of instance variables such as beliefs (including beliefs about the world, about themselves, and about one another), capabilities, and decisions. A computation consists of these agents informing, requesting, offering, accepting, rejecting, competing, and assisting one another. These interaction patterns can be described in a programming language by specifying objects and their interactions (Figure 1).

Message based interaction is translated into the possibility to invoke operations on other objects. In order to express a message based interaction the sender must specify the recipient of a particular message. Most programming models employ a name-based scheme to indicate the recipient(s). This paper indicates the pitfalls of pure name-based interaction. Currently, our work does not focus on the issue of how beliefs, capabilities, and decisions are expressed and maintained as state variables of objects[1]. Essentially, this paper introduces powerful language constructs to specify coordinated object interaction [2].

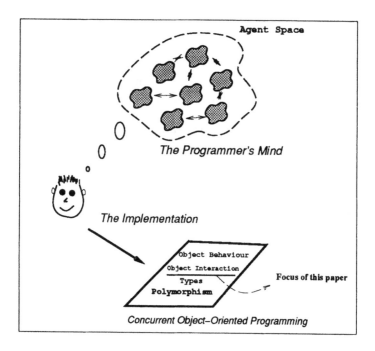

Fig. 1. From a model to an executable program

Both pattern-based group communication and multi-object synchronization constraints are supported by the language. Pattern-based group communication is a facility to specify sender-initiated coordination towards a group of recipients based on some of their properties. Multi-object synchronisation is a facility to specify receiver-initiated coordination by expressing proper synchronisation constraints for restricting the inherent concurrency that results from the programming model. These constructs result in a flexible framework to specify dynamic interaction schemes between cooperating autonomous agents.

To indicate the expressive power of the language constructs for coordination, we model a complex application in the area of molecular dynamic simulation[BJB+94].

---

[1] These issues are extensively described by Shoham [Sho93] and Poggi[Pog94].

[2] In our opinion, the language constructs for expressing agent interaction are orthogonal to the language constructs for expressing individual agent behaviour.

Indeed, this application domain is an excellent example: particles are modelled as autonomous agents that have to obey the laws of Newtonian mechanics. The interaction patterns between these agents are highly dynamic.

This paper is structured as follows: section 2 introduces the computational model of our language. Section three presents a case study of a molecular dynamic simulation and indicates two kinds of coordination: sender-initiated versus receiver-initiated. Section 4 describes the proposed language constructs for expressing the coordination. Section 5 briefly describes the implementation. We summarize in section 6 and indicate some future research tracks.

2 The programming environment

Developing concurrent software for distributed memory machines is a difficult task. In order to assist the programmer, we have defined different views during program development. This enables a clean separation of concerns, and generates a lot of opportunities for software reuse. The separate views (Figure 2) are:

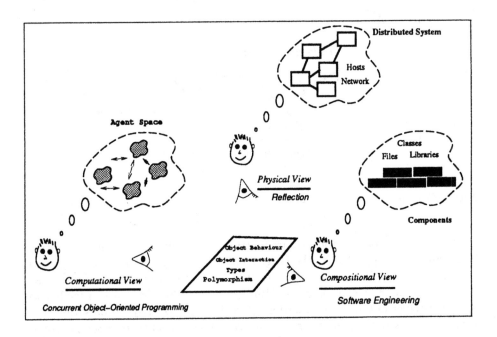

Fig. 2. Three different views during program development

1. Computational View:
   In this view, the programmer specifies his problem (the application) by implementing object behaviour and object interaction. Concurrency is explicit

but distribution is transparent by means of location independent object invocation.

2. Physical View:

In this view, the programmer is concerned with the efficient mapping of the object space on a distributed memory machine. The programmer can use the language's meta-level features (e.g. object migration, object replication) to achieve, for example, an optimal load balance or fault tolerance.

3. Compositional View:

In this view, the programmer is concerned with code management, software reuse and version control.

The next paragraph gives a detailed overview of the computational view of our programming environment.

2.1 Computational View

Programming languages that support the notion of autonomous behaviour are inherently concurrent. Some concurrent object-oriented languages keep the concept of a "process" as a separate entity (like in Emerald [RTL91] or Ada [ANSI83]); other models [Ame87] [Agh86][Yon90] integrate objects and processes into one concept: active objects. This is a natural approach since objects and processes have a lot in common: encapsulation, communication through message passing, protection of private data, etc. In our computational model an agent is modelled as an autonomous active object. An active object can have one or more autonomous operations. An autonomous operation is iteratively scheduled (if the synchronisation constraints allow the scheduler to do so). In this way, an active object owns computational power independently from other objects. An object's behaviour is reflected into its state and operations, and state changes can only be caused by the execution of operations. Our programming model supports two kinds of behavioural specifications.

1. Autonomous Behaviour: The associated operations are autonomously invoked by the object itself.
2. Reactive Behaviour: The associated operations are invoked by other objects. The execution of these operations are triggered by incoming messages.

Object interaction occurs when objects invoke operations on each other. Our model offers two semantics for operation invocation:

1. Synchronous object invocation. The sender's activity is blocked until the operation is executed completely in the receiver object and the result of the operation is returned. Of course, all pure sequential object-oriented languages only support synchronous message passing.
2. Asynchronous object invocation. In order to maximise concurrency, the model supports asynchronous object invocation by avoiding the sender to wait for the operation to complete. Many of the concurrent object-oriented computational models state asynchronous message passing as the fundamental communication model (Actors [Agh86]).

Synchronisation is needed to manage concurrent activities -that is acceptance and computation of requests- within an object. A concurrent object interface can be considered as a set of correlated operations with only a subset available for execution at a particular moment [Nie93]. In a sequential environment, the sequence of operation invocations is under the programmer's control. In a parallel environment, an object may be operated upon by different active objects, which may invoke arbitrary operations at arbitrary times. In this context, simple sequential control becomes inadequate. Thus, a realistic programming approach has to consider an object as a finite state machine which accepts or delays the execution of an operation according to the object's internal state.

We have defined some language extensions for C++ to integrate concurrency into an existing object-oriented language. The extensions are summarized:

- Autonomous operations: An active object can have one or more autonomous operations. These operations are iteratively executed (when the concurrency control specifications are satisfied). In a class definition, autonomous operations are specified after the "autonomous" keyword. Different scheduling policies for the autonomous operations can be expressed at the language's meta-level. Reflective facilities even allow to change the scheduling policies dynamically.
- Asynchronous object invocation. A new invocation operator is defined for asynchronous invocation (the @ operator).
- State based concurrency control. An active object behaves like a finite state machine. Dependent on the current value of the state, a specific operation may be executed (precondition). The abstract state can change when the request is accepted for execution (preaction) or after the execution of the operation (postaction). In a class definition, this behaviour specification must be described after the "behavior" keyword.

3 Atoms, Molecules, and Newtonian Mechanics

Particle simulations are used to observe the macroscopic behaviour of a physical system by simulating that system at the microscopic level. The physical system is then considered as a large collection of particles (e.g. atoms, molecules, electrons and nuclei...). One specific class of such simulations is molecular dynamics.

The fundamental aim of molecular dynamics is to predict the behaviour of condensed matter from a knowledge of the forces acting between the component atoms. This is done by numerically solving the Newtonian equations of motion to obtain the time evolution of the molecular trajectories.

A challenging molecular dynamics application is the simulation of protein molecules, for example in the context of drug design. A protein molecule can be thought of as a complex flexible mechanical system subject to a number of forces between parts of itself and the environment. For each type of force, specific force calculation algorithms have been developed by application domain experts. A particle is modelled as an autonomous agent and such an agent has to obey the laws of Newtonian mechanics. These laws are expressed in terms of forces between particles. We summarise the forces below to illustrate the complexity of the interaction patterns between the communicating agents.

The resulting language framework is called Correlate [Bij94], an acronym for Concurrent Object-oRiented Reflective LAnguage TEchnology.

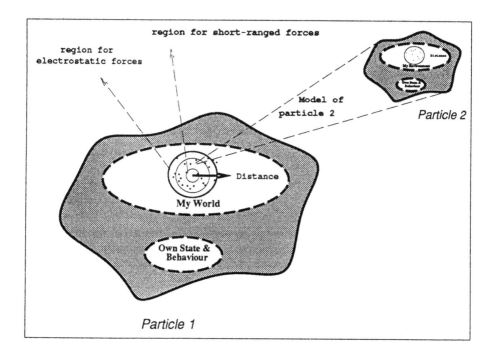

Fig. 3. A particle agent and its local view of the world

1. Short ranged forces. These forces which act between any pair of atoms are actually the combination of very short-ranged repulsions which prevent overlap of atoms and van der Waals attractions. Neighbouring particles are those particles that are within a sufficiently small distance so that the force of interaction on the given particle is non-negligible. The typical way to organise the calculations is by maintaining, for each particle, its list of neighbours. These lists evolve because particles will move in and out of the environment of a given particle. Thus neighbour lists have to be updated frequently.

2. Forces of constraint. A complex molecule consists of a collection of atoms connected together by chemical bonds which constrain the distances between the connected atoms. In some circumstances, bond angles can also be constrained in a similar way.

3. Electrostatic forces. These forces are caused by the interaction between charge distributions. Electrostatic forces between pairs of particles are proportional to and thus exist between a pair of particles with a relatively long distance.

4. Thermostatic forces. These forces adapt the simulation to different environments. The thermostatic forces arise from the desirability of computing the trajectories at constant average temperature, rather than at constant total energy which would be the case for a conservative mechanical system. The thermostatic forces thus express the coupling of the system to an external energy source.

Each time step, the new position and velocity of a particle will be computed from all the forces acting on that particle. In order to enable a particle to compute its next position, it should have knowledge of its environment e.g. position and mass of neighbouring atoms (see Figure 3). Thus, after each time step, there is a need for communication between particle objects. A particle has to keep track of its environment in order to be able and compute all the forces acting upon it. One of the complexities, however, is that the communication patterns are different for each type of force calculation.

This results in cumbersome book-keeping of name-lists to other particles[3] if the language does not support high-level constructs to express these interaction patterns. The next subsection shows that the interaction patterns, even for a single force calculation (short-ranged forces), are hard to manage in a traditional concurrent object-oriented language.

3.1 A simplified Version

This simplified version considers atoms with no chemical bonds and only short-range forces. Objects of type Atom are the basic building blocks of the simulation. An object instantiated from class Atom (see Figure 4) has one autonomous operation: *Step()*. This operation can be scheduled if the object is READY, this means that all the positions of other atoms are received. The autonomous operation (1) computes the forces acting upon the particle, (2) computes its new position and velocity, and (3) sends (*Delivers*) its new position to the other Atoms. After the execution of the *Step()* operation the object becomes WAITING. The object becomes READY again if the positions and mass of the neighbouring atoms have been received. The forces between two atoms is a function of the distance between them. The longer the distance the less important the force will be in the force field. Therfore real applications consider a cutoff range in which atoms interact. A particular atom will only consider neighbouring atoms which

---

[3] These lists will be called neighbour-lists in the sequel of this paper.

```
class Atom : public Agent{
autonomous :
    Step() { //autonomous operation
            ComputeForces();
            ComputeVelocityAndNewPosition();
            //Deliver new position to all atoms in the range
            for ( all_neighbours^a ) neighbour @ Deliver(x,y,z, mass);
    };
public :
    Atom(Position position, Mass mass, Velocity velocity ) {//Constructor
            //Deliver new position to all atoms in the range
            for ( all_neighbours ) neighbour @ Deliver(position, mass);
    }
    Deliver(Position position, Mass mass){
            //invoked by neighbouring Atoms
            PutDataInReceiveList(position,mass);
    };
behavior:
    AbstractState = { READY, WAITING};
    Atom() postaction become WAITING;
    Step() precondition READY; postaction become WAITING;
    Deliver() precondition WAITING;
            postaction if( everything_received_from_neighbours^b ) become READY;
private:
    Mass mass;
    Position x,y,z;
    Velocity velocity;
    Acceleration acceleration;
    List receivelist; //to store the received information from neighbours
    ... }


   ─────────────────
   ^a This list is called the outgoing neighbourlist
   ^b This list is called the incoming neighbourlist
```

Fig. 4. The Atom Class without coordination constructs

reside in this range. Of course, as particles are moving, these neighbour-lists change at run-time.

In this simplified example, each active object has two neighbour-lists:

1. The first one (the outgoing neighbour-list) is consulted when the atom *Delivers* its own position and mass to its neighbours.
2. The second one (the incoming neighbour-list) is consulted when the scheduler checks the synchronisation constraints to see whether all position and masses

of all atoms in the range have been received. (Note that these two lists do not have to be equal.)

How can we implement these lists if the language does not support coordination primitives?

- A naive implementation incorporates ALL atoms in every list. This results in broadcasting the invocation message to every Atom object. For performance reasons this is unacceptable.
- Another solution is to change the neighbour-lists dynamically by keeping track of the atoms within a particular cutoff range. But the management of such a list results in cumbersome book-keeping, and thus in a complex coding effort. This will finally result in unreadable code which will most likely contain bugs.

This study indicates that coordination primitives are required. The expression of other types of forces are even more complicated. For example, in protein simulation, atoms make chemical bonds. Typically, in drug design [BJB+94] such molecules can consist of thousands of atoms. Chemical bonds are modelled as constraint forces between atoms. A large molecule can curl (folding) dynamically during simulation. This results in an enormous change in the members of a neighbour-list.

As mentioned above the needed communication between particles is different for every force type. In other words, every particle has a number of different neighbour-lists (two for every force type), and all these lists change dynamically.

In conclusion, the complexity of this case study shows that coordination primitives are necessary to express the interaction between the application objects.

4   Definition of coordination constructs

The case study has indicated two (different) requirements :

1. *Pattern-based group communication.*
   It should be possible to specify a group of recipients of an invocation based on some properties of the recipients. This way plurality is encapsulated. For example, an Atom object wants to send a message to all other Atom objects within a specified range. The range is based on the position attribute of the other objects.
2. *Multi-object synchronisation constraints.*
   Traditionally, synchronisation constraints of an object are expressed in terms of some state properties of the object itself. The case study showed that there is a need to express synchronisation constraints of an object in terms of some state properties of other objects. Another example where multi-object synchronisation constraints are needed is for example the dining philosophers problem. A philosopher can be modelled as an active object with an autonomous operation "Eat()". The philosopher acts as a finite state machine

and can either be EATING or THINKING. The synchronisation constraints for the operation Eat() do not depend on the philosopher's own state, but depend on the state of the two neighbouring philosophers. The two neighbours must have the state THINKING.

In this section, we propose language constructs for both kinds of coordinated interaction.

```
const float Radius = 5.0;
class Atom : public Agent {
autonomous :
      Step() { //autonomous operation
              ComputeForces();
              ComputeVelocityAndNewPosition();
              //Deliver new position to all atoms in the range
              Atom [ InRange(this→x, Atom→x, Radius)
                     ∧ InRange(this→y, Atom→y, Radius)
                     ∧ InRange(this→z, Atom→z, Radius) ] @ Deliver(x,y,z,mass);
      };
...

attribute:
      Position x,y,z;
private:
      Mass mass;
      Velocity velocity;
      Acceleration acceleration;
      Boolean InRange(Position mine, Position the_other, const float radius) {
              if ( abs(mine - the_other) < Radius)
                     return True;
              else return False;
      }
      ...
}
```

Fig. 5. The Atom Class with sender-initiated coordination

4.1 Pattern-based group communication

In our language framework a sender can specify the set of objects to which a group invocation should be forwarded, based on some properties (values of attributes) of the recipients. The primary characteristic of this facility is that it is type based. A pattern is applied to all objects of the global object space of a particular type and this pattern identifies a group of potential receivers of a message. A pattern is specified in first-order logic, and a receiving object must explicitly make some state properties visible. These state variables are called attributes, and are specified after the *attribute:* keyword. A pattern specification consist of conjunctions and disjunction of boolean-expressions using attributes and constants. Receiver objects must explicitly indicate which of his - normally private - local variables will be promoted to attributes. The syntax of an invocation is expressed in Figure 6.

A clear semantic for type-based group communication is very important. For example, if the languages allows inheritance then the question is : "Should an object instantiated from a subtype of $< Type >$ be part of the pattern matching process?". In our opinion it should, since subtyping corresponds to an "is a" relation with its supertype. It is, however, unclear at the moment whether there exist some examples that indicate possible conflicts between our coordination constructs and inheritance.

4.2   Multi-object Synchronisation Constraints

In our example, the synchronization constraints of the Step() operation must be expressed in such a way that the operation can only be scheduled if the information of all the neighbours is received. In other words, the number of items in the receivelist must equal the number of atoms in the specified range. Therefore we have introduced the possibility to get the exact number of objects that match a particular pattern, called the cardinality operator (*Cardinality(* $< Type > \ "[" < Pattern > \ "]" \ ))$.

$< Invocation >::= < Destination >< Inv\_op > MethodName"(" < Param > *")"$

$< Destination >::=$
    $< Reference >$ //Name-based interaction
    $| < Type > "[" < Pattern > "]"$ //Pattern-based interaction

$< Pattern >::=$
    BooleanFunctionName "(" $< Attributes > *"," < Constants > *")"$
    $| < Pattern > " \vee " < Pattern >$
    $| < Pattern > " \wedge " < Pattern >$

$< Inv\_op >::=$
    $" \rightarrow "$ // Synchronous object invocation
    $|"@"$ // Asynchronous object invocation

Fig. 6. Syntax for object invocation in Correlate

Figure 7 revisits our example in the area of molecular dynamics simulation.

5 Implementation

In this section, we will only focus on the realisation of the language constructs for coordination[4]. An efficient implementation of coordination constructs is the big challenge. In order to obtain such an efficient implementation, application specific semantics must be exploited in the realisation of the language run time. For example, in our case study, due to application specific semantics the results of a molecular dynamic simulation is not incorrect if the set of Atom objects that exactly match the pattern at a particular moment in time, and the set of objects that is computed by the language run-time to match the pattern are not equal. In this situation, for example, an atom can receive information from another atom which is not in the range of the receiving atom. This does not result in an incorrect behaviour, though it causes some useless sending of messages. On the other hand, in other application areas the exact members and the computed members of a pattern-based group invocation must be the same. For example when security is involved. This issue is closely related to consistency. A strict consistent system results in poor performance. On the other hand, non-strict consistency has a much better performance on a distributed memory platform (see caching in section 5.2).

Thus the implementation of the coordination constructs must provide some hooks to enable the advanced application programmer to incorporate some application specific knowledge. But, this may not result in the same difficult book-keeping problems that we were trying to avoid in the first place. Therefore, our language has an open character by introducing a meta-level. At the meta-level computations about other computations can be specified. For example, the membership computation of a pattern is a meta-computation. The problem domain of the membership-computation is the (application) object computation itself.

Basically, the implementation is based on the concepts presented in [BJV94]. In this paper a class hierarchy of Reference objects was presented. These reference objects reify the interaction [Fer89] between objects and reside in the meta-level of the run-time system. The reference objects realize: location independent invocation, transparent group invocation, and transparent object migration and replication. An application programmer can specialise the reference class hierarchy to add new functionality.

Reference objects intercept all object interactions, and their implementations are automatically generated from the application object's class interfaces (cfr. proxy generation). In order to realize the coordination constructs, the language architecture adds two functionalities to the reference concept :

---

[4] The Correlate language run-time uses the Xenoops [BJP+93] execution environment for issues like distribution and load balancing. Xenoops is an object-riented run-time support layer for distributed memory machines.

```
class Atom : public Agent {

...

behavior:
    AbstractState = { READY, WAITING};
    Atom() postaction become WAITING;
    Step() precondition READY postaction become WAITING;
    Deliver() precondition WAITING
        postaction if(NumberofItems(receivelist) == Cardinality(Atom [
            InRange(this→x, Atom→x, Radius)
            ∧ InRange(this→y, Atom→y, Radius)
            ∧ InRange(this→z,Atom→z, Radius) ]) become READY;

attribute:
    Position x,y,z;
private:
    Mass mass;
    Velocity velocity;
    Acceleration acceleration;
    List receivelist
    ...
}
```

Fig. 7. The Atom Class with receiver-initiated coordination

1. Attribute variables are shifted to the meta-level. The meta-level completely controls the attribute variables. This way efficient implementations can be realised (e.g. by caching) on distributed system.
2. The run-time support enables to change an attribute variable (assignment operator) in a atomic way for providing consistency.

5.1 Region reference Object

A new reference object called Region object is introduced. It's a specialisation of the GroupReference class. A GroupReference object reifies plurality at the meta-level: it performs intelligent forwarding of an invocation to all members of the group. At the base level the group of objects (the invocation must be forwarded to) has a single identity which means that a group invocation is completely transparent.

For every type of application object, a Region object exists in the meta-level on every node of the distributed system. A Region object (for type Atom) has four important data members:

1. a list of pointers to LocalReference objects representing the application object (of type Atom) on its node.

2. a list of pointers to the Region objects of all subtypes of Atom.

3. a list of pointers to RemoteReference objects representing the Region objects of type Atom on other nodes.

4. the attribute values of all objects (on its node) of type Atom that are shifted to the meta-level.

Every pattern-based group invocation initiated on node X, is intercepted by the Region object of the specified type on node X. In the case of a sender-initiated coordination primitive, the Region object performs the (intelligent) forwarding of the invocation. In the case of a receiver-initiated coordination primitive, the Region object performs the correct multi-object synchronisation.

5.2 Realisation of pattern matching

Two optimisations are essential to achieve an acceptable performance :

1. Caching of attribute values in different Region objects at different nodes of the distributed memory machine. To avoid network communication, attribute values can be cached in the Region object on another node. Different algorithms can be used to achieve cache consistency. A trade-off exists between the quality of the algorithm and its performance. Since our language framework is open, the application programmer can select a particular specialisation of the Region class. Apart from the ability to reuse different implementation strategies, the application programmer can even refine an existing implementation to incorporate application specific knowledge.

2. First-order logic gives opportunities for an early decision whether a particular object matches the pattern. In a conjunctive clause, if the first boolean expression is negative all other boolean expressions must not be evaluated. In a disjunctive clause, if the first boolean expression is positive all the other expression must not be evaluated. The application programmer can –with his superior knowledge of the application's behaviour– explicitly express the sequence of pattern matching. In particular, the boolean expression that has the biggest change to fail should be annotated first in a conjunctive clause.

6 Conclusion and Future Work

Powerful language constructs are proposed for specifying dynamic agent interaction. Agents are modelled in a concurrent object-oriented language. This paper presents two kinds of coordination semantics in the object space, and a language framework for expressing these interactions is proposed.

1. Sender-initiated coordination by means of pattern-based group communication. The primary characteristic of this facility is the fact that it is type based.

2. Receiver-initiated coordination by means of multi-object synchronisation constraints.

This paper only described the language constructs for agent interaction. Future work will focus on language constructs for describing agent behaviour. Our programming environment will provide a set of base classes which abstract different kinds of agent behaviours. These base classes will provide operations for informing, requesting, ... and offering information.

One of the major advantages of using our framework to develop multi-agent application is the ability to map the agent space on a distributed memory machine in a transparent way. As a result, the simulation time will be reduced dramatically.

Acknowledgements

The authors would like to thank J.W. Perram at Odense University for the fruitful discussions on the research area of molecular dynamics simulation and multi-agent systems.

This text presents research results of the Belgian Incentive Program "Information Technology" - Computer Science of the future, initiated by the Belgian State - Prime Minister's Service - Science Policy Office. Our research has also been sponsored by the ESPRIT Parallel Computing Action.

The scientific responsibility is assumed by its authors.

References

[Agh86] G. Agha. *ACTORS: A Model of Concurrent Computation in Distributed Systems*. The MIT Press series in artificial intelligence, 1986.

[Ame87] Pierre America. Pool-T: A Parallel Object-Oriented Language. In M. Tokoro and A. Yonezawa, editors, *Object-Oriented Concurrent Programming*, pages 199–220. The MIT Press, Cambridge, Massachusetts, 1987.

[ANSI83] Inc. American National Standards Institute. The Programming Language Ada Reference Manual. *Lecture Notes in Computer Science*, 155, 1983.

[Bij94] S. Bijnens. The Correlate Language Definition and Architecture. Technical Report 94-4SB, Dept. of Computer Science, KULeuven, 1994.

[BJB+94] Bob Bywater, Wouter Joosen, Stijn Bijnens, Pierre Verbaeten, Thomas Larsen, and John Perram. Parallel Simulation Software for Drug Design. In *HPCN Europe 94*, pages 189–196. Lecture Notes in Computer Science 796, Springer Verlag, 1994.

[BJP+93] Stijn Bijnens, Wouter Joosen, Jan Pollet, Yolande Berbers, and Pierre Verbaeten. Active Objects, Message Passing and Concurrency Control in XENOOPS. In *Proceedings of the TOOLS EUROPE'93 Workshop on Distributed Objects and Concurrency*, March 1993.

[BJV94] Stijn Bijnens, Wouter Joosen, and Pierre Verbaeten. A Reflective Invocation Scheme to Realise Advanced Object Management. In R. Guerraoui, O Nierstrasz, and M. Riveill, editors, *Object-Based Distributed Programming*, Lecture Notes in Computer Science 791, pages 139–151. Springer-Verlag, 1994.

[Fer89] Jacques Ferber. Computational Reflection in class-based object-oriented languages. In *Proceedings of OOPSLA '89*, pages 317–326. ACM Sigplan Notices, October 1989.

[Nie93]   Oscar Nierstrasz. Regular Types for Active Objects. In *Proceedings of OOP-SLA '93*, pages 1–15. ACM Sigplan Notices, October 1993.

[Pog94]   A. Poggi. Agents and Resources Management with CUBL. In *Proceedings of the 27th Hawaii International Conference on System Sciences*, pages 112–121. IEEE Computer Society Press, January 1994.

[RTL91]   Rajendra K. Ray, Ewan Tempero, and Henry M. Levy. Emerald: A General-Purpose Programming Language. *Software: Practice and Experience*, 21(1):91–92, January 1991.

[Sho93]   Y. Shoham. Agent-Oriented Programming. *Artificial Intelligence*, (60):51–92, 1993.

[ST90]   T. Sueyoshi and M. Tokoro. Dynamic Modeling of Agents for Coordination. In *Proceedings of the European Workshop on Modeling Autonomous Agents in a Multi-Agent World (MAAMAW'90)*, August 1990.

[Yon90]   A. Yonezawa. *ABCL: An Object Oriented Concurrent System*. The MIT Press series in artificial intelligence, 1990.

A Distributed Approach to
Partial Constraint Satisfaction Problems

Khaled GHEDIRA

Institute of Computer Science and Artificial Intelligence
University of Neuchâtel
Emile Argand, 11
2007 Neuchâtel, Switzerland.

Abstract

First we present, in this paper, a multi-agent approach for the partial constraint satisfaction of overconstrained problems. The approach comes from the Eco-problem solving ideas based on interactions between agents, each of them trying to reach its own satisfaction. It works by displacements within the set of possible states searching for a state satisfying the greatest number of constraints. These displacements are guided by stochastic and heuristic local repairs distributed on each variable. Each variable performs its repairs by using its own simulated annealing process combined with a min-conflicts heuristic; one of the originalities lies in the distributed implementation of the latter process. The approach also focus on the termination, completeness and optimisation problems, which are difficult to be dealt with by distributed approaches.
Then we describe the implementation of the approach and provide experimental results. Additionally we test the effectiveness of the min-conflicts heuristic.

Context and Motivations

Informally, a Constraint Satisfaction Problem (CSP) consists of a set of variables, their associated domains (i.e. the set of values the variable can take) and a set of constraints on these variables. A solution is found when each of the variables has been instantiated (assigned a value from its domain) such that all constraints are satisfied.

Because constraint satisfaction problems are generally NP-complete, peoples have been interested in them and various algorithms have been developed to solve them. These algorithms can be classified into three categories: tree search algorithms, local consistency techniques (arc consistency, path consistency and others) and hybrid tree search/local consistency algorithms. Many improvements of these algorithms have also been suggested namely learning and use of heuristics; see [Nadel 89] [Jegou 91] for more details. Other methods by reasoning about the topology of constraint networks associated to CSP have been also proposed notably the cycle-cutset [Dechter & Pearl 87] and the tree-clustering [Dechter & Pearl 89] methods.

Recent works in multi-agent systems have considered the Distributed Constraint Satisfaction Problem in which variables of a CSP are distributed among agents. Each agent has a subset (one or more) of the variables and tries to instantiate their values. Constraints may exist between variables of different agents and the instantiations of the variables must satisfy these inter-agent constraints. Various models of assigning variables to agents have been investigated [Kuwabara & al 90] [Liu & Sycara 93]. Most of them are based on tree search/arc-consistency algorithms.

All these centralised or decentralised methods deal with problems where there exists at least one solution: an instantiation of all variables that does not violate any of the constraints. Unfortunately, there are some cases where such a solution does not exist or it is costly to get it. In such cases, [Freuder & Wallace 92] proposes to find a partial solution, i.e. an instantiation of all variables that satisfies a sub-set of constraints. Such problems are called PCSP for Partial Constraint Satisfaction Problems.

The approach we propose, has the same objective than PCSP. It is also close to iterative repair methods [Minton & al 92] [Verfaillie 93] [Liu & Sycara 93] that consist in starting with a possible inconsistent configuration (i.e. a configuration that possibly contains constraint violations) and incrementally repairing constraint violations until a consistent assignment is achieved. These repairs are guided, in our approach, by a stochastic optimisation tool, the simulated annealing, whose objective is to reach an optimal state that satisfies the greatest number of constraints. Note that our approach is also close to GSAT [Selman & Kautz 93], which is a randomised local search procedure for solving propositional satisfiability problems that are equivalent to CSP.

The proposed approach does not only benefit from the use of simulated annealing process but also multi-agent techniques that have opened a natural and pleasant way to solve diverse problems in terms of cooperation, conflict and concurrence within a society of agents. Each agent is an autonomous entity which is asynchronously able to acquire information from its environment and/or from other agents, to reason on the basis of this information and to act consequently. Within the large domain of multi-agent systems, our approach is inspired by the principles of Eco-Problem Solving

[Ferber & Jacopin 90]: satisfaction, flight, aggression, ..., which offer a general framework to easily express a problem with reactive and simple agents.

A first version of the approach was developed for the resource allocation problem [Ghedira & Verfaillie 91] [Ghedira & Verfaillie 92a] [Ghedira & Verfaillie 92b] [Ghedira 92]. The good experimental and theoretical results encouraged us to deepen the approach and to generalise it to Constraint Satisfaction Problems. A basic approach was presented in [Ghedira 94a]. A theoretical formulation with Markov chains was made and the asymptotic convergence was proved. Improvements to speed-up and consequently to put into practice simulated annealing were proposed and their impact on the previous theoretical results discussed. First this paper summarises the ideas used to improve the basic approach, namely the distributed simulated annealing and the fast cooling scheme, and then provides experimental results. The other purpose is to focus on termination, optimisation and completeness problems, which are difficult to be dealt with by distributed approaches.

There are mainly three expected outcomes:

• To be able to deal with the dynamic aspect of CSP, i.e. the problem modifications such as addition or deletion of constraints, in a simple way, starting from a previous solution and being very likely to reach a new solution not very far.

• Naturally deal with inherently distributed problems such as multi-site scheduling, network control, distributed databases, ... where a centralised approach cannot be considered because it is impossible or difficult to gather the information at the same place.

• To open the way to use parallel architecture in order to solve hard and/or large CSP with the prospect of a decreased run time.

1 The Approach

First we introduce the basic dynamics; then we focus on termination, completeness and optimisation problems, which will lead us to

• use the simulated annealing algorithm in order to deal with the optimisation and completeness problems, and

• introduce a forced termination mechanism to ensure the termination.

Finally, we detail the approach taking into account the three latter problems. Note that we associate to each agent a graph of states in order to better cope with the global dynamics.

1.1 The Basic Dynamics

The basic model involves Constraint and Variable agents in direct interactions, each of them seeking its maximal satisfaction. Following the Eco-Problem solving ideas, each agent has a simple structure: acquaintances (the agents that it knows), a local memory composed of its static and dynamic knowledge and a mailbox where it stores the received messages it will later process one after one.

In order to simplify, we have defined the agent's general behaviour independently of its type. This one is based on the search for satisfaction giving priority to message processing:

if mailbox not empty
then   process-first-message
else   if satisfied
*   then satisfaction behaviour (nothing)*
*   else unsatisfaction behaviour*

A constraint is satisfied if its associated relation is satisfied. Each unsatisfied constraint chooses one of its variables and asks it to change its value. A variable is satisfied when it is instantiated and not asked to change its value. Each unsatisfied variable chooses a value and informs its constraints.

1.2 Termination, Completeness and Optimisation

As expected, difficulties come from the distributed aspect of the approach and the asynchronous behaviour of agents. Here we focus on difficulties that concern the termination and optimisation (or completeness) properties:

• The first property could be expressed as follows: is the dialogue between constraints and variables likely to go on indefinitely without reaching the satisfaction of the agents, or an acceptable compromise between them.

• The second is: if one or several solutions exist, does the result belong to these solutions (completeness)? if no solution exists, is the result (partial solution) optimal, in the sense of the targeted objective (optimisation)?

These two questions are closely connected and call for a single technical solution. We are looking for a mechanism guaranteeing the termination and offering the best chances to terminate with a solution, if such a solution exists, or at an optimal partial solution otherwise.

For example, a "first in, first out" mechanism applied by each variable on the demands of its constraints ensures the termination but does not ensure the completeness or the optimisation since the final configuration depends on the arrival order of constraint messages (stochastic).

At the level of one variable, an improvement would be to accept to change value, provided that it increases the number of satisfied constraints. Unfortunately, the satisfaction maximisation at the variable level doesn't guarantee the global maximisation and the risk remains to be blocked into a local maximum of satisfaction. This type of algorithms called "greedy algorithms" is efficient only in the case of convex objective functions.

This leads to the idea to use the simulated annealing algorithm [Aarts & Van Laarhoven 87] [Weisbuch 89] and to adapt it to a multi-agent world. This algorithm comes from the statistical physics and has successfully been applied to connectionnist model [Aarts & Korst 89] and to other famous problems like the travel salesman problem [Kirkpatrick &al 83] [Bonomi & Lutton 84].

Integrated into the basic dynamics, the simulated annealing consists in

• allowing local deterioration of satisfaction at the variables level, hoping to improve the global satisfaction and

• controlling this possibility (so as to avoid a roaming behaviour) with a stochastic process that is guided by a parameter, the *tolerance*, which is usually called temperature: when the process starts, there is a high tolerance to local satisfaction deterioration, and this tolerance progressively decreases until it reaches a zero-level, where only changes leading to an increase of the local satisfaction are accepted.

In relation to classical implementation of simulated annealing, the originality of our approach lies in the tolerance parameter control. Indeed, the multi-agent idea offers the possibility of a local control of this parameter, at the level of each variable. So, each variable has got its own simulated annealing that it controls. According to both its goals and knowledge, it sets its own initial tolerance and its evolution in time. This alternative was applied in the framework of connectionnist model [Aarts & Korst 89] where each unity has its own simulated annealing that it locally controls. It gave good experimental results but suffers from the lack of theoretical basis.

With this totally distributed implementation of simulated annealing, we keep the notions of locality and autonomy defined in eco-problem solving.

Another mechanism, which we call *the forced termination mechanism*, is added to make sure that the process terminates:

• At zero-tolerance, a variable accepts only changes leading to a strict increase of the local satisfaction.

• A change, in other words a value, rejected at this level, becomes forbidden.

• If all its values, except the current instantiation value, are forbidden, a variable is locked. Therefore, it is no more required by its constraints to change its value.

If a constraint is unsatisfied and all its variables are locked, it becomes itself locked and does not seek to be satisfied any longer. The overall process terminates when all constraints are either satisfied or locked. Consequently, we are near the required result: guaranteed termination and best likelihood to reach a global maximum.

As the simulated annealing could lead the system to move from a good state to a worse one, the two types of agents are not sufficient and an interface is necessary between these agents and the user in order to:

• detect that the CSP has been resolved and

• especially inform the user of the best partial solution reached during the dialogue.

Thus, a third and last type called Machine has been created, which contains only one instance.

1.3 The Detailed Approach

1.3.1 The Constraint agents

A constraint has as acquaintances its variables, i.e. the variables that it constrains, and the Machine agent. The static knowledge of a constraint consists of its associated relation. Its dynamic knowledge concerns its variables: the current instantiation values and the locked or unlocked states. Each unsatisfied (and unlocked) constraint chooses one of its unlocked variables and requires it to change its value.

According to the agent's general behaviour, the unsatisfaction behaviour is the following:
if not-locked
then
  choose-variable (among the unlocked)
  variable <- change-value

The associated graph of states consists of four basic states (fig.1): not-instantiated, instantiated-satisfied, instantiated-unsatisfied and waiting. The first state corresponds to a situation where the constraint is not yet instantiated (i.e. one at least of its variables is not instantiated), the second one to a situation where the constraint is both instantiated and satisfied and the third one to a situation where the constraint is instantiated but not satisfied. The last one corresponds to a situation where the constraint waits for a decision of a variable after having answered to its demand-opinion message. In this state, the constraint does nothing except queuing the incoming messages in its mailbox. Once it leaves this state, it resumes its activity and executes its standard behaviour defined in §1.1. Moreover, the forced termination mechanism implies a new state: locked, which is generated by the *inform-decision* message.

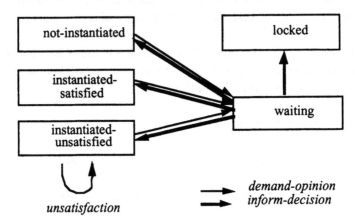

Fig. 1. Graph of constraint's states

A constraint can receive only the two following messages:

  • *inform-decision*
  store-decision
  update-own-memory (eventually locked variables, ...)
  change-state (see fig.1)

  • *demand-opinion*
  if waiting-state
  then store-message (this one)
  else
    state:= waiting
    evaluate-satisfaction (satisfied or unsatisfied about the selected value)
    variable (in question) <- answer-opinion

1.3.2 The variable agents

A variable has as acquaintances its constraints, i.e. the constraints that constrain it, and the Machine agent. The static knowledge of a variable consists of its domain of values. Its dynamic knowledge consists of its current instantiation value, its satisfaction level, its current tolerance and its forbidden values. Each unsatisfied variable randomly chooses a value among its authorised (not forbidden) values, asks its constraints for their opinion* about the selected value and waits for their answers. After receiving the answers of all its constraints, the variable takes its decision to whether accept or reject this problem by using its own simulated annealing as follows: Let v be the considered variable, let i denotes its current state, let j be its new state generated by the selected value, let S(i) be the number of its satisfied constraints in the state i (ditto for j), let T(k,v) be its tolerance at the time k, the probability to accept j is defined by:

$$A_{ij} = \begin{cases} 1 & \text{if } S(j) \geq S(i) \\ 1 & \text{if } \left[(\text{random}[0,1] < \exp(\frac{S(j) - S(i)}{T(k,v)})) \wedge (S(j) < S(i)) \right] \\ 0 & \text{otherwise} \end{cases}$$

Finally it informs, on one hand its constraints, which were all in the waiting state for its decision, and on the other hand the Machine agent of its decision.

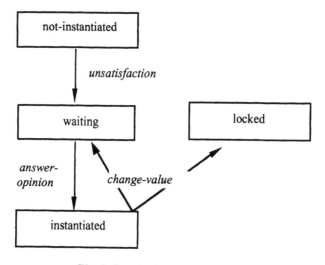

Fig. 2. Graph of variable's states

According to the agent's general behaviour, the unsatisfaction behaviour is the following:
choose-value
state := waiting
Constraint acquaintances <- demand-opinion

---

* When a constraint is requested to give its opinion about a selected value, it evaluates its satisfaction state, answers "satisfied" or "unsatisfied" about the selected value and waits for the decision of the variable, which asked it.

The associated graph of states consists of three basic states (fig.2): not-instantiated, instantiated and waiting. The first state corresponds to an unsatisfaction situation, the second one to a satisfaction situation and the third one to a situation where the variable has chosen a value and is waiting for the opinion (satisfied or unsatisfied) of its constraints about this choice. Moreover, the termination mechanism implies another state: locked, which is generated by the *change-value* message.

A variable can receive only the two following messages:
  • *change-value*
  if not waiting
  then unsatisfaction-behaviour
  else ignore-message

  • *answer-opinion*
  store-opinion
  if all-opinions-received
  then   take-decision (by using its simulated annealing)
    state := instantiated
    update-own-memory (forbidden values, tolerance, ...)
    Constraint acquaintances <- inform-decision (eventually locking)

1.3.3 The Machine agent

The Machine agent has as acquaintances both variables and constraints. It knows the state of each constraint, which is communicated either by the variables (satisfied or unsatisfied after value change) or directly by the constraints themselves (locking situation). Note that this agent does not interfere with the problem resolution process, i.e. in the dialogue between constraints and variables. It is only an intermediary between the agents and the user.
It is satisfied when all the constraints are either satisfied or locked. In unsatisfaction case, it does not do anything. In the satisfaction case, it informs the user of the results choosing the best configuration reached during the agents dialogue (the dialogue history is kept by the Machine).

2 Experimentation

2.1 Simulated annealing in practice

The idea is to find a finite-time implementation of the simulated annealing algorithm resulting in a compromise between a good quality of solution (the nearest possible from global optimal solutions) and an acceptable run time. To achieve this one must specify a set of parameters that governs the convergence of the algorithm. These parameters are combined in a so-called *cooling scheme*, which specifies: an initial tolerance, a tolerance decreasing profile and a stopping criterion. We propose the following scheme, we have empirically developed:

• Initial tolerance: The best would be to have, for each transition from a state i to a state j, an initial acceptance probability equal to 1; but such a value would generate an infinite initial tolerance. Let v be a variable, its initial tolerance T_{init} (v) is, in practice, chosen such that the exponential part of the acceptance probability is greater than 1/2 [Aarts & Korst 89]: $\exp(\Delta S_{ij}/T_{init}$ (v)) $\geq$ (1/2), $\forall$ the transition ij. This condition is equivalent to: $|\Delta S_{ij}| / \text{Log}(2) \leq T_{init}$ (v), $\forall$ ij.
Let card-const(v) denotes the number of V's constraints, we have: $|\Delta S_{ij}| \leq$ card-const(v) - 1, $\forall$ ij;
from which the condition for the initial tolerance of a variable v is given by:
T_{init} (v) $\geq$ (card-const (v) - 1) / Log(2).
This condition is strongly linked to the considered variable, it depends on the number of its constraints.

• Decreasing profile: Whenever a variable v accepts to change its value in spite of a satisfaction decrease, it decrements its tolerance of one: T_{n+1} (v) = T_n (v) - 1.

• Stopping criterion: According to forced termination mechanism, when a variable is locked, it is no more requested by its constraints.

2.2 Experiment design

The implementation was developed with Actalk [Briot 89], an Object-Based Concurrent Programming language in the Smalltalk-80 environment. In this language framework, an agent is implemented as an actor having the smalltalk object structure enriched by an ability to send/receive messages to/from its acquaintances, buffering the received messages in its own mailbox.

The experimentation is performed on binary CSP-samples randomly generated. The generation is guided by two parameters: constraint density and constraint tightness. Constraint density is a number between 0 and 100% indicating the ratio between the number of the problem effective constraints to the number of all possible constraints (i.e. a complete constraint graph). Constraint tightness is a number between 0 and 100% indicating the ratio between the number of pairs of values forbidden (not allowed) by the constraint to the size of the domain cross product.

Having chosen the following values {0.1, 0.3, 0.5, 0.7, 0.9} for the previous parameters, we obtain 25 density-tightness combinations. For each combination, we randomly generate 5 examples. Each of these examples uses 10 variables, each variable having a domain size among 5 and 10. Therefore, we have 125 examples. Moreover and considering the random aspect of simulated annealing, we have performed 5 tests per example and taken the average. For each combination density-tightness, we also take the average of the 5 generated examples.

2.3 Completeness

In order to evaluate the completeness, we compare the proposed model with a tree search method, the forward-checking algorithm [Haralick & Elliot 80]. We choose this algorithm because it is enough known in the CSP domain for its reasonable complexity comparatively to other search methods. It particularly is exact: it finds all solutions satisfying all constraints.

Figure 3 presents the satisfaction levels of the proposed model by squares and the forward checking results by crosses. Of course, the results of the last one are presented only if there are solutions. In figure 3, whenever the forward checking finds a solution, this one is also reached by our model; which experimentally shows the model completeness in the case of problems with solutions. But it is not sufficient to assert that the model is really complete because we don't know whether the other partial solutions are optimal or not (family of most strongly constrained and very tight problems). In order to further evaluate the optimality for this family of problems, it would be better to do comparisons with algorithms, which aim at the same objective than our model such as [Minton & al 92], [Freuder & Wallace 92], ...

Moreover, we will introduce in the next paragraph the use of an heuristic in order to further improve the model especially in the case of problems without solution.

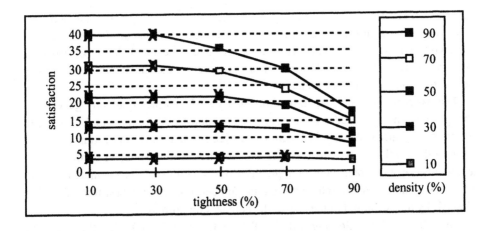

Fig. 3. Quality of partial solutions

2.4 Effect of the min-conflicts heuristic

2.4.1 Introduction

In CSP, various heuristics for finding good value/variable ordering has been investigated [Haralick & Elliot 80]. These heuristics are very efficient especially in the case of backtracking algorithms. The asynchronous backtracking, developed for Distributed CSP [Kuwabara & al 90], has used successfully this type of heuristics [Kuwabara & al 91].

Because our approach is close to iterative repair methods [Johnston & al 92], we are interesting in min-conflicts heuristic that has been used in this type of method. Indeed, this heuristic has been successfully applied to the n-queens problem by [Chabrier & al 91] [Johnston & al 92] and in other various fields by [Johnston & al 92]. In addition, this heuristic fits very well our objective, which consists in maximising the number of satisfied constraints.

This heuristic is guided by a simple ordering for repairing constraint violations: select a variable that is currently participating in a constraint violation, and choose a new value that minimises the number of outstanding constraint violations.

The application of this heuristic to our approach results in the following: A variable, not instantiated or requested by one of its constraints to change its value, sends to all its constraints a *demand-opinion* message attached with its domain of values. Each of its constraints checks its associated relation for each value and answers "satisfied" or "unsatisfied" for each value. After receiving all answers from its constraints, it chooses the value that minimises the number of its unsatisfied constraints, it takes decision to whether accept or reject this value (by help of its own simulated annealing) and then informs its constraints and the Machine agent of its decision.

2.4.2 Experimental results

In order to make comparisons, we compute ratios of WH-H (the proposed model with heuristic) and WT-H (the proposed model without heuristic) performance using the number of state changes (by analogy with the number of backtracks in the tree search algorithms), the number of constraint checks, the cpu time and the satisfaction level. This allows a quick assessment of the relative performance of the two methods WH-H and WT-H being compared. Thus WT-H performance is the numerator when measuring state changes, constraint checks and cpu time ratios, and the denominator when measuring satisfaction ratio. Any number greater than 1 indicates superior performance by WH-H.

Figure 4 shows the performance ratios from which we draw out the following results:

• From the point of view of the state changes, WH-H never requires more than WT-H. For the most strongly constrained and most weakly tight set of examples, WH-H requires up to five orders of magnitude less.

• From the point of view of the constraint checks, WH-H never requires more than WT-H. For the most strongly constrained and most weakly tight set of examples, WH-H requires up to seven orders of magnitude less.

• From the cpu time point of view, WH-H requires up to four orders of magnitude less for the most strongly constrained (i.e. overconstrained) and most weakly tight set of examples. Nevertheless and in some problems especially for the most strongly tight set of examples, the cpu time ratio is less than 1, suggesting that WH-H pays little overhead penalty to check values of a given domain one per one. This weak sub standard performance is compensated by the result quality. Let us mention that the cpu time includes the cost of communication.

• From the satisfaction point of view, WH-H always finds more or same satisfaction than WT-H. It finds about 1.5 orders of magnitude more for the most strongly tight and most strongly tight set of problems.

2.5 Summary

The without-heuristic approach is complete with respect to CSP with complete solutions. For PCSP, we cannot conclude although the curves present satisfaction levels relatively close to the corresponding total numbers of constraints. As it has the same objective than the various simulated annealing processes, the min-conflicts heuristic has been added. Globally, it considerably improves the results especially for the most strongly constrained and/or most strongly tight set of problems.
Furthermore, the min-conflicts heuristic still keeps the completeness for CSP with complete solutions since WH-H satisfactions are always better than those of WT-H.
To evaluate the completeness in the general case (with or without complete solution), it would be better to do comparison with appropriate approaches, i.e. that deal with PCSP.

Perspectives and first conclusions

Further precise comparisons have to be done with other approaches dealing with partial constraint satisfaction problems, on the basis of stronger experiments. Nevertheless, it appears that:

• On these particular CSP, the multi-agent approach improved by some extensions related to the introduction of distributed simulated annealing (a simulated annealing per variable), has shown its viability and its capacity to give some answers to termination and completeness questions.

• Contrary to other works (see [Liu & Sycara 93]) that didn't show so good results, the min-conflicts heuristic has given quite promising results particularly concerning problems where no configuration, satisfying the set of all constraints, exists. We think that these good performances result from the fact that the min-conflicts heuristic fits very well the use of simulated annealing.

Our short purpose is to apply the proposed approach to real-world problems. We have already begun with the scheduling of assembly workplants and the design of assembly installations.

Our further studies will put the stress on experimental and theoretical issues:

• first, we will continue our experimental comparative studies involving the other approaches (dealing with PCSP) mentioned in this paper;

• then, we intend to deepen some works about the CSP dynamic aspect, which were already developed in [Ghedira 94b], and

• finally, we will implement the proposed approach into parallel architecture.

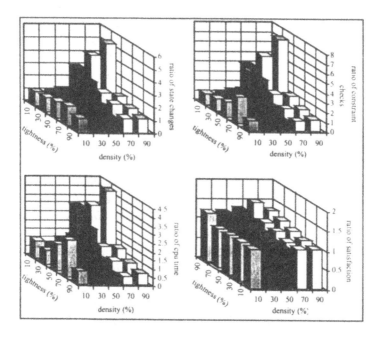

Fig. 4. Effect of the min-conflicts heuristic

Moreover, it is known that local consistency techniques are very efficient to reduce the domains of values and consequently both the set of states and the overall run time. Unfortunately, our approach does not use such techniques because they risk to prevent the simulated annealing from converging to optimal solutions by removing states that might lead to optimal states.

REFERENCES

[Aarts & Van Laarhoven 87] E.H.L. Aarts and P.J.M. Van Laarhoven: "Simulated Annealing: Theory and Applications", D.Reidel Publishing Company, 1987.

[Aarts & Korst 89] E.H.L. Aarts and J.Korst: "Simulated Annealing and Boltzmann Machines: A stochastic approach to combinatorial optimization and neural computing", A Wiley Interscience Publication, 1989.

[Bonomi & lutton 84] E.Bonomi and J.L. Lutton: "The N-city Travelling Salesman Problem: Statistical Mechanics and the Metropolis Algorithm", SIAM Rev, 26, 1984.

[Briot 89] J.P.Briot: "ACTALK: a testbed for classifying and designing actors languages in the SMALLTALK environment", *ECOOP*, 1989.

[Chabrier & al 91] J.Chabrier, J.J.Chabrier et F.Trousset: "Résolution efficace d'un problème de satisfaction de contraintes: le millions de reines", *International Conference of AI, KBS, ES and NL*, Avignon, 1991.

[Dechter & Pearl 87] R.Dechter and J.Pearl: "The cycle-cutset method for improving search performance in AI applications", *Proc. third IEEE Conference on AI applications, Orlando*, 1987.

[Dechter & Pearl 89] R.Dechter and J.Pearl: "Tree clustering for Constraint Networks", *Artificial Intelligence, 38*, 1989.

[Ferber & Jacopin 90] J.Ferber et E.facopin: "The framework of Eco Problem Solving", *Y.Demazeau et J.P. Müller, v. 1, Decentralized Artificial Intelligence, Editions North Holland, 1990.*

[Freuder & Wallace 92] E.C.Freuder and R.J.Wallace: "Partial constraint satisfaction", *Artificial Intelligence, 58*, 1992.

[Ghedira & Verfaillie 91] K.Ghedira and G.Verfaillie: "Approche multi-agents pour le problème d'affectation", *International Conference of AI, KBS, ES and NL*, Avignon, 1991.

[Ghedira & Verfaillie 92a] K.Ghedira and G.Verfaillie: "Approche multi-agents d'un problème de satisfaction de contraintes: optimalité et réactivité", *International Conference of AI, KBS, ES and NL*, Avignon, 1992.

[Ghedira & Verfaillie 92b] K.Ghedira and G.Verfaillie: "A multi-agent model for the resource allocation problem: a reactive approach", *ECAI 92, Vienna*, 1992;
also published in: *"Scheduling of Production Process", Edts by Y.Dorn and K.A.Froeschl, University Vienna,* 1993.

[Ghedira 92] K.Ghedira: "A reactive and distributed approach to the revision problem in the framework of the resource allocation problem", *ETFA, Melbourne*, 1992.

[Ghedira 94a] K.Ghedira: "Partial Constraint Satisfaction by a Multi-Agent-Simulated Annealing approach", *International Conference of AI, KBS, ES and NL*, Paris, 1994.

[Ghedira 94b] K.Ghedira: "Dynamic Partial Constraint Satisfaction by a Multi-Agent-Simulated Annealing approach", *workshop CSP-ECAI*, Amsterdam, 1994.

[Haralick & Elliot 80] R.M.Haralick and G.L.Elliot: "Increasing tree search efficiency for constraint satisfaction problems", *Artificial Intelligence, 14*, 1980.

[Jegou 91] P.Jégou: "Contribution à l'étude des problèmes de satisfaction de contraintes: algorithmes de propagation et de résolution, propagation de contraintes dans les réseaux dynamiques", *PHD-Thesis, LIRMM-USTL Montpellier II*, 1991.

[Johnston & al 92] S.Minton, M.D.Johnston, A.B.Philips et P.Laird: "Minimizing conflicts: a heuristic repair method for constraint satisfaction problem and scheduling problems", *Artificial Intelligence*, 1992.

[Kirkpatrick & al 93] S.Kirkpatrick, C.D.Gelatt, Jr.M.P.Vecchi: "Optimisation by simulated annealing", *Science, 220*, 1983.

[Kuwabara & al 90] M.Yokoo, T.Ishida and K.Kuwabara: "Distributed Constraint Satisfaction for DAI Problems", *Proc. 10th International Workshop on Distributed Artificial Intelligence*, 1990.

[Kuwabara & al 91] Y.Nishibe, K.Kuwabara and T.Ishida: "Effects of Heuristics in Distributed Constraint Satisfaction: Towards Satisficing Algorithms", *Proc. 10th International Workshop on Distributed Artificial Intelligence*, 1990.

[Liu & Sycara 93] J.Liu & K.Sycara: "Emergent Constraint Satisfaction through Multi-agent Coordinated Interaction",

K.Ghedira & F.Sprumont: *proc of MAAMAW'93, Neuchatel, Switzerland*, 1993.

[Metropolis & al 53]   N.Metrolpolis, A.W. Rosenbluth, M.N. Rosenbluth, A.H. Teller and E.Teller: "Simulated Annealing", *J. Chem. Pys. 21*, 1953.

[Minton & al 92]   S.Minton, M.D.Johnston, A.B.Philips and P.Laird: "Minimizing conflicts: a heuristic repair method for constraint satisfaction problem and scheduling problems", *Artificial Intelligence*, 1992.

[Montanari 74]   U.Montanari: "Networks of constraints: fundamental properties and applications to picture processing", *Information Sciences, 7*, 1974.

[Nadel 89]   B.A. Nadel: "Constraint satisfaction algorithms", *Search in artificial intelligence, Editions L.Kanal et V.Kumar, Springer Verlag*, 1989.

[Selman & Kautz 93]   B.Selman & H.Kautz: "Domain-Independent Extensions to GSAT: Solving Large Structured Satisfiability Problems", *IJCAI, 1993*.

[Verfaillie 93]   G.Verfaillie: "Problèmes de satisfaction de contraintes: production et révision de solution par modifications locales", *International Conference of AI, KBS, ES and NL*, Avignon, 1993.

[Weisbuch 89]   G.Weisbuch: "Dynamique des systèmes complexes: une introduction aux réseaux d'automates", *Intereditions/Editions CNRS*.

A Collaboration Strategy for Repetitive Encounters

Kei Matsubayashi * Mario Tokoro **

Department of Computer Science, Keio University.
3-14-1 Hiyoshi, Kohoku-ku, Yokohama 223 Japan

Abstract. Agents might interact more than once. In other words, agents have opportunities to reach good agreements (solutions) which could not have been achieved in only one collaboration (game). This paper proposes a *Collaboration Strategy*, that is, a policy for choosing a strategy in a repetitive but changing game, which takes the chance of meeting again into consideration.

There are two main collaboration strategies. One, using FSM, considers only the history but not the payoff, and another, that selects the most rational strategy in each game, considers only the payoff but not the history. Both together are essential to repetitive collaboration. Therefore, our collaboration strategy for repetitive encounters among n agents utilizing positive relations between plans takes both into account.

Simulation results are also given so that the necessary conditions for a collaboration strategy for reaching better agreements between agents than here to fare can be discussed.

1 Introduction

Agents might interact more than once. In other words, agents might be presented with opportunities to reach good agreements (solutions) which would not have been achievable in an earlier collaboration (game). This paper proposes a *Collaboration Strategy*, that is, a policy for choosing a strategy in a repetitive but changing game, which takes the chance of meeting again into consideration.

The following are the two main collaboration strategies proposed up to now. Each has its limitations.

1. The first one is the collaboration strategy represented by FSMs which use the history of previous strategies as input in finding the new strategy.
   While choosing a strategy depends on the history of previous strategies, the payoffs in the game cannot be taken into account. Thus, this cannot be used in a domain where the payoffs of a game change.

---
* *kei@mt.cs.keio.ac.jp*. This research is supported by Research Fellowships of the Japanese Society for the Promotion of Science for Young Scientists.
** *mario@mt.cs.keio.ac.jp*. Also affiliated with Sony Computer Science Laboratory Inc.

2. The second is the collaboration strategy which selects the most rational strategy for each game.

   Choosing a strategy depends on the payoff of each game, but history is not taken into consideration. Thus, cooperative solutions cannot occur if agents meet again.

In cases where the communication costs are not negligible, the number of agents collaborating changes or the payoff matrix is inconsistent, these collaboration strategies are insufficient. Therefore, we are proposing a collaboration strategy that considers the positive characteristics of both: the payoff and the history.

Although it has been shown by Axelrod that there can be no one best way of choosing a strategy [1], it is important to compare the collaboration strategy proposed in this paper with the above mentioned ones. Here, we concentrate on the collaboration of positive relationships between plans so as to test collaboration between agents using our collaboration strategy and agents using the collaboration strategy 2 above (where Nash solution is selected in each game), in various situations with different proportions of each kind of agent. By discussing the results from the viewpoint of ESS (Evolutionarily Stable Strategy) [8], we demonstrate the necessary conditions for parameters using our collaboration strategy to have an agent that is capable of reaching a better agreement.

We describe the domain and the assumptions in our research in Sect. 2. In Sect. 3 and 4, we propose our collaboration strategy and give the simulation results. In Sect. 5, we discuss computation costs and compare our work with related works. The conclusion follows in Sect. 6.

2 Domain

In order to concentrate on collaboration strategy, we assume the following:

1. Each agent has a plan which satisfies its goal but does not know the plans of other agents.
2. Unambiguity of meaning and equality of cost of an action for all agents.
3. Agents collaborate on the positive relations [5] of their plans.

   A positive relation is the relationship that exists between overlapping plans. If agents can merge their plans, and so remove redundancy, their plans will be more efficient.

4. Merged plan can be executed by only one agent.

   If a merged plan could be split up into m plans which ideally need m agents to fulfill the tasks most efficiently, agents must negotiate m times to assign those plans.

5. Agents can find n other agents ($n \geq 1$) to participate in the collaboration.

   This can be realized by an agent using Contract Net Protocol, for example, to announce its intention to collaborate.

6. The agent strategy that is proposed in a collaboration is denoted as the agent that receives the merged plan.

   If the strategy of an agent is denoted as that agent itself, we call the strategy, a 'reception' strategy. In the same manner, if the strategy of an agent is denoted as an other agent, we call the strategy, a 'delegation' strategy.

7. Agreement is reached if an agent, *i.e.* A, proposes the delegation strategy, 'agent B', and B proposes the reception strategy, 'agent B'.

3 The Collaboration Strategy

The current agent's strategy has an influence on the future strategy of other agents. When selecting a strategy, an agent has not only to consider the history of previous strategies and the payoffs of the current game, but also to predict and consider the future strategies of other agents. To perform this prediction, we utilize the notion of *social law* [7] in our collaboration strategy:

For example, when agents collaborate on positive relation between plans, they decide through negotiation which of them will execute the merged plan. If an agent receives the execution, it has to execute more actions than before, so that rational agents take only delegation strategies. In other words, only benevolent agents can collaborate on positive relation. However, even rational agents can expect future benefits from choosing a reception strategy in the current game and a delegation strategy in some future game, if the future is predicted using a social law such as "If an agent delegates the plan execution now, it cannot delegate a plan in the future".

Agents can avoid conflicts over delegation strategies by considering the social law and its benefits and considering the downside also. However, other agents might use a social law that contradicts with the former, or they might not utilize any social law. This kind of situation can occur very frequently since Multi-Agent Systems can be seen as open distributed systems.

In order for agents to predict future benefits accurately even under such situations, we have introduced to our collaboration strategy a *reliability*, or the probability that another agent abides by a law that doesn't contradict with the agent's law.

3.1 Notations

Henceforth, we use the following notations.

- π_A

  Plan of agent A.
- $\text{Merge}(\{\pi_1, \ldots, \pi_n\}, \text{Agent}_e, \text{Agent}_i)$

  Plan of agent i $(i = 1, \cdots, n)$ when the subplans of $\text{Agent}_1, \ldots, \text{Agent}_n$ are merged so that Agent_e $(e = 1, \ldots, n; e \neq i)$ has to execute $\{\pi_1, \cdots, \pi_n\}$

- Cost(π_A)

    Cost of agent A's plan

- U(Merge($\{\pi_1, \ldots, \pi_n\}$, Agent$_e$, Agent$_j$),π_j)

    Agent j's utility when it executes Merge($\{\pi_1, \ldots, \pi_n\}$, Agent$_e$, Agent$_i$).

3.2 Social Law

We utilize the social law that was formalized by Shoham [7]. We use the particular law for collaboration on positive relation.

If the social law is something like "If an agent delegates the plan execution now, it cannot delegate a plan in the future" then when two agents negotiate, they can select even a reception strategy and expect some future benefit. However, when n agents negotiate at one time, the law is insufficient and might not enable them to reach unanimous agreement.

In this paper, we assume that the agents abide by the following law.

Social law:
The agent that has delegated its executions most, which means, whose payoff sum (benefit sum - loss sum) is the highest among the agents participating in the collaboration, is forbidden to choose delegation strategy in the current game.

3.3 Payoff Matrix

In the following, the use of $\mathcal{A}$, $\mathcal{B}$, $\mathcal{C}$ does not refer to the agent itself, but to the strategy which denotes 'the agent that receives the execution', according to assumption 6 in Section 2. For instance, the payoff matrix of agent A, when agent A and B collaborate and both of them abide by the law (reception strategy), is shown in Table 1.

		B	
		$\mathcal{A}$	$\mathcal{B}$
A	$\mathcal{A}$	U(Merge($\{\pi_A, \pi_B\}$, A, A),π_A)	–
	$\mathcal{B}$	–	U(Merge($\{\pi_A, \pi_B\}$, B, A),π_A)

Table 1. A's payoff matrix (2 participating agents)

The '–' in Table 1 represents 'undefined', which means that this state is not possible if both agents abide by the law.

If three agents, *i.e.*, A, B and C, participate in a collaboration, the payoff matrix is not like the above matrix any more. it now has three dimensions. Generally speaking, the matrix needs n dimension to express a game of n agents.

Here in this paper, we express the matrix as follows in order to express n dimensions. The example shows the collaboration between agents A, B and C. ($\mathcal{A}$,$\mathcal{A}$) represents that B's strategy is $\mathcal{A}$ and C's strategy is $\mathcal{A}$.

Next, we calculate each element of the matrix. Suppose that there are n participating agents $(1, 2, \ldots, n)$ and the strategy of agent i is $s(i)$, each element

		(B,C)		
		$(\mathcal{A},\mathcal{A})$	$\cdots$	$(\mathcal{C},\mathcal{C})$
$\mathcal{A}$	A	U(Merge($\{\pi_A,\pi_B,\pi_C\},A,A),\pi_A$)	$\cdots$	$-$
B		$-$	$\cdots$	$-$
C		$-$	$\cdots$	U(Merge($\{\pi_A,\pi_B,\pi_C\},C,A),\pi_A$)

Table 2. A's payoff matrix (3 participating agents)

of the matrix of agent i is $Payoff(s_i,(s(1),\cdots,s(i-1),s(i+1),\cdots,s(n)))$, and so payoff can be calculated as follows.

$Payoff(s(i),(s(1),\cdots,s(i-1),s(i+1),\cdots,s(n)))$

$$= \begin{cases} U(\text{Merge}(\pi_\Sigma \cup \{\pi_i\},s(i),i),\pi_i), & s(s(i))=s(i)=s(k),\ k\in\Sigma,\ k\neq i \\ & \text{where } \pi_\Sigma = \{\pi_k|k\in\Sigma\} \\ 0, & \text{otherwise.} \end{cases}$$

The payoff is the utility U if the strategy of agent i, $s(i)$, is the same strategy of agent $s(i)$, $s(s(i))$. Set Σ represents the plans of those agents whose strategy is the same as $s(i)$.

In this paper, we use the cost of executing a merged plan as the utility. The utility is not just the execution cost of a single plan, because the current strategy influences the future strategies of other agents. Thus, the utility contains a prediction of future costs. This is shown for particular examples.

Utilities when all agents abide by the law

The utility of agent i is as follows, supposing that all agents abide by the law.

$U(\text{Merge}(\pi_\Sigma \cup \{\pi_i\},s(i),i),\pi_i)$

$$= \begin{cases} \text{Cost}(\pi_i) - \text{Cost}(\text{Merge}(\pi_\Sigma \cup \{\pi_i\}),i,i) & \\ \quad + \sum_{k\in\Sigma}(\text{Cost}(\pi_k) - \text{Cost}(\text{Merge}(\pi_\Sigma \cup \{\pi_i\}),k,i)), & s(i)=i \\ \text{Cost}(\pi_i) - \text{Cost}(\text{Merge}(\pi_\Sigma \cup \{\pi_i\}),s(i),i) & \\ \quad +(\text{Cost}(\pi_{s(i)}) - \text{Cost}(\text{Merge}(\pi_\Sigma \cup \{\pi_i\}),i,i)), & s(i)\neq i \end{cases}$$

In the first case, the utility represents the case where agent i receives the execution $(s(i)=i)$. In this case, the utility is decreased by the second term, the current costs. Using the social law, agent i can predict that it can have the same plan as agent k whose plan is received by i, and i will be able to delegate the plan to k in the future. Thus, the predicted costs in the third term, which represents future outcome, increase the utility.

In the second case, the utility represents the case where agent i delegates its execution to agent $s(i)$. In this case, the second term (cost) is nearly equal to zero. According to the law, agent i can predict that in the future, agent $s(i)$ can have the same plan as i has in the current collaboration, and i will have to receive the execution. This is represented in the third term.

Utilities when some agents do not abide by the law

Because Multi-Agent Systems can be seen as Open Distributed Systems, there might be agents that do not abide by the law, so we have to consider the influence of these agents. In this case, the utility is represented as follows. $\Sigma - \sigma$ means the set whose elements are members of the set Σ and not of set, σ.

Utility if agents in a set, $\sigma(\subseteq \Sigma)$ do not abide by the law :
$U(\mathrm{Merge}(\pi_\Sigma \cup \{\pi_i\}, s(i), i), \pi_i)$

$$
= \begin{cases}
\mathrm{Cost}(\pi_i) - \mathrm{Cost}(\mathrm{Merge}(\pi_\Sigma \cup \{\pi_i\}), i, i) & \\
\quad + \sum_{k \in \Sigma - \sigma}(\mathrm{Cost}(\pi_k) & \\
\quad - \mathrm{Cost}(\mathrm{Merge}(\pi_{\Sigma-\sigma} \cup \{\pi_i\}), k, i)), & s(i) = i, \quad s(i) \notin \sigma \\
\mathrm{Cost}(\pi_i) - \mathrm{Cost}(\mathrm{Merge}(\pi_\Sigma \cup \{\pi_i\}), i, i) & s(i) = i, \quad s(i) \in \sigma \\
\mathrm{Cost}(\pi_i) - \mathrm{Cost}(\mathrm{Merge}(\pi_\Sigma \cup \{\pi_i\}), s(i), i) & \\
\quad + (\mathrm{Cost}(\pi_{s(i)}) - \mathrm{Cost}(\mathrm{Merge}(\pi_\Sigma \cup \{\pi_i\}), i, i)), & s(i) \neq i, \quad s(i) \notin \sigma \\
\mathrm{Cost}(\pi_i) - \mathrm{Cost}(\mathrm{Merge}(\pi_\Sigma \cup \{\pi_i\}), s(i), i) & s(i) \neq i, \quad s(i) \in \sigma
\end{cases}
$$

In the case where agent i delegates/receives the execution to/from agents that abide by the law ($s(i) \notin \sigma$), the utilities are the same as before. However, utilities for $s(i) \in \sigma$ consists of only the current costs.

3.4 Modelling other agents

The opponent agents are modeled from two points of view: strategy and probability of obeying the law.

Strategy

If the agents abide by the law, their strategies are modeled according to the law. In the same way, if agents do not abide by the law, their strategies are modeled differently from the ones obtained using the law. Here, we use a mixed strategy, with probability $q_k(l)$, for the model of agent k's strategy when k chooses strategy l from among strategies $\{1, \cdots, n\}$.

If k abides by the law:

$$
q_k(l) = \begin{cases}
1 & \text{if } l \text{ has delegated the most} \\
1/n & \text{if the costs of plans delegated by each agent is the same} \\
0 & \text{otherwise}
\end{cases}
$$

If k does not abide by the law:

$$
q_k(l) = \begin{cases}
0 & \text{if } l \text{ has delegated most} \\
1/(n-1) & \text{otherwise}
\end{cases}
$$

Reliability

We define P_k, the probability of agent k abiding by the law, as *reliability*. Reliability is defined by the constants α, β and the history h_k that indicates how many times the model of the strategy for agent k has been the same as the actual strategy of k.

$$P_k = \begin{cases} 0 & h_k < 0 \\ 1 - \exp(-\beta h_k) & h_k \geq 0 \end{cases}$$

$$h_k = \begin{cases} h'_k + 1 & s'(k) = s(k) \vee q(s(k)) = 1/n \\ h'_k - 1 & s'(k) \neq s(k), \end{cases}$$

The initial value of h_k is α. h'_k is the former value of h_k and $s'(k)$ is the actual strategy of k.

Constants α and β represent the characteristics of n agents and define each agent. α corresponds approximately to 'the reliability of the opponent for the first collaboration' and β to 'sensitivity to the alternation in reliability'.

3.5 Expected Utility

Expected utility E, that is, the expected value of utility, is given as follows, when agent i takes strategy $s(i)$ with probability, $q_i(s(i))$.

$$E = \sum_{\sigma \subseteq \Sigma} \{ P_\sigma \times \sum_{s(i)=1}^{n} (Payoff(s(i), (s(1), \cdots, s(n)))) \times \prod_{k=1}^{n} q_k(s(k))) \}$$

$$P_\sigma = P_1 \times \cdots \times (1 - P_l) \times \cdots \times P_n, \quad l \in \sigma$$

Each payoff matrix corresponds to the state of an agent abiding or not abiding by the law. This gives the number of payoff matrices as 2^{n-1}. E is obtained by summing up the expected utility of each payoff matrix. Finally, agent i can choose the rational strategy $q_i(s(i))$ if it maximizes E.

4 Simulation

Here, we distinguish between the following two collaboration strategies.

1. Collaboration Strategy for Single Encounter (CSSE)

   Agent selects the strategy that maximizes its payoff in the current game.

2. Collaboration Strategy for Repetitive Encounter (CSRE)

   Agent selects the strategy that maximizes both the sum of the payoff in the current game and the future payoff predicted using both the history of previous strategies and the social law.

Defined in these terms, we call the previously proposed collaboration strategy, which is based on game theory, CSSE, and the new one, that takes account of social law, CSRE.

For collaboration on positive relation, CSSE uses Nash solution in the game: agents with CSSE propose only strategies that involve delegating the plan executions. Agents with CSRE, however, propose both strategies that involve delegation and reception of the executions. Therefore, we have to investigate whether agents with CSRE benefit more than those with CSSE or not, and clarify the neccessary parametrical conditions for our collaboration strategy.

In the experiment, we have to be careful about two points: the experimental environment and the index. Environmentally, there will be many situations where the proportion of the number of agents with CSSE and that of agents with CSRE differ. It is realistic to assume that there exist many kinds of agents in Multi-Agent Systems. In relation to the index, it is better to use the notion of Evolutionary Stability (ES) [8]. In ES, certain individuals can continue to dominate an environment when there is a selection process natural selection based on a fitness value such as the effectiveness of the behaviour of an individual, even if a small number of individuals whose type is different enter the environment. Multi-Agent Systems are systems like this since agents can be seen as software, and small numbers of new agents from some vendor enter the system. Finally, users select the agents with high fitness values (effective software) and kill the agents with low fitness values (poor software). Thus, agents need to have the characteristics of Evolutionarily Stability if they want to survive in the systems.

Here in this experiment, we investigated the neccessary conditions for the parameters in our collaboration strategy from the viewpoint of ES in various, dynamic situations using different proportions of each kind of agent.

4.1 Configurations

The agent's plan used in the simulation is depicted in Figure 1(a). Associated numbers represent the costs of execution which are changing with every agent, and every collaborations. The central part of the plan (gray colored section) is the core part that is executed by other agents, if it is delegated. For example, when two agents have the following kinds of plans, the merged plan (Figure 1(b)) is executed by the agent that chose reception.

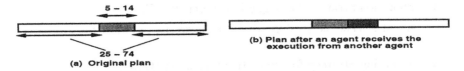

(a) Original plan

5 – 14

25 – 74

(b) Plan after an agent receives the execution from another agent

Fig. 1. Plans used in simulation

We simulated a situation where there were 20 agents, and from 2 to 5 participants per collaboration were randomly selected from them. The horizontal axis of the experimental results represents 'The Number of Collaborations' and the vertical axis represents 'The Cost Reduction'. This is defined as the proportion of the costs needed if agents collaborated against the costs needed if agents did not collaborate. All the results were obtained from 10 simulations.

4.2 The Results

There are 3 parameters in this simulation: parameters for reliability (α, β) and the number of agents with CSSE. Figure 2 shows the decrease of in execution costs for each agent when they continue to collaborate where there are 5 agents using CSSE and $\alpha = 1, \beta = 0.1$. This shows that the cost reductions for both kinds of agents (those with CSSE and those with CSRE) are less than 1. That is, the execution costs are lower as compared to the case where there is no collaboration. Specifically, agents with CSRE decreased their costs more than agents with CSSE.

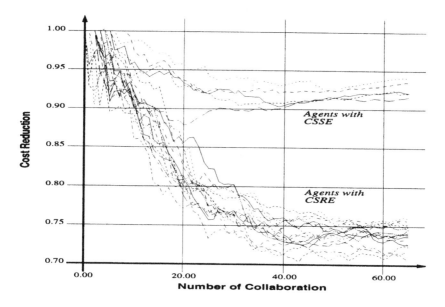

Fig. 2. Five agents using CSSE and $\alpha = 1, \beta = 0.1$

Furthermore, as the number of collaborations increase, the cost reductions seem to converge to certaion values. These values can be calculated from the execution costs of plans, the type and proportion of agents.

Next, we investigated whether agents with CSRE could reduce their costs more than those with CSSE or not even for the other parameters. To do that, we took the minimum number of collaborations and parameters (α, β) when agents with CSRE lower the cost reduction more than agents with CSSE and compared them using two curves, each of which represents the average of the results of the same type of agents.

The lower the minimum number is, the better the agents survive if the interval of selection is earlier. Thus, they are more evolutionarily stable.

Figure 3 depicts the case where 3 of the 20 agents use CSSE. When α is between -2 and 0 approximately, agents with CSRE can reduce their costs more than those with CSSE within only a few interactions. However, the more α

132

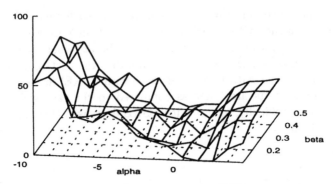

Fig. 3. When 3 agents use CSSE

increased, the more the interactions were needed. This arises from the fact that α represents the reliability when an agent meets another agent for the first time, so that agents with high α are more inclined to receive executions from agents with CSSE. Another thing that can be seen from the result is that when α increased the results do not disimprove linearly with α. This shows that there is a limit for disimproving because there are only 3 agents using CSSE. Bad results were obtained with decrements of α. This arises from the fact that agents with CSRE behave like those with CSSE even interacting with the same kind of agents when α is less than 0. The results disimproved a little with increments in β.

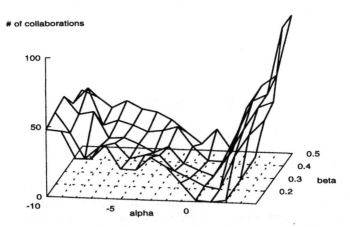

Fig. 4. When 9 agents use CSSE

Figure 4 depicts the case where 9 agents use CSSE. The greater the number of agents with CSSE, the worse were the results when α is bigger than 0. This is because agents with CSRE are more inclined to receive the executions.

This tendency grew with increment ofs in the number of agents with CSSE. When there were 15 agents using CSSE, about 100 interactions were needed when $\alpha < 0$.

From these results, the following conditions are neccessary for agents with CSRE to reach better agreements than those with CSSE from the viewpoint of evolutionary stability.

- α must be around 0 when there are small number of agents with CSSE.
- α must be less than 0 when there are large number of agents with CSSE.
- β must be approximately 0.1.

5 Discussion

First, let us discuss the computational costs required for the selection of a strategy. The size (number of elements) of the payoff matrix is n^n when n agents collaborate. 2^{n-1} payoff matrices must be considered as each payoff matrix corresponds to a state representing which agents abide by the law and which agents do not.

If more agents participate in the collaboration, more plans are optimized, but the computational costs increase disproportionally and they cannot be compensated for the decrease in costs from plan optimization. Thus, there appears to be an appropriate number of agents (size of coalition) for participation in the collaboration. Since this number depends on the plans of the agents, it changes with the situation. If agents can establish an appropriate cooperation size, the appropriate agents are then chosen by evolutionary computation, and agents might be able to keep an appropriate coalition size and the Multi-Agent System efficient even in dynamically changing situations.

An alternative way to keep the system efficient is to decrease the computational costs themselves. The payoff matrix would be very empty, so that the number of elements that must be considered can be decreased. If agents can neglect some payoff matrices that have low probability for that state (P_σ), the computational costs will be greatly decreased. In other words, computational costs can be reduced by bounded rationality.

We treated the collaboration as an n-person non cooperative game. However, if sufficient communication is possible when reaching an agreement, and the utility can be divided and transferred to the opponents, it can be seen as a cooperative game. From this perspective, even better solutions can be obtained using the Sharpley value to share the benefit of collaborations as seen in [4][10][9]. The Sharpley value is calculated for each agent. It is the sum of the increased benefits from all possible coalitions if an agent participates in a collaboration (coalition). If agents use Foulser's algorithm [3] for optimization of their participants plans when they calculate the increase in their benefit, their computational costs are the product of the length of all plans, $\prod_{i \in S} |\pi_i|$ (where S is a set of agents in coalition). This increase in benefits is summed for all possible coalitions, so that the computational costs are $O(\sum_{S \subset N} \{\prod_{k \in S} |\pi_k|\})$ (where N is a set of all agents). This shows that the costs are exponential to n and corresponds to the result of our method.

Axelrod studied policies for selecting a strategy for the game "the iterated Prisonor's Dilemma" [1]. He described some conditions for survival that have more general application. Those conditions correspond to the reliability P_i and the social law, if we think of the defection strategy in the iterated Prisonor's Dilemma as that strategy which goes against the social law in our domain.

Based on the high number of different programs in the computer competition that was held by Axelrod, there might be many different social laws. However, for each situation, at least one suitable "best law" can be found. Therefore, the law might be able to evolve using evolutionary computation in future implementations.

6 Conclusions

In this paper, we proposed a collaboration strategy for repetitive encounters that takes the probability of repeated interactions into account. Using social law and reliability, agents can predict the opponents' strategies so that they can choose a rational strategy taking into account the payoffs (costs). We also simulated a situation where agents using our collaboration strategy (CSRE) and those using only delegation strategy (CSSE) exist in various proportions. These results show that agents with CSRE can reduce their costs more than agents with CSSE if there are multiple agents using CSRE whose reliability is neither too low nor too high.

We plan to evolve the law for each situation, and to use higher level models of reliability.

References

1. Robert Axelrod. *The Evolution of Cooperation*. Basic Books, 1984.
2. David Fogel. Evolution of Strategies in Iterated Prisoners' Dilemma. *Evolutionary Computation*, 1(1), 1993.
3. David E. Foulser, Ming Li, and Qiang Yang. Theory and Algorithms for Plan Merging. *Artificial Intelligence*, 57, 1992.
4. Steven P. Ketchpel. Coalition Formation Among Autonomous Agents. In *Pre-proceedings of MAAMAW-93*, 1993.
5. Frank Von Martial. *Coordinating Plans of Autonomous Agents*. Lecture Notes in Artificial Intelligence, Subseries of LNCS. Springer-Verlag, 1992.
6. K. Matsubayashi and M. Tokoro. A Collaboration Mechanism on Positive Interactions in Multi-agent Environments. In *Proceedings of IJCAI-93*, 1993.
7. Y. Shoham and M. Tennenholtz. On the synthesis of useful social laws for artificial agent societies (preliminary report). In *Proceedings of AAAI-92*, 1992.
8. J.M. Smith. *Evolution and the Theory of Games*. Cambridge University Press, 1982.
9. Gilad Zlotkin and Jeffrey S. Rosenschein. A Domain Theory for Task Oriented Negotiation. In *Proceedings of IJCAI-93*, 1993.
10. Gilad Zlotkin and Jeffrey S. Rosenschein. One, Two, Many: Coalitions in Multi-Agent Systems. In *Pre-proceedings of MAAMAW-93*, 1993.

ASIC: An Architechture for Social and Individual Control and Its Application to Computer Vision

Olivier Boissier[*][1] and Yves Demazeau[**][2]

[1] ENSMP, 60 Bd. Saint Michel 75272 Paris Cedex 06, France
boissier@cc.ensmp.fr
[2] LIFIA-IMAG, 46 av. Félix Viallet 38031 Grenoble Cedex, France
Yves.Demazeau@imag.fr

Abstract. Most of the work done until now in computational vision deals with the construction of independent visual processing methods that implement a specific subtask of the whole process. In this paper, we are proposing a control architecture, ASIC, based on a multi-agent approach. It has been used to build the MAVI system which integrates different visual modules and makes them cooperate. We demonstrate its use to study local and global control in a vision system.

1 Introduction

Until recently, most of the work done in computational vision has focused on the development of processing methods dedicated to particular subtasks of the visual process. Their integration in a complete system is a very important, difficult task. Initiated in the seventies as presented in [16], the construction of such systems is appearing more often especially within the active and purposive vision paradigms [1] [2]. The main issues involved in this construction include, firstly, deciding how the processing methods and the data that are used should be grouped into modules and, secondly, deciding how these separate components should interact and which problem they should solve. A multi-agent approach is well founded to ground this construction. Coming from the Artificial Intelligence field with the idea of distributing knowledge and process, this approach proposes models to facilitate cooperation between heterogeneous modules, called *agents*.

Firstly, we present the foundations that led us to use a multi-agent approach to design our system. Its control architecture (ASIC[3]) is then described. This architecture allows us to compose an integrated vision system (MAVI[4]) from a number of independent modules designed around the same agent model. Each agent is a continuously operating system, that maintains a description of the

---

[*] Maitre Assistant à l'Ecole Nationale Supérieure des Mines de Paris (ENSMP). This work was done while the author was at LIFIA-IMAG
[**] Chargé de recherche au Centre National de la Recherche Scientifique (CNRS).
[3] Architecture for Social and Individual Control
[4] Multi-Agent sytem for Visual Integration

scene at a particular level of representation. The control of the system is designed along two dimensions : a global one, called *social control* and a local one, called *individual control*. Before concluding with some perspectives, some experiments done with the MAVI system are presented.

2 Foundations

The first issue involved in the construction of an integrated vision system deals with deciding how the processes and data of the system should be grouped into modules. The latters are numerous and heterogeneous (e.g. combining numeric and symbolic information, related to physical, geometrical aspects of the world or to the objects present in the scene). In [3], we have defined two main criteria : *levels of representation* and *focus* to help this decision. The *levels of representation* define a hierarchy of abstractions that are the media of interaction between the processes. The *foci* organize the control activity of the system along the levels of representation (e.g. object models, regions of interest, tasks, shape from methods). Their intersection defines, implicitly or explicitly, the basic units of the system.

The second issue deals with the control of the system. An integrated vision system interprets the environment continuously. Every time, each module has to select both the data to exchange and the actions to execute in order to interpret the scene, given the perceived data from the environment (e.g. images). In a computational system, the control architecture is a crucial issue to obtain a flexible solution to this control problem. In existing systems, the integration process is often made in a restrictive way by fixing cooperation modes between modules (e.g. hierarchy in [11], central control in [1]) and by fixing the global behaviour of the system (e.g. top-down processing in [11]). The different control cycles that are reported in [18] demonstrate the complexity of the definition of a control architecture for a vision system that could encompass all of them. Moreover these cooperation modes need to be modified dynamically during the processing, taking into account the information sources that are available or the incoherences between the results that would need feedback loops between the modules.

Our objective is to implement an integrated vision system (cf. Fig. 1) that is composed of several independent visual modules which dynamically maintain a description of the scene at a given level of representation for a given focus. So, the system has to be *open* and *flexible* :

1. Work in vision is often incremental and we have to be able to integrate future visual methods without the need to redesign the entire system. The openness of the control architecture will be guaranteed by its independence from the observed environments (i.e. scenes) and from the domain knowledge (e.g. types of objects).

2. The control has to be modified whenever the global functioning of the system is changing according to the evolution of the scene and according to

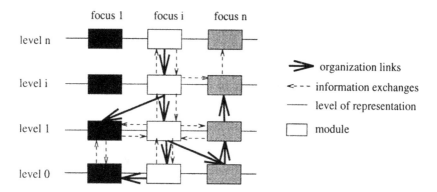

Fig. 1. Objective guiding the implementation of the ASIC control architecture. Modules are schematic. In fact one module could cover several levels of representation or foci.

the global goals to satisfy. To ensure this possibility without rebuilding the system, the control is divided into two aspects : social control (i.e. global control, definition of the cooperation modes in the system) and individual control (i.e. local control of the behaviour of each module given the existing social control). The social control will be expressed by explicit, dynamic organizational links and chaining of interactions between modules. Taking them into account, each module will be able to define its goals, to react to the evolution of the scene and to take care of the interaction with the other modules.

3 The ASIC Control Architecture

In order to satisfy this objective, a multi-agent approach has been used. Its models aim to make heterogeneous modules cooperate. They are called *agents* because of their capacity to define their goals and activity and interact with others by exchanging information. In order to allow a more flexible control of the system we choose a *decentralized* control approach.

All the agents have been designed using the same model. The latter had to cover the different processing problems of the high and low levels of representation of a vision system. The defined agent model (cf. Fig. 2) is a cognitive one inspired by [15] [13] [7]. It is composed of two submodels (cf. Fig. 2) : the *individual control model* (in white on Fig. 2) [4] and the *social control model* (in gray on Fig. 2) [4]. It is defined by the following 10-tuple :

$$Agent = < PS, RS, DS, CS, ES, KR, L, Pr, Or, PM >$$

Different *representation states* (shown as circles) structure the processed data into : perceived data (PS), data involved in the reasoning process (RS), intentions (DS), commitments (CS), data to send (ES). KR, L, Pr, Or (shown as rounded rectangles) are, respectively, the agent's *knowledge*, the *interaction*

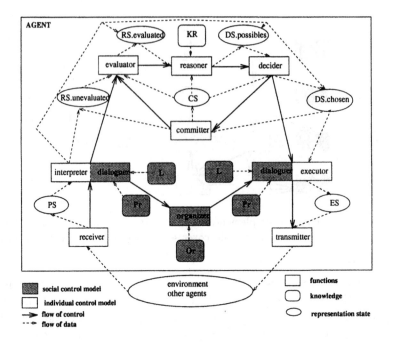

Fig. 2. The Asic control architecture. *PS*, *RS*, *DS*, *CS*, *ES* are the perception, reasoning, decision, commitment and execution states; *KR* knowledge, *L* interaction language, *Pr* interaction protocols and *Or* organizations. The individual control model (shown in white) is organized along a control hierarchy that is shown in Fig. 3. in order not to overload the schema.

language, the set of *interaction protocols* and the set of *organizations* used to define and structure the information exchanges between the agents. *PM* is the set of *processing functions* (shown as rectangles) that build the agent architecture. They use *KR*, *L*, *Pr* and *Or* to update the representation states. These functions are called in sequence by a scheduler as shown in Fig. 2. *PM* is the following 11-tuple[5] :

$$PM \; = \; < receiver, \; interpreter, \; evaluator, \; reasoner, \; decider, \; committer,$$
$$switcher, \; executor, \; transmitter, \; dialoguer, \; organizer >$$

The individual control model defines the architecture to use *KR* and to update the *representation states*. The social control model is added to it to keep the modularity of the system and to control the behaviour of the agent in the society. Its architecture (*dialoguer* and *organizer* functions) is defined in reference to: *L*, *Pr* and *Or*.

---

[5] We use *switcher*, *committer* and *dialoguer* to denote respectively the switch manager, the commitments manager and the dialogue manager.

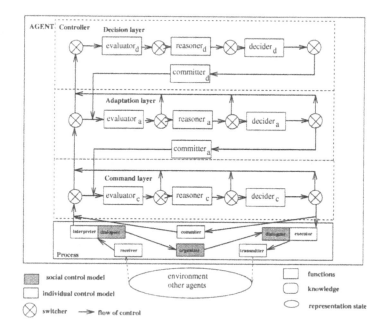

Fig. 3. Control cycle of the ASIC individual control model. The processing functions related to *evaluator, reasoner, decider* and *committer* are decomposed along the control hierarchy. Each layer composes the controller of the lower layers of the agent. The knowledge and representation states that are on each layer are not represented in order not to overload the figure.

3.1 Individual Control Model

To perform its behaviour, each visual module uses control methods which reinforce the heterogeneity that exists in a vision system. Modules that act on the low levels of representation implement their control with technics from the control theory, whereas, those of the high levels use Artificial Intelligence technics (e.g. planning). The resulting behaviour of the former lacks flexibility whereas the latter's lacks repetitivity and reactivity. As shown in [9], approaches combining repetitive and planning techniques would be useful in modules acting on the low levels.

In order to capture these different aspects, the *individual control model* (cf. Fig. 3) defines and structures the knowledge KR and the representation states RS, DS, CS along the following control hierarchy: decision layer, adaptation layer and command layer (indexed by the letters d, a, c on Fig. 3). This architecture is close to other approaches which combine planning and control of execution [10].

Knowledge. The agent's knowledge KR is composed of the *skills* (KR_c), the *tactics* (KR_a) and the *strategies* (KR_d). Skills are managed on the command layer. They represent the actions that an agent can execute. Tactics act on the adaptation layer and strategies act on the decision layer. Tactics are used to build the different plans that the agent will execute and the strategies are used to choose the goals to satisfy.

Representation States. The *perception state PS* (resp. *execution state*) gathers all the incoming (resp. outgoing) data. The *reasoning state RS* represents all the information which is manipulated by the agent, expressed in its knowledge representation language. These are *goals*, *plans* and *hypothesis*.

The *decision state DS* groups the possible and chosen *intentions* that express all the agent's ongoing activity. Depending on the layer, intentions are : a possible or chosen strategy (on the decision layer DS_d), a possible or chosen plan (on the adaptation layer DS_a) and a possible or chosen skill (on the command layer DS_c).

The *commitment state CS* is the set of the *commitments* which control the agent activity. The commitments are used by the *reasoner* and the *decider* functions, respectively, to set a strategy, a tactic or a skill as possible or chosen in *DS*. Repetitive behaviours are set by the use of the same commitments during several cycles. Each commitment has a validity condition that is tested by the *switcher* (see below). When it is invalidated it causes the switch from a repetitive behaviour into a deliberative one which aims at defining new commitments.

Processing Functions. The *receiver* collects the incoming messages and stores them in *PS*. The *interpreter* translates these messages into the agent's internal representation language and writes them in *RS* or *DS*. This function uses the *dialoguer* (see below in the social control model) to perform the translation. The control hierarchy is then activated to produce the action, goal or plan to be executed locally or by other agents. In case it has to be sent, the *executor* translates this information in a message to be exchanged. It receives the help of the *dialoguer*. The messages are then sent to the other agents by the *transmitter*.

Each layer x of the control hierarchy defines the commitments (expressed in CS_{x-1}) governing the processing of the lower layer $x - 1$. The following functions are present on each layer x: $evaluator_x$ that detects conflicts in RS; $reasoner_x$ that builds the possible intentions written in $DS_x.possibles$, given RS and KR_x; $decider_x$ that updates $DS_x.chosen$ with the intentions picked out of $DS_x.possibles$ according to the current commitments in CS_x; $committer_x$ that updates CS_{x-1} from the content of $DS_x.chosen$. Between each of these functions, $switcher_x$ (cf. Fig. 3) checks the validity condition of the commitments written in CS_x against RS and DS_x. The processing is repetitively done on the command layer until some commitment is invalidated. In this case the processing returns to the upper layer $x + 1$ where the same process is applied in order to define new commitments and goes down again.

3.2 Social Control Model

In the ASIC architecture, each agent can interact with every other agent, if it wants to. The social control model defines what has to be sent, when and how in order to make the system converge to a solution, given the global goals to satisfy and the local processing done by each agent. This model is based on the assignment of controller and process roles on the agents of the system that make clear the structure and the information exchanges in the system. A *controller* defines the command acting on other agents by using observations on their activity. A *process* executes this command.

This controller/process structure is defined by the organizations grouped in *Or*. The interaction language *L* and the interaction protocols *Pr* implement the information exchanges that consist of observations and commands.

Interactions Language. The common language *L* defines the common vocabulary and the semantics in the system. It is used to build the *interactions* that express exchanges of actions, plans, goals or hypotheses between the agents. *L* defines an interaction with the following syntax (see [14] for more details) :

$$< interaction > ::= < communication > < mas > < content >$$

1. $< communication >$ contains information which is used by the communication layer of the system for the routing of the message.
2. $< mas >$ gathers all the information which is related to the multi-agent system and that is independent of any application domain. Three kinds of informations are defined : $< type >$, $< nature >$ and $< strength >$. The $< type >$ implements the basic interaction types used by the agents : request, answer or inform. The $< nature >$ implements the command and observation exchanges seen above : dec (goals to solve), ada (plans to execute), com (actions to execute) and obs (goals, plans, actions and hypothesis). The last-mentioned nature permits an agent to make the others aware of its current goals, plans, actions whereas the other natures express command exchanges. The $< strength >$ defines the priority of the exchanged information contained in the message. We borrow the terms for filling this field from the Speech Act theory [17] : comm (commanding, high priority) to info (informing, low priority).
3. $< content >$ defines the semantics of the message. It is dependent on the application domain (see [6] for a detailed description).

Interaction Protocols. The set of interaction protocols *Pr* restricts the different interactions that the agents can chain to solve a problem. A *protocol* is a transition network (cf. Fig. 4) that defines, a priori, the set of possible transitions (shown as straight lines) which link a set of states (shown as circles) that the agents will occupy alternately according to the exchanged interactions. A transition expresses constraints on the filling of the format of the interaction that we presented above.

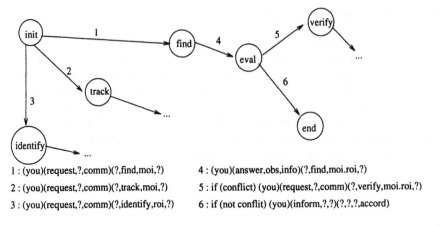

1 : (you)(request,?,comm)(?,find,moi,?)   4 : (you)(answer,obs,info)(?,find,moi.roi,?)

2 : (you)(request,?,comm)(?,track,moi,?)   5 : if (conflict) (you)(request,?,comm)(?,verify,moi.roi,?)

3 : (you)(request,?,comm)(?,identify,roi,?)   6 : if (not conflit) (you)(inform,?,?)(?,?,?,accord)

Fig. 4. Example of interaction protocol. States are in circle. Transitions are represented by arrows.

Organizations. Protocols define for all the agents what can be sent. It is necessary now to restrain the possibilities of the agents in the system according to their role in the global behaviour. This is why we have organisations (grouped into Or) that define links "controller-process" between the agents. Several links exist in an agent because of its ability to be simultaneously the controller with respect to certain agents and a process with respect to others. These relations express a filter which acts on the inputs and outputs of the agent. This filter is used to constrain fullfilling of the interactions permitted by the interaction protocols. For example, a controller-agent may send command-interactions to its process-agent whereas this agent may only send observation-interactions to it. For the moment, these links have the following definition:

$$< link >::=< type > < kind\text{-}of\text{-}link > < content >$$

The $< type >$ has the value individu (resp. **social**) in case the filter has to force the agent to send (resp. receive) some kind of interaction. The $< kind\text{-}of\text{-}link >$ consists in the $< nature >$ and $< strength >$ fields which mark the nature and strength of the interaction that can pass through the filter (see above). The $< content >$ expresses the restrictions on the interaction's contents. It is defined the same way as the content field of interaction language.

Processing Functions. The *dialoguer* (see Fig. 2) uses Pr and L to handle the interactions which take place between the agents. When receiving messages, it translates the message into internal representation using L. When sending a message, it chooses an interaction taking into account the current state of the protocol in use and translates the information into an interaction, using L.

The *organizer* (see Fig. 2) defines the current organization which takes place in the society in order to constrain the interaction and the resolution between the agents, given the global goal.

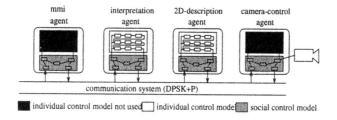

Fig. 5. Example of use of the Multi-Agent system for Visual Integration MAVI

4 The MAVI System

We have used the ASIC architecture to compose an integrated vision system, MAVI, and study different strategies : global ones (use of the social control model) and local ones (use of the individual control model).

4.1 Global Overview of the System

We have integrated some of the visual processing modules of the active vision system VAP [11] in ASIC to validate our approach. The testbed (cf. Fig. 5) is composed of four agents. Each agent is a continuously running cyclic process implemented as a separate Unix process that builds the scene description at one level of representation and one focus (in our case, the focus is on image features and particularly intensity). These agents are : *camera-control agent* that feeds the system with sequences of images to be interpreted and controls the camera, *2D-description agent* that builds the 2D features (contrast edges and perceptual grouping) from the images, *interpretation agent* that builds the symbolic description of the scene from the 2D features, *mmi agent* that manages the interaction with the user.

4.2 Example of Individual Control in the 2D-description Agent

We have mainly studied the control in the *2D-description* and in the *interpretation* agents. The requirements of these agents are quite different in the sense that the *2D-description* agent has an a-priori deterministic behaviour with few control parameters whereas the *interpretation* agent has more knowledge and needs at each step to choose the action to execute. Throughout this model, we have been able to define several strategies that install continuously working visual process with explicit interruption conditions that were expressed by the validity condition of the commitments acting on each layer. We illustrate this with experiments in the *2D-description* agent.

Knowledge. All the knowledge of a MAVI-agent is represented by condition/action rules. The conditions express the required configuration of RS to execute the actions.

```
ex : (skill edge-extractor (layer command)
         (condition (hypothesis image (status unprocessed) (value ?image-ptr)))
         (action (bind ?pyramid (build-pyramid ?image-ptr))
              (bind ?gradient (compute-gradient ?pyramid))
              (bind ?segment-ptr (segment-extract ?gradient
                                        ?roi ?high-threshold ?low-threshold))
              (hypothesis-create segment ?segment-ptr
                                     (compute-quality ?segment-ptr)))))
```

Skills (KR_c) define the visual processing methods building the scene description on one representation level (e.g. fusion, hypothesis generation). Tactics and strategies express the knowledge related to the different visual tasks that the agent can solve (e.g. identification, watching).

In the *2D-description* agent, the skills are : edge-extractor and a set of grouping procedures. Some tactics (KR_a) were defined to set and monitor the region of interest within the description of the scene according to the task and to the region of interest defined by the decision layer. For instance, the behaviour of the region of interest in Fig. 6 is achieved by a tactic that defines the center of the region of interest as the center of gravity of the segments extracted in the region of interest of the previous image. Other tactics choose the better level of the resolution pyramid. Some tactics set the value of the parameters for the edge-extractor and for the grouping procedures according to the kind of task and to the quality defined by the decision layer.

Strategies (KR_d) were defined for choosing the task to achieve and to define the primitive region of interest and the quality factors for the features.

Representation States. The scene description which is built by a MAVI-agent is expressed as hypotheses about the world in *RS*. According to the representation level on which the agent acts, they will be images, 2D descriptions (segments and grouping), 3D descriptions (volumetric descriptions) or symbolic descriptions. Goals and plans define the tasks to be executed taking into account the focus in which the agent acts.

In the *2D-description* agent, the hypotheses consist of the following types : image, segments, perceptual groupings (e.g. parallel, junctions, Y-junctions). The goals are a combination of a *task* (e.g. find, identify), a *model* (e.g. segment or perceptual grouping) and maximal *region of interest* in which to search for the features matching the chosen model. The plans are expressed as sets of parameters or regions of interest.

Commitments can be regions of interest, processing parameters, thresholds to control the processing methods expressed in the skills or the functions of the architecture themselves. In this agent, the commitments expressed on the decision layer, CS_d, are : quality, region-of-interest. Depending on the layer, the region of interest is defined as a rectangle in the image (x, y, dx, dy) to which can be added the level of the resolution pyramid to consider.

ex : (commitment MOI (layer decision) (end-when eq-quality-p 0.9)

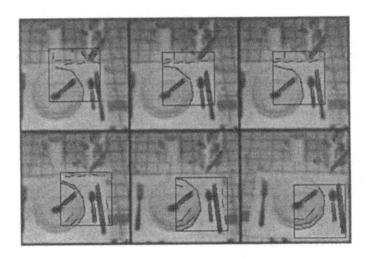

Fig. 6. Example of the execution in the *2D-description* agent. The images represent from left to right and top-down : image at time 0, image at time 1, image at time 2, image at time 4, image at time 7, image at time 12. The region of interest is changed in the images 1, 4, 7 and 12 because of the invalidation of the condition of the region of interest commitment. Each time this condition is not satisfied, the adaptation layer is triggered in order to define a new region of interest.

(value find segment quality 0.9))
(commitment ROI (layer command) (end-when gc-in-roip 4) (value 0 0 3 30 30 1))

On the adaptation layer of the *2D-description* agent, CS_a contains: **parameters** for the procedures producing the searched feature expressed in the skills KR_c (see above), **region-of-interest**. The region of interest takes place within the one defined by the decision layer and adds the level(s) (k and dk) of the resolution pyramid on which to compute the features : (x y k dx dy dk). Each one has a validity condition. For instance, the region of interest which controls the processing done on the command layer as shown in Fig. 6 has a validity condition (gc-in-roip) that implements a motion tracking the segments in the sequence of images: each time it is evaluated, it computes the center of gravity of the segments found in the region of interest. If the center of gravity is far from a number of pixels (4) of the center of the region of interest, the validity is not satisfied.

Processing. The processing is done according to the description made in section 3. Each layer defines the region of interest and the parameters for the lower layer. This process is iterated until the validity condition of the commitments (parameter or region of interest) are not satisfied. The reasons could be either because the search is successful or because something happens in the scene that prevents to continue the processing.

Other validity condition have been used to break the cyclic process taking

place on a layer with a defined region of interest by taking into account the number of segments found. This architecture enables us to envision improvements of the control in visual modules which are usually implemented in a way that prevents such a study.

4.3 Example of Social Control

In MAVI, *L*, *Pr* and *Or* are used to express the structure and the information exchanges according to the particular behaviours of a vision system: *recognition* (global goal satisfaction) and/or *interpretation* (no global a priori goal). They reflect the structure expressed through the representation levels and from the privileged relations which exist between agents belonging to the same focus. To illustrate the social control of our system, we have defined the control for a recognition process (cf. Fig. 7).

Interaction Language for the Application. The interactions are composed of *commands* (region of interests, processing parameter like thresholds) and *observations* (the scene description built through the use of the command). The < *content* > field of the interaction language has been defined from the visual information managed on the levels of representation (see [6] for details).

Interaction Protocol. Interaction protocols express predict and verify loops. These basic interactions are chained along the levels of representation into more or less complex control cycles expressing bottom-up and/or top-down processing for agents that belong to the same focus or fusion/competition modes for agents that belong to different foci within the same level of representation.

To implement the recognition behaviour, we built the interaction protocol presented in Fig. 4. Each agent uses its local copy to know which interaction to send given the current state of the protocol. The trace of message passing between the agents is shown in Fig. 7.

At the begining of the exchange, the *mmi-agent* (step 1 on Fig. 7) is in state init of the protocol. According to the first transition of the protocol shown in Fig. 4, it is constrained to use a **request**, addressing whatever control layer it wants (?) but using a high priority strength (comm) and asking for the solving of the task (find) related to whatever model (moi) the agent wants (?). On receiving the interaction the *interpretation* agent has to initiate a new dialogue with other agents to fulfill the request of the *mmi* agent. It starts a dialogue with the *2D-description* agent using the protocol. It is in state init (step 2 on Fig. 7) for this exchange, whereas it is in the **start** state dealing with the exchange with the *mmi* agent. When it has the results, it will only be able to send an interaction message (step 8 in Fig. 7) following the transition 4 in Fig. 4 (state start in Fig. 4).

The use of such declarative expressions of protocols enables us to test global strategies that implement different control cycles in the system without having to rebuild it. This is a work that we have started to explore in [14].

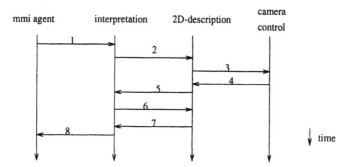

1 : (request dec comm) (mmi-level find moi cube) cube)

2 : (request dec comm) (interpretation-level find moi segment)

3 : (request dec comm) (2D-level find moi image)

4 : (answer obs info) (image-level find moi.roi image image-content)

5 : (answer obs info) (2D-level find moi.roi segment segment-content)

6 : (request dec comm) (interpretation verify moi.roi segment segment-content roi-content)

7 : (answer obs info) (2D-level verify moi.roi segment segment-content roi-content)

8 : (answer obs info) (interpretation find moi.roi cube cube-content roi-content)

Fig. 7. example of social control. In this example, we present just the content of field $< mas >$ and $< content >$ of the interaction.

Organization. No global law exists for structuring the agents into controller or process in a vision system. We can just say that the representation levels and the foci play an important role : for agents belonging to the same focus, one agent acting on one level is often the controller of the agent(s) acting on the lower level(s).

A hierarchical organization implementing the recognition behaviour has been tested. Each agent that is placed on one level of representation can control all the agents that are placed on the lower levels. This is, from top to down : *mmi* agent, *interpretation* agent, *2D-description* agent, *camera-control* agent. The field $< content >$ of the links defining the organization, has been instanciated by our application domain. For instance some relations holding in the *2D-description* agent are the following :

```
ex: (relation (type social) (kind-of-link ada comm)
          (content (level interpretation-level) (action ?) (kind roi) (parameter ?)))
    (relation (type individu) (kind-of-link ada info)
          (content (level interpretation-level) (action ?) (kind roi) (parameter ?)))
```

The first relation tells that the *2D-description* agent is controlled by any agent (i.e. must accept any interaction coming from these agents) being on the interpretation level, for any action concerning a region of interest with any parameter. These interactions can concern at most the decision and adaptation layers (**ada**) with any strength (**comm**).

The second relation tells that the *2D-description* agent has to interact with agents laying on the interpretation level in order to define the region of interest on the adaptation layer. This relation prevents this agent to use its decision and adaptation layers for information related to region of interest : the agent cannot control itself to define its region of interest.

5 Conclusion and Perspectives

A prototype implementing ASIC has been written in CLIPS 5.1. The distributed execution of the system on several Sun stations has been realized through the use of the DPSK+P system [8]. This system offers a message passing communication mode. The visual processing methods building the agents of MAVI are written in C.

The presented experiences have enabled us to validate the control models. We avoid the centralized control bottleneck by building a decentralized control system. Each agent is an independent process, running continuously in order to satisfy its own goals and to react to the evolution of the scene. It controls its behaviour and the behaviour of other agents given the global control that is expressed by the interaction protocols and the organizations. The modularity of the system is kept by the definition of a common interaction language. The global control of the system is realized, on one side, by the use of a declarative structure of the agents in the system (organizations) and on the other side, by the use of the declarative interaction chaining (protocols). Our approach favours the flexibility of the entire system rather than its computing performance in terms of "real time".

However, it is necessary, first, to develop other agents and to explore different local control strategies with the individual control model. Dealing with the global control, we must go on the development of organizations and protocols while writing of benchmarks to test their efficiency. In our validation we have only studied the "vertical" control between agents belonging to different representation levels and to the same focus. We have to broaden these experiences in order to study the control between agents acting on the same representation level in different foci. An ongoing project MAGIC[6] [5], [14] takes place in the context of these further developments. Its aim is the enrichment of both the social control model and the agent model to integrate visual modules for the building of a scene interpretation system.

Acknowledgment

The authors wish to thank Uma Garimella for her constructive suggestions.

---

[6] This research is supported by French National Project "PRC Communication Homme Machine".

References

1. Aloimonos, J.Y.: Purposive and Qualitative Vision. ECCV Esprit Workshop on Control of Perception, (1990)
2. Bajcsy, R.: Active Perception. IEEE Proceedings, 8 (76), (1988) 996–1005
3. Boissier, O., Demazeau, Y.: A Distributed Artificial Intelligence View on General Purpose Vision Systems. in Decentralized Artificial Intelligence, Elsevier Science Publishers B.V. (North Holland), Werner, E., Demazeau, Y., editors, (1992) 311–330
4. Boissier, O.: Control Problem in an intergrated vision system. Use of a multi-agent approach (in french). Phd Thesis, Institut National Polytechnique de Grenoble, (1993)
5. Boissier, O., Demazeau, Y., Masini, G., Skaf. H.: A multi-agent architecture for the implementation of the low level of a scene understanding system (in french). Actes des secondes journées francophones sur l'IAD et les systèmes multi-agents, Voiron, AFCET-AFIA-Pleiad, (1994) 293–304
6. Boissier, O., Demazeau, Y.: MAVI : a Multi Agent system for Visual Integration. Proceedings of the 1994 IEEE International Conference on Multisensor Fusion and Integration for Intelligent Systems, Las Vegas, NE, October 2-5 1994, 731–738
7. Burmeister, B., Sundermeyer, K.: Cooperative problem solving guided by intentions and perception. in Decentralized Artificial Intelligence, Elsevier Science Publishers B.V. (North Holland), Werner, E., Demazeau, Y., editors, (1992) 77–92
8. Cardozo, E., Sichman, J.S., Demazeau, Y.: Using the active object model to implement multi-agent systems. In Proceedings of the IEEE conference on Tools with AI, Boston, (november 1993)
9. Clark, J.L., Ferrier, N.J.: Control of Visual Attention in Mobile Robots. Robotics and Automation, (1989)
10. Clement, V., Thonnat, M.: A knowledge approach to integration of image processing procedures. CVGIP : image understanding, vol. 57, n. 2, (1993) 166–184
11. Crowley, J.L., Chehikian A., Kittler, J., Illingworth, J., Eklundh, J.O., Granlund, G., Wiklund, J., Granum, E., Christensen, H.I.: Technical Annex for ESPRIT Basic Research Action 3038 : Vision As Process., Aalborg, (1989)
12. Crowley, J.L., Zoppis, B., Calvary, G., Boissier, O.: Perceptual grouping for scene interpretation in an active vision system. In proceedings of Stockholm Workshop on Computational Vision, (1991)
13. Demazeau, Y., Müller, J.P.: Decentralized Artificial Intelligence. in Decentralized Artificial Intelligence, Elsevier Science Publishers B.V. (North Holland), Demazeau Y., Müller, J.P., editors, (1990) 3–13
14. Demazeau, Y., Boissier, O., Koning, J.L.: Using Interaction Protocols to Control Vision Systems Proceedings of SMC conference, San Antonio, (October 1994)
15. Georgeff, M.P., Lansky, A.L.: Reactive Reasoning and Planning. AAAI Conference, (1987) 677–682.
16. Hanson, A.R., Riseman, E.M. editors : Computer Vision Systems. Academic Press publishers, (1978)
17. Searle, J.R.: Speech Acts. Cambridge University Press, (1969)
18. Tsotsos, J.K.: Image Understanding. The Encyclopedia of Artificial Intelligence, S. Shapiro and D. Eckroth editors, Wiley and Sons, (1987)

Hierarchical Model and Communication by Signs, Signals, and Symbols in Multi-Agent Environments

Brahim Chaib-draa and Pascal Levesque
Département d'informatique, Faculté des Sciences
Université Laval, Sainte-Foy, QC, G1K 7P4, Canada

December 8, 1995

Abstract

This paper describes a general framework for designing agents for a multiagent systems. A hierarchical agent model is described, structuring an agent according to different types of situations. It has to deal with: routines, familiar and unfamiliar situations. Then, an idea is developped for the coordination between agents: agents should prefer low levels (i.e. routine and familiar situations) than the high level (i.e. unfamiliar situations). The reason is that low levels are fast, effortless and are propitious for coordinated activities between agents, whereas the high level is slow, laborious and can lead to conflicts between agents. To achieve this, we develop the idea of using communication by signs and signals (and not by symbols) in order to allow agents to rely on their low levels. Finally, implementation and experiments demonstrated, on some scenarios of urban traffic, the applicability of concepts developed in this article.

1 Introduction

In a multiagent environment, the agents are autonomous, potentially preexisting and typically heterogeneous. Research here is concerned with coordinating intelligent behaviors among a collection of autonomous agents, that is, how these agents can coordinate their knowledge, goals, skills, and plans jointly to take action and to solve problems [1, 3]. In this type of environment, the agents may be working toward a single global goal, or toward separate individuals goals that interact.

Coordination is central to multiagent systems (MAS), without it any benefits of interaction vanish and the group of agents quickly degenerates into a collection of individual with a chaotic behavior. To produce coordinating behaviors in MAS, most research has concentrated on developing groups in which both control and data are distributed. Distributed control means that agents are autonomous (to some degree) in their actions. This autonomy of course can lead to uncoordinated activities because of the uncertainty of each agent's actions. In this context, a number of coordination techniques have been deployed. However, no technique investigated the relation between uncertainty and the situation addressed by agents. Indeed, the uncertainty decreases when the degree of familiarity of the addressed situation increases.

Our work presented in this paper is a step toward remedying this problem by providing a framework for designing multiagent systems in which agents are capable of coordinating their activities in routine, familiar and unfamiliar situations. We begin in Sect. 2 by motivating our framework. We then outline basic elements of our framework relative to three levels of cognitive control in Sect. 3. Section 4 presents a new model of communication based on signs, signals and symbols, and corresponding to the skill level, the rule level and the knowledge level respectively. Section 5 provides technical details on our implementation and presents results of our experiments. Finally, Sect. 6 discusses issues about our framework and the underlying concepts and concludes with some open problems.

2 Coordination between Agents: Guiding Principles

Our work has been motivated by our efforts to coordinate intelligent agents in domains like air traffic control [4] or urban traffic (see Sect. 5). The framework presented in this paper reflects an effort that has extended over several years. In this section we summarize the guiding principles which have led us to develop this framework.

2.1 Coordination is Easier in Routine than in Unfamiliar Situations

In MAS, agents should coordinate their distributed resources which might be physical (such as communication capabilities) or informational (for instance, information about goals, skills and plans). Clearly, agents must find an *appropriate technique for working together in harmony* [15]. In fact, if all agents had complete knowledge of the goals, actions and interactions of their members, it would be possible to know exactly what each agent is doing at the present moment and what it is intending to do in the future. In this context, it would be possible to avoid conflicting and redundant efforts, agents could be perfectly coordinated and the effort of achieving this state would not be prohibitively high.

However, such complete knowledge about actual actions and reactions is only feasible in routine situations. In real-world domains, there are also familiar and unfamiliar situations. In familiar situations, agents can generally coordinate their behaviors since individual acts are carried out under expectations of future actions of other agents' actions and beliefs. In unfamiliar situations however, the coordination between agents is difficult to obtain and maintain because agents

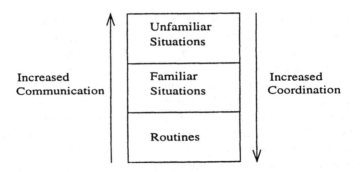

Figure 1: Coordination in different situations in a multiagent environment

need to be constantly informed of all developments in order to elaborate their decisions. In fact, a complete analysis to determine the detailed activities of each agent is impractical in unfamiliar situations, and agents should have the capability to reason about others.

In multiagent systems, we are therefore interested in three kinds of interactions between agents: interaction in routine situations, interaction in familiar situations and interactions in unfamiliar situations. For these categories of interactions, the coordination between agents is generally more attainable in routines than in unfamiliar situations. Whereas the communication between agents is generally more invoked in unfamiliar situations than in routines (Fig. 1).

A goal of our research is developing an architecture of agents with the conceptual models to investigate the three kinds of interactions. Generally, conceptual models have a hierarchical structure defined by the skill-rule-knowledge (S-R-K) levels (Figure 2) of Rasmussen [17]. In the S-R-K perspective, the skill-based level denotes almost routines performances. At this level, agent performance is governed by stored patterns of predefined procedures, that map directly from observation (i.e. perception) to an action. The rule-based level represents more conscious behavior when handling familiar situations. The rule-based behavior is conventionally described by a set of heuristics, that is by a set of stocked rules. The knowledge-based level accounts for unfamiliar situations for which know-how or rules are not available. Indeed, for these situations the control of performance must move to a higher conceptual level, in which behavior is controlled by goal and utility and more generally by the reasoning about others.

2.2 Communication by Signals and Signs Lead Agents to Prefer their Lower Cognitive Levels

Generally, a skill-based behavior refers to "automated" behavior typical in frequently encountered situations. At this level, the external information should act as signals which define the space-time relations, deviations, variations, etc. from the environment. The rule-based behavior is governed by a set of rules or associations, which are known and followed. At this level, the external infor-

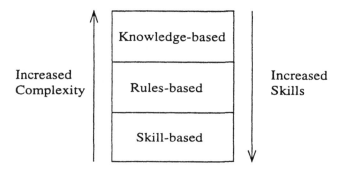

Figure 2: Hierarchical model of human behavior and reasoning techniques

mation serves as signs both to identify the situation and to be able to associate the appropriate set of rules. Consequently, signals and signs refer to low levels of cognitive control where the coordination between agents is easier and where agents' behavior is expected to be less prone to mistakes or misjudgments. In this case, the communication by signals and signs between agents should be preferred when it is possible, in order to allow agents to rely on low levels of their cognitive control.

2.3 A Knowledge Representation for Increasing Coordination

In conformity with interactions in routine, familiar and unfamiliar situations, the mode of knowledge representation adopted should have the following characteristics:

- it should represent mental constructs, models or structures for skill, rule and knowledge-based reasoning,
- it should make *abstraction* easy, particularly abstracting behaviors that can represent goals or objectives representing *what* is being achieved, and plans, procedures or tasks representing *how* the results are being achieved [8]. A behavior in this context can also have dimensions for *when* and *where* activities are taking place, for *who* are involved in the activities, and for *why* the behavior has been adopted. Notice that a hierarchical behavior with these dimensions allows agents to improve their coordination, and can propose alternative behaviors that lead to better coordination.
- it should make case-based reasoning possible in order to reflect *adaptation* to an unfamiliar situation from similar situations or cases. In this way, agents use their own experience if they have a relevant one, or they make use of the experience of others to the extent that they can obtain information about such experiences. This adaptability allows a flexible reconfiguration and consequently help agents to coordinate their activities, particularly in unfamiliar situations.

We have taken a step in this direction by adopting a knowledge representation based on memory organized packages (MOPs). Further details on this representation are given in [5, 6].

3 An Agent Model based on Hierarchical Model of Human Behavior

It is becoming widely accepted that neither purely reactive nor purely planning systems are capable of producing the range of behaviors required by intelligent agents in a dynamic, unpredictable multiagent environment. Indeed, in these environments, agents require skills to respond quickly to familiar situations or routines, while simultaneously being able to carry out unfamiliar situations such as conflicts. Furthermore, in multiagent environments, an unfamiliar situation for an agent can be a familiar situation for another, and the former can request the latter to carry it out. Therefore, agents in complex, real-world domains need to combine the benefits of reactive and planning systems to control their behaviors. Recently, some approaches try to integrate these two levels [7, 10, 11, 16]. However, these approaches still seem incomplete to us since they do not incorporate the decision making process that is important in multiagent environments [20]. As a result, our effort has gone into determining an agent model which combines advantages of reactive, planning and decision-making systems. Precisely, the proposed model in this work has been influenced by the skills, rules and Knowledge (S-R-K) levels of Rasmussen [17].

The skills, rules and knowledge-based processing proposed by Rasmussen reflects differences in consistency of response and conscious control of human behavior. Skill-based behavior refers to fully automated activities such as tracking or guiding, rule-based behavior to stereotyped actions such as test point checking in troubleshooting electronic circuit, and knowledge-based behavior to conscious activities involving problem solving or decision making. We believe that this differentiation between the three cognitive levels is also applicable for multiagent environments where it is important to analyze the behavior of many agents with reference to their cognitive levels. Furthermore, we should concentrate on developing groups of agents in which both control and data are distributed. Distributed control means that agents are autonomous to some degree in their actions. This autonomy can however lead to uncoordinated activities because of the uncertainty of each agent's actions. To reduce this uncertainty, agents should have the propensity for skill-based and rule-based behaviors rather than knowledge-based behavior.

These considerations have led us to adopt Rasmussen's conceptual model as a framework to develop an agent architecture that evolves in a world inhabited by other agents. This model is driven by the goal of combining the complementary advantages of reactive, planning and decision-making systems in order to take into account different situations which arise in multiagent environments: routines, familiar and unfamiliar situations. First, it needs to be reactive to be

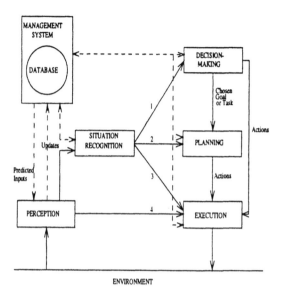

Figure 3: An agent model based On S-R-K framework: 1 corresponds to an unfamiliar situation that needs decision-making; 2 is a situation recognized in terms of a goal; 3 is a situation recognized in terms of an action; 4 is a situation perceived in terms of patterns to execute (i.e. stimulus)

able to quickly respond to changes in its environment. Secondly, it should be capable to plan its activities for a recognized task or goal. Finally, the model must also allow reasoning about others since agents should be capable of making decisions that take into account their own intentions and also others' intentions.

The proposed model (Fig. 3) includes the following phases. First, perceived information from the environment leads the agent to execute an action if the corresponding situation is perceived in terms of action. If this is not the case, the agent tries to recognize the situation. It can recognize the considered situation in terms of an action or in terms of a goal. In the first case, it tries to execute the corresponding action, and in the second case it invokes the planning module. Finally, if the agent faces an ambiguity and cannot come to a decision, or faces many alternatives, then it invokes the decision-making module (based on cognitive maps) to make a decision in order to commit to achieve a goal or an action. A goal leads an agent to plan, that is to produce a sequence of actions that achieve the chosen goal. The reader interested by the details of this architecture can refer to [5, 6]. Finally, we can summarize in table 2, the relationship between the proposed model and the three levels of control of human behavior.

Table 1: The relationship between the proposed model and the three levels of control of human behavior

Knowledge	perception - recognition - decision - planning - execution
	perception - recognition - decision - execution
	perception - recognition - planning[a] - execution
Rules	perception - recognition - planning[b] - execution
	perception - recognition - execution
Skills	perception - execution

[a]the planning process adapts old cases to the new situation, and the adaptation is significant.

[b]the planning process adapts old cases to the new situation, and the adaptation is generally minor

4 Communication by Signals, Signs and Symbols

In previous research in DAI environments, the possible solutions to the communication problem ranged between those involving no communication to those involving high-level, sophisticated communication. Solutions between these two extremities were: use of primitive communication, plan and information passing, information exchanges through a blackboard and finally, message passing. In the *no communication* case, an agent rationally infers other agents' plans without communicating with them. To achieve this, researchers [12, 19] have used game-theoretic approach characterized by pay-off matrices that contain agents' payoffs for each possible outcome of an interaction. In the *primitive communication* case, the communication is restricted to some finite set of fixed signals (usually two) with fixed interpretations. Georgeff [13] has applied this work to multiagent planning to avoid conflicts between plans involving more than one agent. In the *plan and information passing* approach, an agent A_1 communicates its total plan to agent A_2 and A_2 communicates its total plan to A_1 [19]. In the case of *exchange through the blackboard*, the agents use a shared global memory on which agents write messages, post partial results and find appropriate information. On the other hand, several works in DAI have used classical *message passing* with a protocol and a precise content [8]. Finally, the *high-level communication* approach focuses on dialogue between agents [21, 23]. This dialogue allows the generation and the interpretation of utterances which are speech actions planned to convey the information that the speaker is in particular mental states (beliefs, commitments and intentions) which consist of inducing a particular mental states in the hearer.

In our work, we adopt a new approach to communication. This approach firstly distinguishes between communications by signals, communication by signs and communication by symbols. Notice that the fact that information or indications going to and from agents can be perceived in different ways is not new [9, 17], but curiously enough, it has so far not been explicitly considered by multiagent systems designers.

Signals can be viewed as data representing time-space variables from a dynamic, spatial configuration in the environment and they can be processed directly by the agents as continuous variables. In communication by signals, the signal delivered by an agent i has the end of simply being a releaser for the receiving agent j – of simply eliciting a reaction by j. That is, the signal generally invokes a stimulus or a reaction, without passing through the memory (or the database in our model). In this case, we have a *non cognitive communication* characterized by

$$perception \longrightarrow action$$

An example of communication by signals in urban traffic is the case where a driver follows the signal delivered by another driver in front of him, in a situation of dense fog.

Signs are another kind of information that agents can exchange. Signs indicate a state in the environment with reference to certain norms for acts. In the case of communication by signs, the sender makes a sign which refers to some state of environment and which has the end of signifying, of letting the receiver knows the same reference. Of course, the sender and the receiver should share a set of signs with their references in order to communicate efficiently. For instance in urban traffic, communication between a driver and a policeman at a crossroad is generally done by signs. The policeman makes a specific sign which refers to a certain action and which is addressed to certain driver(s). The addressee(s) recognize(s) the reference of this sign and activate(s) stored patterns of behaviors. Note that information perceived at the rule level (see table 1) acts generally as signs activating familiar situations. Furthermore and conversely to signals, signs pass through the memory (or the database in our model). In this case, the communication can be viewed as a *cognitive communication*.

Finally, agents can also communicate by symbols. *Symbols* represent variables, relations and properties and can be formally processed. They are abstract constructs related to and defined by a formal structure of relations and processes, which according to convention can be related to features of the external world [17]. In urban traffic for instance, a dialogue between a policeman and a driver in natural language reflects a symbol-based communication.

Information at knowledge and rule levels can act as symbols depending on the situation and the language used for communication. In familiar situations corresponding to the rule level, agents can use a specific language (derived or not from a natural language). This language is generally constructed from repeated activities. When unfamiliar situations occur, agents do not dispose of any operative knowledge nor of any specialized language. They must then make use of a non specialized language (for example natural language), which is less concise but more flexible than their operative language used in familiar situation.

In summary, with signals and signs, agents do not force their cognitive control to a higher level (i.e. the knowledge level) than the demands of the situation requires. In contrast, agents have a propensity for behaviors based on skills and

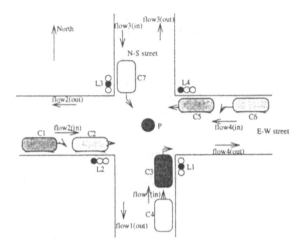

Figure 4: A multiagent scenario in urban traffic: the crossroads (C denotes a car, L traffic-lights, and P the place of a policemen)

rules. These behaviors are generally fast, effortless and propitious to a better coordination between agents.

5   The Urban Traffic As Illustrative Example

Building on major ideas developed in this work, we now give details about an illustrative example and its implementation using the hierarchical architecture and the communication by signs, signals and symbols developed in this paper. Urban traffic is generally a highly interactive task between various agents. These agents can be people (drivers, policeman, pedestrians, etc.) or machines (vehicles, traffic-lights, etc.) and have to continuously adjust their actions in order to avoid conflicts such as traffic-jams, and in severe cases, crashes.

The urban traffic application is a relevant area of research for multiagent paradigm. Consequently, we might demonstrate the applicability of the major concepts developed in this article for this application. We particularly focus on investigation of global aspects such as interaction between agents in routine and less routine situations and communication between agents using signs, signals and symbols. More precisely, in this section we investigate a multiagent scenario showing traffic situations at an intersection (Fig. 9).

Our scenario captures: 1) agents' behaviors in routine and familiar situations (e.g. the agents' behaviors are coordinated by traffic lights); 2) agents' behaviors in complex situations (e.g. the agents' behaviors are coordinated by a policeman); 3) agents' behaviors in unfamiliar situations (e.g. the agents' behaviors are coordinated by social laws, because traffic lights are off).

5.1 Implementation

The architecture presented in Fig. 3 depicts a general model and can be adapted to a vast number of fields. We implemented each component of the architecture (in Common Lisp) while keeping in mind this idea of generality. In order to validate this architecture in a multiagent environment, we have implemented the crossroads scenario using our architecture and the communication based on signs signals and symbols. The crossroads scenario has been simplified and instead of striving for a comprehensive simulation of reality, emphasis has been put on the applicability of the major multiagent system aspects developed in this work. One type of agent used to model the considered scenario is the human agent and more particularly drivers and policemen (pedestrians are not yet modeled since they are not considered in this first work). This type of agent is implemented using the architecture presented in Fig. 3. Notice that drivers use cars as prosthesis that widen the range of human senses by providing information to other agents. More precisely, in our scenario, each association driver-car is represented by a car (e.g. C1, C2, etc.) whose flow of information adheres to model presented in Fig. 3. In these conditions, a car $\in$ {C1,C2 etc.} has to pass the traffic-lights by coordinating his activities with other cars. He can communicate with others through signals and signs, particularly the signals and signs delivered by other cars (parking-lights, turn-lights, brake-lights, stop-lights, etc.), signs and symbols delivered by a policeman (go-ahead, turn-right, stop, etc.) and signs delivered by traffic lights.

To represent a car, we have adopted the following properties: f_s_e (i.e. the frontal surrounding environment); b_s_e (i.e.the back surrounding environments); dir (i.e. the direction of the car's next move that might be turn_left, turn_right, straight_ahead). These properties are represented by MOPs and those relative to surrounding environment are periodically updated to reflect any change.

We have implemented a simple model of a crossroads in order to simplify the sequencing of traffic-lights (which is generally very complex) and the process of decision-making when the traffic-lights do not work . In this model (adopted from Lux's model [14]), the intersecting streets are represented simply as a pair of queues. This simplification allows to do without traffic lights showing arrows for the different directions of traffic flow, and simplifies light sequence control considerably. Furthermore, a crossroads is assumed to have no *capacity* and consequently flows of Fig. 9 adhere to:

$$\sum_{I=1}^{I=4}(\texttt{flowI(in)} - \texttt{flowI(out)}) = 0.$$

In this simplified crossroads model, traffic-lights L1, L2, L3 and L4 (see Fig. 9) are interdependent since opposite directions always switch in synchrony. Thus, opposite flow volumes, flow2(in), flow4(in) and flow1(in), flow3(in) are controlled by exactly the same sequence. Furthermore, when L1 and L3 show green the L2 and L4 must show red and vice versa. For the control regime reflecting the functionality of the Crossroads, there are different strategies, each with its own set of rules to follow. The objective is to control the flow so that all directions are served equally. Based on our simple model of crossroads and on what we seek to achieve, we have adopted the following strategy:

As long as no significant differences in traffic flow volumes are detected, L1, L2, L3 and L4 adhere to a standard value. When the traffic flow in one of the intersection streets becomes extremely small, the lights of the busier direction stays green until one or more cars approach the intersection in the less busy street. Then the light turns green in the latter direction as needed, up to a predetermined maximum time.

In our scenario, each car has a RoutePlan determining its route. Guided by this RoutePlan, the agent finds its way and turns the desired direction at a crossroads. To do this, the agent periodically interrogates its RoutePlan to know what to do. For example, being in street N-S at traffic-light L1 and knowing the direction of the next step suffices to determine which street to enter next.

Finally, all agents implicated in our scenario share common knowledge including social laws about the highway code and other social behaviors.

5.2 Experiments

As stated previously, there are three levels (S-R-K: skills, rules and knowledge) of cognitive control in multiagent systems (MAS). These three levels can be grouped together into two general categories [18]. K is concerned with analytical problem solving based on symbolic representation, whereas S and R are concerned with perception and action. S and R levels can be only activated in routine and familiar situations because these low levels require that agents know the perceptual features of the environments and the knowledge relative to these situations. The K level, on the other hand, is only activated in unfamiliar situations. These considerations have been taken into account in designing our agents.

With these agents, we have developed implementations and experiments in urban traffic to verify our intuitions about the distinction between the two modes of processing: perceptual processing (i.e. S and R levels) and analytical problem solving (i.e. K level) [22]. Perceptual processing is fast, effortless and is propitious for coordinated activities between agents, whereas analytical problem solving is slow, laborious and can lead to conflicts between agents. To this end, we are conducting a series of experimental studies on three policies of the crossroads scenario. The policy 1 refers to a routine of urban traffic. In this routine, agents' activities are coordinated by traffic lights. Policy 3 refers to an unfamiliar situation of the crossroads scenario. In this situation, agents should rely on social laws to make decisions because traffic lights are off, and there is no policeman to coordinate their activities. Finally, the policy 2 refers to a complex situation where agents' activities are coordinated by a policeman, that is by a knowledgeable agent.

Table 2: Experiments summary for the cars (these results are averaged across 10 scenarios)

Performance\Policies	Policy 1	Policy 2	Policy 3
Communication (i)	1.9	3.1	5.3
Proc. time for S (ii)	140	145	30
Proc. time for R (iii)	17	130	17
Proc. time for K (iv)	6	60	420
Waiting time (v)	163	335	467
Errors (vi)	0.2	2.7	4.1

Table 3: Experiments Summary for the Policeman (Parameters in this table are measured during the total waiting time per car)

Performance\Policies	Policy 2
Communications	8.7
Proc. time for S	40
Proc. time for R	90
Proc. time for K	205

(i)mean messages (signs and/or symbols) sent per car while waiting to pass,

(ii) mean Sun Sparc cpu seconds per car for reasoning at the skill level, while waiting to pass,

(iii) mean Sun Sparc cpu seconds per car for reasoning at the rule level, while waiting to pass,

(iv) mean Sun Sparc cpu seconds per car for reasoning at the knowledge level, while waiting to pass,

(v) mean Sun Sparc cpu seconds per car for the total waiting time at crossroads,

(vi) mean number of near misses or collisions for all cars in a scenario.

We examined for the cars three performance indices when comparing the policies: communication, processing time for each mode of reasoning (skills, rules and knowledge), and task effectiveness. The effectiveness is specified by two distinct parameters: errors and waiting time. A summary of the main experiments is given in table 2. For the policeman who intervenes in the policy 2, we examined two performance indices: communications and processing time for each level of the agents' cognitive control. The results about these indices are given in table 3.

As we had anticipated, our implementation and experiments successfully demonstrated that perceptual processing is fast, effortless and is propitious for coordinated activities between agents. Policy 1 is in this case, since it is considered (in our implementation) as routine of urban traffic.

More precisely, *policy 1* which reflects a routine, performed best overall. Particularly, this policy allows agents to have the best waiting time and there is no effort since the processing time at the skill level is much higher than at other levels. As we had anticipated, our implementation and experiments successfully demonstrated that with a routine, the number of near misses or collisions between cars is the fewest. In addition, the number of messages sent per car in this routine is also the fewest. Consequently, our expectation that coordination at the skill level is more easy to obtain and to maintain than at knowledge level, is proved true. In the same context, our expectation that routines are not generally communication intensive is also proved true. What happens in this routine is that agents share social laws that allow them to respect traffic lights, and therefore to coordinate their activities without communicating intensively.

The *policy 3* is considered (in our implementation) as an unfamiliar situation where agents reason at the knowledge level to elaborate their decisions. In this context, we had also expected that the analytical problem solving, that is the knowledge level, would be slow and effortful. These expectations are proved true as indicated by our results. Precisely, policy 3 performed worst overall. Indeed, agents have the worst waiting time and their major processing time is at the knowledge level where reasoning is about itself and about others. This reasoning mode is considered as requiring effort since it needs knowledge about others' intentions in order to predict dimensions relative to actions or plans such as for instance what (to do) and who (is the actor). By doing this, agents try to improve their coordination. Finally, with the policy 3, the number of near misses or collisions between cars is the greatest. This result is also in accordance with what we had expected, that is that the analytical level is more propitious to errors and therefore to poor coordination between agents.

Finally, the *policy 2* is a complex situation where cars are coordinated by a knowledgeable agent who is the policemen. In this type of situation, we had expected that cars reason at low levels and the policeman at a high level. Our implementation and experiments confirm this expectation. Precisely, processing times in table 2 indicate that agents consider the situation relative to policy 3 as a situation which is more familiar than policy 3 but less routine than policy 1. In the same context, processing times in table 3 show that the same situation is considered by the policeman as a unfamiliar situation with a certain degree of familiarity. These considerations led in the context of cars, to a policy which is intermediate in performance as shown in table 2, since the waiting time of policy 2 is intermediate between the waiting times of policies 1 and 3.

Our implementation and experiments demonstrated also that the presence of policeman improve the coordination between cars since the number of near misses or collisions is lower than the number of near misses of the policy 3 where there is no coordinator. The number of messages sent per cars is also lower than the number of messages of policy 3 since cars in policy 2 only follow indications given by the policeman. However, implementation and experiments show that the coordination in the case of policy 2 is not as efficient as the coordination in the case of policy 1.

Collectively, our implementation and results are consistent with what we had expected.

6 Discussion and Open Problems

There are two characteristics of realistic multiagent environments that it is worthwhile to note. First, agents in complex work domain need to be highly skilled as for instance operators of such systems which have extensive experience in controlling the environment. Second, agent design for these environments consists of specifying an agent for a single, specific application. In this case, we do not need to design a general agent. Thus, issues associated with transfer between various applications do not play a significant role in MAS because we will almost always be dealing with the same agents for the same application.

These two considerations make perceptual processing, (i.e. skill and rule levels) an attractive possibility for the designer of MAS. This recommendation does not mean that perception is always better than knowledge but that the characteristics of multiagent domains are generally propitious for perceptual processing. In other words, if one can design agents that effectively take advantage of perceptual processing, then the benefits can be great. In particular, communication is minimized and coordination is easier to obtain and maintain. However, to be truly effective, a MAS should also support higher levels of cognitive control in order to reason about others to be able to reduce negative interactions between agents in the case of an unfamiliar situation.

In summary it is important to note that for MAS design:

1. lower levels are easier for efficiency interactions and consequently agents should be designed in a way that allows them to rely on low levels in routine and familiar situations (greater the skills, lower the level),
2. complex tasks including routines, familiar and unfamiliar situations require all levels and consequently all levels (skills, rules and knowledge) need to be supported.

Finally, communication by signals and signs allow agents to rely on low levels.

7 Conclusion

The framework described in this paper was motivated by a problem: how to permit agents to coordinate their activities in routine, familiar and unfamiliar situations. The first step taken toward solving this problem was to determine what model of agent was associated with these situations. Common sense revealed that coordination is generally more easy to obtain and maintain in routine than in unfamiliar situations. Conversely, unfamiliar events must face the problem of reasoning about others and consequently agents which are in this situation can use communication intensively if they do not succeed in making a decision about what to do next with other agents. In addition, for unfamiliar situations, agents are more propitious for making negative interactions. In these conditions, a viable approach to agent design for multiagent systems must be able to combine benefits of reflexive, planning and decision making systems in order to produce skill-based behaviors, goal-oriented behaviors and commitment-based behaviors as required by real multiagent environments. To this end, we have proposed an architecture for agents that reflects three levels of cognitive control as specified by Rasmussen's taxonomy: a skill-based behavior, heuristic-based behavior, and knowledge-based behavior. We also argued that communication by signals and signs allow agents to rely on low levels since these levels are easier for efficiency interactions. In the remainder of the paper, we showed how our proposed model can be used in multiagent environments. Finally, our implementation and experimentation was consistent with what we had expected, in particular: the lower levels (i.e. skills and rules levels) are easier for efficiency interactions.

Acknowledgements

The results presented in this paper reflect an effort that has extended over several years. Many people have contributed ideas in a variety of ways. This research was supported by the Natural Sciences and Engineering Research Council of Canada (NSERC) and by the Fonds pour la Formation des Chercheurs et l'aide à la Recherche (FCAR) du Québec.

References

[1] A. Bond and L. Gasser, eds.*Reading in Distributed Artificial Intelligence*, San Mateo, CA, Morgan Kaufman, 1988.

[2] R. A. Brooks. A robust layered control system for a mobil robot. *IEEE Jour. of Robotics and Autom.*, vol. 2, 1986, pp. 14-23.

[3] B. Chaib-draa, B. Moulin, R. Mandiau et P. Millot. Trends in distributed artificial intelligence. *Artificial Intelligence Review*, vol. 6, 1992, pp. 35-66.

[4] B. Chaib-draa, and P. Millot. A framework for cooperative work: an approach based on the intentionality. *Int. Jour. of AI in Engineering*, vol. 5, 1990, pp. 199-205.

[5] B. Chaib-draa. Coordination between Agents in Routines, Familiar and Unfamiliar Situations. Rapport de Recherche du département d'Informatique, DIUL–RR–9401, 1994.

[6] B. Chaib-draa. Coordination between Agents in Routines, Familiar and Unfamiliar Situations. *Int. Jour. of Intelligent & Cooperative Information Systems*, (to appear), 1996.

[7] P. R. Cohen. M. L. Greenberg, D. H. Hart and A. E. Howe. Trial by fire: understanding the design requirements for agents in complex environments. *AI Magazine*, vol. 10, 1989, pp. 34-28.

[8] E. H. Durfee and T. A. Montgomery. Coordination as distributed search in a hierarchical behavior space. *IEEE Trans. Syst., Man, Cybern.*, vol. 21, Dec. 1991, pp. 1363-1378.

[9] U. Eco. *A Theory of Semiotics*. Bloomington Indiana Univeristy Press, 1979.

[10] I. A. Ferguson. Touring-machines: autonomous agents with attitudes. *IEEE Computer*, vol. 25, 1992.

[11] J. R. Firby. An investigation into reactive planning in complex domains. *Proc. of AAAI-87*, Seattle, WA, 1987, pp. 202-206.

[12] M. R. Genesereth, M. L. Ginsberg and J. S. Rosenschein. Cooperation without communication. *Proc. of AAAI-86*, Philadelphia, PA, 1986, pp. 51-57.

[13] M. P. Georgeff. Communication and interaction in multiagent planning. *Proc. of IJCAI-83*, Karlshure, Germany, 1983, pp. 125-129.

[14] A. Lux, F. Bomarius, D. Steiner. A model for supporting human computer cooperation. *Proc. AAA-92 Workshop on Cooperating Heterogeneous Intelligent Systems*, San Jose, CA, July 1992.

[15] T. W. Malone. Toward an interdisciplinary theory of coordination. CCS TR #120, MSA Center for Coord. Sc., MIT, Camb., MA, April, 1991.

[16] J. P. Müller and M. Pishel. An architecture for dynamically interacting agents. *Int. Jour. of Intelligent and Cooperative Systems*, 3(1), (1994), 25-45.

[17] J. Rasmussen. *Information Processing and Human-Machine Interaction: An Approach to Cognitive Engineering*, North Holland, 1986.

[18] J. Reason, *Human Error*. Cambridge, UK: Cambridge Univ. Press, 1990.

[19] J. S. Rosenschein. Rationnal interaction: cooperation among intelligent agents. Ph.D. Thesis, Computer Science Department, Stanford University, 1986.

[20] A. P. Sage. Information systems engineering for distributed decisionmaking. *IEEE Trans. Syst., Man, Cybern.*, vol. SMC-17, 1987, pp. 920-936.

[21] M. P. Sing, M. N. Huhns, and M. Stephens. Declarative representation for multiagent systems. *IEEE Trans. Know. and Data Eng.*, vol. 5, 1993, pp. 721-739.

[22] K. J. Vicente and J. Rasmussen. Ecological interface design: theoretical foundations. *IEEE Trans. Syst., Man, Cybern.*, vol. SMC-22, 1992, pp. 589-606.

[23] S. T. C. Wong. COSMO: communication scheme for cooperative knowledge-based systems. *IEEE Trans. Syst., Man, Cybern.*, vol. SMC-23, 1993, pp. 809-824.

Plan Recognition:
from Single-Agent to Multi-Agent Plans

Rino Falcone and Cristiano Castelfranchi

Finalized Project "Information Systems and Parallel Computation", U.O.:
Istituto di Psicologia-CNR
Viale Marx, 15 - 00137 ROMA - Italy
E-mail: cris@pscs2.irmkant.rm.cnr.it or falcone@vaxiac.iac.rm.cnr.it

Abstract

The ability of recognizing a multi-agent plan - a plan which has been generated for multiple executing agents - implies the skill of recognizing the plan underlying a collective activity in which a group of agents is involved. Multi-agent plan recognition is a necessary and useful extension of current PR systems in some domains.
In this work starting from CHAPLIN (CHart Applied to PLan INference, a chart-based plan recognition system) we discuss how extending this system to the multi-agent world, many problems arise. More in general we consider the challenges that the multi-agent domains produce for the plan recognition systems. In fact this extension involves non-trivial problems and it calls for a general theory of the relationships between single-agent plans and multi-agent plans.
CHAPLIN shows how the chart allows an effective representation of the structural organization of plans.
Some of the main problems arising in MAP recognition are identified and discussed (iterative decomposition, virtual actions, virtual plans). We show how Multi-CHAPLIN - the extension of the CHAPLIN system - can partially manage those problems.
Finally, we will call for the necessity of a theory of "plan transformation": from single-agent plans to multi-agent plans. Such a theory is claimed to be very advantageous both for the generality and abstraction of plan formalization, and for the economy of plan memory.

1 Introduction

Our research program, starting from the study and implementation of a single-agent plan recognition system named CHAPLIN (CHart Applied to PLan INference) [Falcone and Castelfranchi, 1993a], is moving to extend this system to the multi-agent world [Falcone and Castelfranchi, 1994, Castelfranchi and Falcone, 1994]. The aim of this work is to discuss the main problems tackled moving from a single-agent plan (SAP) to a multi-agent plan (MAP) recognition system and to specify its necessary properties. Relevant issues of the affect of multiple agents on plan recognition, as well as some problems and solutions, will be viewed.
Let us consider that, on the one hand the MAPs are becoming more and more important in AI systems, and on the other hand the general theories of plan (and particularly PR models) remain mainly focused on single-agent plan representations. In particular, the relationships between SAPs and MAPs are not explained and a theory of their reciprocal transformations does not exist.
The ability of recognizing a MAP - a plan which has been generated for multiple executing agents [Bond and Gasser, 1988] - implies the skill of recognizing the plan underlying a collective activity in which a group of agents is involved. MAP

recognition is a necessary and useful extension of current PR systems in some domains.

On the one hand, there is a trend extending the interactive single-user systems to network facilitators and to systems supporting conversation and cooperative work. Research in Computer Supported Cooperative Work (CSCW) contains everything in Human Computer Interaction (HCI) plus. There is a need for theories and models of the users. With group work, theories must additionally encompass the conversations among the participants, the roles they adopt, and the organizational setting: "Simply stated, we need to understand the nature of group work" [Olson *et al.*, 1993]. Our claim is that the understanding of the nature of group work necessarily encompasses MAPs recognition ability.

On the other hand, also within the DAI and MAS fields the growing issues concerning team-work, coalition formation, and conflicts, will require MAP recognition ability by the agents.

CHAPLIN and Multi-CHAPLIN (the MA extension of CHAPLIN) use a chart-based parsing approach to plan recognition [Vilain, 1990; Falcone and Castelfranchi, 1993b].

In section 2, we will introduce CHAPLIN, and we will show how the chart allows an effective representation of the structural organization of plans.

In section 3, we will identify some of the main problems that arise in MAP recognition (*iterative decomposition, virtual actions, virtual plans*). We will claim the necessity of a theory of "plan transformation": from SAPs to MAPs and vice versa, or from an unspecified scheletal plan to a SAP or to a MAP. Such a theory is claimed to be very advantageous both for the generality and abstraction of plan formalization, and for the economy of plan memory. The main problem we identify in "plan transformation" is the *Insertion Problem* and the *Transfer* of knowledge, resources and products among the agents in MAPs.

In section 4 we will describe Multi-CHAPLIN and we will show how it can partially manage those problems thanks to the introduction of some structural modifications in CHAPLIN basic mechanism.

2 The CHAPLIN System

CHAPLIN (CHart Applied to PLan INference) is a chart-based system for plan recognition [Falcone and Castelfranchi, 1993a] whose aim is the reconstruction of the plan of a single main agent (the agent which is responsible of the actions), starting from the description of actions visualized by sequences of vignettes of simple stories (that is to say stories with several actors including just one protagonist).

The actions are represented within a formal structure - the chart - in order to realize an analysis mechanism about these actions, turning out to be quite similar with the one realized in chart-parsing [Stock *et al.*, 1989].

The chart as directed acyclic graph represents at any time the state of the plan recognition. Given a sequence of actions, their bounds are called vertices and they are represented as nodes in the chart. The vertices define a temporal scanning of the actions: given the vertices $V_1,..., V_n$ it is possible establish that $t_{V_i} < t_{V_j}$ if $V_i < V_j$ (with $1 \leq i,j \leq n$). Each vertex has an arbitrary number of arcs, called edges, entering and leaving it. An edge is therefore a link between two vertices and it represents a possible plan-based interpretation of the input portion between the vertices. In other terms, the vertices represent the temporal bounds the action is carried out within.

An edge may be of two types: inactive or active. An inactive edge stands for a recognized constituent. An active edge represents a partially recognized constituent. More definitely any inactive edge detects, in the area set below it, or an observed action, or a set of elements and a set of relationships between these elements representing a plan. An active edge, on the contrary, represents a plan not having some of its component.

An inactive edge will be, in its main components, specified by:
- starting vertex (*from*); - arrival vertex (*to*); - constituent's category (*category*).

In the case of an active edge:
- starting vertex (*from*); - arrival vertex (*to*); - a plan's library's rule (*rule*); - a rest (*res$_i$*) indicating the right part of the rule which has not yet been recognized; the *i* index indicates the position in the right part of the rule up to the point where the components have been recognized.

The main rule of the chart plan recognition (CPR) is:

Given an active edge A between the vertices V_a and V_b and an inactive edge I between the vertices V_b and V_c, then if A refers to the edge with R *rule* and the *res$_i$* rest, and the I category is rightly C_{i+1}, (i+1)th symbol of the R right part, therefore a new edge E can be introduced into the chart. This edge will go from the V_a vertex to the V_c vertex and if C_{i+1} is the last symbol in the right part of R, E will be an inactive edge having the same category as the symbol in the left part of R, otherwise it will be an active edge with R rule and *res$_{i+1}$* rest (Fig.1).

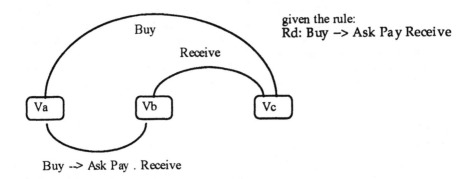

given the rule:
Rd: Buy --> Ask Pay Receive

Buy --> Ask Pay . Receive

Fig. 1

Following Kautz hierarchical representation [Kautz, 1987], it is possible to think of organizing the plans according to two relationships: abstraction and decomposition. We have two different tables of rules:
• one containing the abstraction (specialization) relationships among the actions:

$$P^a_1 \rightarrow A_1 \qquad P^a_2 \rightarrow A_2 \qquad .... \qquad P^a_n \rightarrow A_n \qquad [1]$$

samples in CHAPLIN domain: *Ask-to-have --> Point-out* ,
Show --> Point-out , To-around --> Walk;
or in the Cooking World:
Make-Pasta-Dish --> Make-spaghetti-marinara,   Make-pasta --> Make-spaghetti.
• and one containing the decomposition (composition) rules among the actions:

$$P^c_1 \dashrightarrow A_{11} \dots A_{1n} \qquad \dots\dots\dots \qquad P^c_m \dashrightarrow A_{m1} \dots A_{mk} \qquad [2]$$

samples in CHAPLIN domain: *Buy --> Ask-to-have Pay Receive*
or in the Cooking World:
Make-Pasta-Dish --> Make-Sauce Make-pasta Boil
The rules' invocation strategy, starting from which the analysis is realized, can be either top-down or bottom-up.

In top-down case, given an active edge with R *rule* and *res$_i$* rest (*(Pay Receive)* in Fig.2), that has reached the vertex V, if there is a R' *rule* having the left part equal to C_{i+1}, (i+1)th symbol of the right part of R (*Pay --> Take-money Give-money* in Fig.2), an empty active edge is introduced into the vertex V, with R' *rule*, (once that such an edge is not yet to be found in the chart).

Pay -> . Take-money Give-money

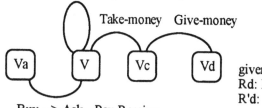

given the rules:
Rd: Buy -> Ask Pay Receive
R'd: Pay -> Take-money Give-money

Buy -> Ask . Pay Receive

Fig. 2

In bottom-up case, once given an inactive edge with *category* C (*Ask* in Fig.3) that starts from the V_a vertex and finishes in V_b vertex, if there is a R rule, having C as the first symbol of its right part, an edge is introduced from the V_a vertex to V_b vertex with R *rule* (once that such an edge is not yet to be found in the chart); this edge will be inactive if C is the only element in the right part of R (therefore always in the case of abstraction rules), while it will be an active edge in the opposite case (having the right part of R as a rest, except C).

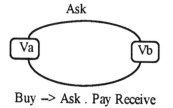

given the rule:
Rd: Buy -> Ask Pay Receive

Buy -> Ask . Pay Receive

Fig. 3

As in Kautz, the action have some parameters (agent, patient, instrument, etc.) and some constraints on these parameters that have to be respected: the three rules described above (main, top-down and bottom-up rules) have therefore to be considered true adding these controls.

For the use of CPR it is necessary consider a main limit: it is not possible to recognize a plan the component actions of which cross with those of another plan which is not included in the plan under consideration. In other words it is possible to recognize either one plan at once or more independent parallel plans, where the time sequence of each plan is uninterrupted.
These constraints will be found also in the MAP case.

3 Challenges for PR in a MA world

In this section we try to point out some of the main problems we met extending PR to a multi-agent world. In particular we describe problems arising in MAP recognition, focusing on the unification of the plan libraries and on the problem of the SAP/MAP transformation; this transformation involves non-trivial problems and calls for a general theory of the SAP/MAP relationships as a crucial part of a general plan theory. Such a theory is claimed to be very advantageous both for the generality and abstraction of plan formalization, and for the economy of plan memory.

3.1 Observation Time vs Action Time

While in traditional PR systems like CHAPLIN it is implicitly postulated that the order in which the actions are "observed" by the system (the input order) coincides with the order of the action execution, this simplification is much more problematic in a MA world. Since both the agents performing the actions of a given plan, and the agents observing and reporting on such actions, are distributed, we cannot anymore assume that the order in which the PR system acquires knowledge about an action coincides with the actual order of that action. This obliged us to make explicit the action time in Multi-CHAPLIN. Thus, the sequence of actions given as input to the system is generated by a reordering procedure which takes into account the proper time of the actions and not the time of their "perception". Suppose that there is a plan P1 composed of three ordered actions Ax, Ay, Az respectively (be it a SAP or a MAP), and that the PR system receives the following news from some observers (O1, O2): at time T1 O1 says "Az happened at Tz", at time T2 O2 says "Ax happened at Tx and Ay happened at Ty ". Because T1 is before T2 the system could be deceived: it could recognize a different plan (Az, Ax, Ay) - if any - or not recognize any plan. This is why the system should not use as input order the order of arrival of information items.

Using a chart-based approach one is obliged to put into a sequence possible simultaneous actions. This problems, that is present also with SAPs, obviously becomes more important with MAPs. However with the explicit time representation the system can preserve this constraint on the actions as well as other constraints.

3.2 Challenges in MAPs recognition

a) For a Unique Plan Library

Most part of planning and plan recognition systems are memory-based: they use some kind of plan library (hierarchical planning, case based and adaptive, etc.) [Kolodner, 1983; Sycara, 1987; Stanfill and Waltz, 1986]. Usually memorized plans, at any arbitrary level of abstraction, are in fact just SAPs.

In the MA domain a further complication arises about what kind (SA, MA, unspecified) of plans there should be in the libraries. In our opinion it is clearly impractical and implausible to always have two plan libraries or two different plans, one for the SA case and another for the MA case. In other words, we assume that

SAPs and MAPs are not two independent and irreducible kinds of mental objects: as a matter of fact cognitive agents are able to generate new multi-agent plans from a scheletal plan or from a SAP example in their plan memory. They could be able also to execute a SAP starting from their plan memory of a MAP, or to recognize a MA execution of a plan that they already know as a SAP. It seems useful to have a theory able to specify the double phenomenon of plan activation and plan adaptation to the SA and MA cases.

In [Retz-Schmidt, 1991] - one of the few examples of MAP recognition - we read: "The knowledge about possible interaction between multiple agents is represented in the domain-specific interaction library. This way, knowledge about plans of individual agents and knowledge about typical interactions between several agents is kept separate. (...) The interaction library contains *interaction schemata*, which each represent aggregations of plans and interactions of multiple agents typically occurring jointly in a situation. The interaction schemata are graphs whose nodes represent plans and whose arcs represent interactions between plans of agents." In this approach plans clearly refer only to single-agent behavior. It is not taken into account the possibility to have exactly the same plan executed either by a SA or by more than one agent. We would like to have a system able to recognize both true plans executed by multiple agents and regular interaction patterns which are not true collective plans.

b) SAP/MAP Transformation

There are two basic procedures for transforming a SAP into a MAP:
- the *Distributive Mechanism*: the different plan actions are assigned as tasks to different agents;
- the *Iterative Decomposition*: the same plan action could be iteratively performed by different agents.

If we allocate the plan actions to more than one agent, regarding the possible constraints, we obtain a MA version of that plan. We call this mechanism of MAP generation Distributive Mechanism since it consists in a task distribution among the agents. Note that the agents will execute different tasks possibly requiring different competencies. This is a well studied DPS problem [Durfee *et al.*, 1992]. Let us examine more extensively the other mechanism which is less considered in the literature.

The introduction of MAPs imposes to cope with a more complex plan grammar with respect to the SAP case. While, in fact, in the latter case the mere description of the structure of every rule is sufficient to get an overall picture of each plan composition, in the MA case it has to be presumed that each component action of the plan can be reiterated by more than one agent (Iterative Decomposition). This is true if the goal of the plan is achievable gradually: the actions of the plan's body must have quantitative results. Quantitative results are represented by states of the world where there are MASS entities (water, people, etc) or plural COUNT entities (students, dishes, etc.): consider, for instance, the preparation of a spaghetti-party for a folklorist celebration: Make-Spaghetti(Gianni) Make-Spaghetti(Nino) Make-Spaghetti(Ugo) Make-Marinara(Mario).

Then we can say that while representing any MAP (and thus when writing the rule representing the same) we do not know (besides, of course, the values of instantiation of the variables as in the case of SAPs) the number of the variables and their distribution into component actions.

Besides the two procedures above mentioned there is a very important problem in "plan transformation" that is *the problem of transferring knowledge and resources among the agents in MAPs.*

SAP/MAP transformation requires the insertion of new actions which were absent in the original SAP case or in the scheletal plan (Insertion Problem). So in fact there is a great number of possible MAP transformation from a single SAP.

The most interesting problem raising in transformation lies precisely on the Insertion Mechanism and its reasons. This problems has just been perceived [Grosz and Sidner, 1990]. In a MAP:
- the knowledge acquired in performing an action,
- the products of the action,
- the involved resources,

which in a SAP are by definition owned by one and the same agent, must be transferred from one agent to the others performing the subsequent actions.

A. Information-Transfer Insertion Rule (*Rule1*):

given a sequence of two actions (simple or complex) A_1 and A_2 in a plan, assigned to different agents, *if* A_2 requires to be successfully executed, as one of its precondition, the results of A_1; *then* insert in between A_1 and A_2 an action A_x (simple or complex) whose goal is that A_2's agent is informed about the execution and the results of A_1.

Notice that we assume the following postulate: if A_2 requires to be successfully executed, as one of its precondition, the results of A_1, then A_2 requires, as one of its precondition, also the knowledge about A_1's execution and results. It is postulated that the execution of an action by an agent implies that that agent knows that the action has been executed.

B. Resource-Transfer Insertion Rule (*Rule2*):

given a sequence of two actions (simple or complex) A_1 and A_2 in a plan, assigned to different agents, *if* A_2 requires to be successfully executed, as one of its precondition, a resource of A_1; *then* insert in between A_1 and A_2 an action A_x (simple or complex) whose goal is that A_2's agent has at his disposal that resource.

A similar rule can accounts for the transfer of products (*Rule3*).

Notice that we didn't specify who should be the agent of the inserted action A_x: this is because it depends on the kind of A_x's plan. In fact, there are many possible plans for the goal that A_2's agent is informed about the execution and the results of A_1. Either A_1's agent communicates to the other agent about his action; or A_2's agent looks at, monitors A_1 to know about its results; or a third agent knowing the A_1 results informs A_2's agent. The same possibilities are held in the transfer of resources and products: A_1's agent or a third agent give A_2's agent the resource or product, or A_2's agent takes by himself the resource or product.

There is a certain redundancy among the above mentioned rules, because in every case you may apply Rule2 o Rule3, you should also apply Rule1. On the contrary, taking advantage from this redundancy, when we apply Rule2 or Rule3 we don't give explicitly the relative information. In other words we consider this information as implicitly given: if A_2's agent receives the product or the resource of A_1, he is intitled to assume that A_1 was successfully performed. Thus, in this case it is superfluous to explicitly insert the information action in the plan.

As for the transformation from MAPs into SAPs, the process seems simpler than the inverse one, implying just the pruning of the transfer actions (information and resources): an agent does not need to inform himself of having done a certain action, or to give himself a permission.

c) Conversation Plans vs Practical Plans

Normally in a multi-agent world the agents before executing a plan are required to negotiate about it, to discuss and to reach some agreement. From the PR point of view, on the one hand, one should be able to recognize also the conversation/negotiation as a MAP; on the other hand one should not mix up the two levels of PR. Of course, we can deal with the negotiation level only if in the plan libraries of the system that plan or protocol already exists.

Multi-CHAPLIN allows the representation not only of practical plans but also of communication and interaction protocols. Notice that these are in fact intrinsically multi-agent plans [Falcone and Castelfranchi, 1994].

d) Virtual Actions

The introduction of a special kind of actions, the communicative actions (such as "to ask for doing", "to accept doing .. if ..", "to report doing..", "to refuse doing ..", "to prohibit to do .." and so on), implies that the actions must accept as parameters the labels or the descriptions of other actions of the same plan (*Virtual Actions*).

We claim that there is no effective MAP representation (and generation or recognition), without the ability of representing such a link between the mention of an action and occurrence of the action itself. For example, if an agent A says to B "give me the bistury", and B gives A a bistury, you did not really recognize this plan if you didn't understand that B's action is the same action mentioned by A.

Analogously, you cannot generate a MAP by a SAP transformation, inserting in it a communicative action like "give me the bistury", without accounting for the relation between this communicative action and the practical action ("giving the bistury") of the same plan.

e) Point of Views in MAPs

The other challenge that MA case put to the PR is about the different or equal plan representation by the cooperative agents. Should we assume that the agents share believes about the plan they are involved in? In other words, if MAP recognition is not only the recognition of sequence of actions but is the recognition of the intention and believes of the agents, should we attribute to them the same mental representation? In our system we use this simplified assumption but clearly more advanced MAP recognition systems should attribute to the agents different perspectives on the plan: not only they could have different representations of the plan but they may not have identical motivations and intentions in participating in that collaborative plan [Kraus, 1994].

4 CHAPLIN and its MAP extension

In CHAPLIN, considering a single protagonist (X) and several other parameters $(y_1...y_L)$ of the plan's actions (SAP case) we will have:

$$P(X;\sigma_0) \rightarrow A_1(X;\sigma_1)...A_N(X;\sigma_N)$$
[3]

where: $\sigma_i \subseteq \{y_1...y_L\}$ with $0 \leq i \leq N$; $(y_1...y_L)$ are never actions.

In the case of a MAP, having several protagonists $(X_1,...,X_M)$, we will be able to write:

$$P(X_1,...,X_M;\sigma_0) --> A_1(\xi_1;\sigma_1)...A_N(\xi_N;\sigma_N) \qquad [4]$$

where: $\xi_j \subseteq \{X_1,...,X_M\}$ with $1 \leq j \leq N$ and $\sigma_i \subseteq \{y_1...y_L\}$ with $0 \leq i \leq N$, and with $\cup \xi_j = \{X_1,...,X_M\}$.

MultiCHAPLIN can deal with the Iterative Decomposition phenomenon.

In [4] we can assume that each component action can be rewritten as follows:

$$A_j(\xi_j;...) --> A_j(\xi_j^1;...) \;\; .... \;\; A_j(\xi_j^q;...) \text{ with } 1 \leq j \leq N;$$

where q is indeterminate, $\xi_j^i \subseteq \xi_j$ with $1 \leq i \leq q$ and $\cup \xi_j^i = \xi_j$ with $1 \leq j \leq N$.

The Iterative Decomposition can be allowed in our system if we introduce a change in the bottom-up invocation rules of the chart edges [Castelfranchi and Falcone, 1994].

Considering Fig. 4 we can see how two identical actions with different protagonists (*Make-Marinara(Mario), Make-Marinara(Pino)*), can be associated with one single edge (*Make-Marinara(Mario,Pino)*).

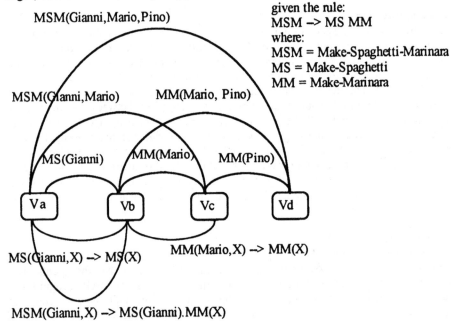

given the rule:
MSM -> MS MM
where:
MSM = Make-Spaghetti-Marinara
MS = Make-Spaghetti
MM = Make-Marinara

Fig. 4

For treating simple or complex actions as arguments of higher level actions (Virtual Actions), we can write:

$$P(X_1,...,X_M;\sigma_0;A_{vir}) --> A_1(\xi_1;\sigma_1)...A_N(\xi_N;\sigma_N) \; EXEC(A_{vir})$$

where: A_{vir} is contained in at least one of σ_i with $1 \leq i \leq N$ and it can represent either a simple or a complex, either a practical or linguistic action and where EXEC expresses the fact that an action forming the plan is the agent counterpart of A_{vir} itself in the plan.

In Fig. 5 you can see Multi-CHAPLIN coping with the Virtual Action problem.

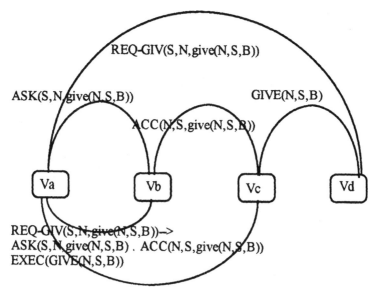

REQ-GIV(S,N,give(N,S,B))-->ASK(S,N,give(N,S,B))
ACC(N,S,give(N,S,B)) . EXEC(GIVE(N,S,B))

given the rule:
REQ-GIV(S,N,give(N,S,B))-->ASK(S,N,give(N,S,B))
ACC(N,S,give(N,S,B)) EXEC(GIVE(N,S,B))
where:
REQ-GIV = Request-Give Plan,   ACC = Accept,   S= Surgeon,
N = Nurse, B = Bistury

Fig. 5

In the field of recognition there is a very remarkable and complex problem: the one of the recognition of the plan on a "virtual" layer. In fact a proper comprehension of a multiagent interaction requires that the system recognizes when the agents argument or negotiate about a series of actions which are parts of a single plan. By "Virtual Plan" we mean a set of virtual actions (within the same discourse) corresponding to the actions forming a plan. For instance, starting from the plan analyzed by [Kautz, 1987]: if A says to B "make pesto and make spaghetti and boil " or if A says to B "make pesto" then he says to him "make-spaghetti" and then he says to him "boil", therefore the system should be able to recognize that A asked B the plan "make-spaghetti-pesto" and its abstraction "make-pasta-dish". This according to the fact that the three actions *Make-pesto*, *Boil* and *Make-spaghetti* are the parts forming the plan *Make-spaghetti-pesto* (part-of) that, in its turn, is an instance of the plan *Make-pasta-dish* (abstraction). In other words, this means that the system must use its plan library by applying it to the virtual actions to recognize merely virtual plans, that is to say plans we talk about. And then it must use the same memorized plan to recognize from the exec actions the same actually executed plan. Let us also assume that without the recognition of virtual plans it would not be possible to compare them with the actually recognized executive plans.

In the first approximation some constraints that control this recognition process of virtual plans in the communication acts can be introduced. A constraint posed by the Chart-based Plan Recognition is that the order in which the virtual actions are mentioned in these communication acts must correspond to the order in which the actions appear in the rewriting rules of plan in the grammar. A second simplifying constraint is that the virtual actions forming a virtual plan be argument of a same meta-action.

We postulate that:

a) if x executes a meta-action on single actions forming a plan, he executes that meta-action on the plan itself; vice versa b) if x executes a meta-action on a complex action it is just like as if he executed the same meta-action on each component action (if exist only one decomposition of that plan). That is to say Ask(A B Make-spaghetti-pesto) corresponds to Ask(A B Make-pesto) and Ask(A B Make-spaghetti) and Ask(A B Boil), and vice versa. Not only we would be able to recognize virtual plans formed by virtual actions being arguments of meta-actions, but we must recognize the same plan if it is argument of different meta-actions (this allows, for example, to reach the agreement in the negotiation between the customer and the performer). Consider this case:

Request[A, B, make-spaghetti-pesto] Commit[B, A, {make-pesto make-spaghetti boil}].

As one can see, the introduction of the notion of virtual actions and virtual plans creates a double level of PR and of matching. On the one hand, the recognition of virtual plans and their match in which other, which implies also the recognition of conversational plans. On the other hand the recognition of the executive plans and their match with the virtual ones.

It is possible to illustrate different matching situations between virtual plans and virtual plans, and between virtual and executed plans.

As for the problem of multiple points of view currently MultiCHAPLIN is not very interesting. However treating plans as complex structure of actions, interestingly enough MultiCHAPLIN is able to recognize not only plans in strict sense but also (and in the same way) MA scripts, routines, interaction protocols, etc. We claim that this is not only quite useful in applying PR to cooperative work, in which procedures, routines and protocols are quite diffused, but also quite relevant from a theoretical point of view. We mean that the basic properties of recognition should apply in general to collective activity indipendently of their nature of true plans or of mere protocols or routines.

5 Conclusions

The capability to recognize plans performed by more than one agent seems to be quite relevant for supporting coordination, negotiation, etc. in distributed and multi-agent systems.

MAP recognition is not a trivial extension for current PR systems. It involves significant technical and theoretical problems. In particular, this is true:

- if one assumes (as we have done) the aim of exploiting *a common plan library* to adapt to the SA and MA cases;

- if one assumes the conception of *plan as a structure of believes and goals*.
A chart-based PR system (CHAPLIN) has been illustrated, and it has been shown
how his MA extension (Multi-CHAPLIN) can cope with some of those difficulties:
iterative decomposition, virtual action, virtual plans.
By the way, even starting from an existing system and from the recognition task our
main aim has been to throw light on some general problems in the SAP/MAP
transformation, such as the *Insertion Problem*, and the problem of *knowledge,
resource and product Transfer* from one agent to the other.

References

[Bond and Gasser, 1988] Bond, A. H., Gasser, L. G., (eds), *Readings in Distribuited Artificial Intelligence*. San Mateo, CA: Morgan Kaufmann, 1988.
[Castelfranchi and Falcone, 1994] Castelfranchi, C., Falcone, R., Towards a theory of single-agent into multi-agent plan transformation. *The 3rd Pacific Rim International Conference on AI*, Beijing, China, 16-18 agosto 1994.
[Durfee *et al.*, 1992] Durfee, E., Lesser, V., Corkill, D., Distributed Problem Solving in Shapiro, S.,C., *Encyclopedia of Artificial Intelligence - Second Edition*, John Wiley & Sons, Inc., 1992.
[Falcone and Castelfranchi, 1993a] Falcone, R., Castelfranchi, C., CHAPLIN: A Chart based Plan Recognizer, Proceedings of the *Thirteenth International Conference of Avignon*, Avignon, France, 24-28 May, 1993.
[Falcone and Castelfranchi, 1993b] Falcone, R., Castelfranchi, C., Plan recognition for Explanation: a Chart-based system, Proceedings of the *8th Int.Conf. of Applications of AI in Engineering* (AIENG-93), Tolose, France, June, 1993.
[Falcone and Castelfranchi, 1994] Falcone, R., Castelfranchi, C. (1994), Multi-CHAPLIN: A Multi-Agent Plan Recognizer. Technical Report, Finalized Project "Information Systems and Parallel Computation", CNR, Italy.
[Grosz and Sidner, 1990] Grosz, B., Sidner, C. Plans for Discourse, P.R., Morgan, J. and Pollack, M.E. (eds), *Intentions in Communication*, MIT press, USA, pp 417-444, 1990.
[Kautz, 1987] Kautz, H. A. (1987). A Formal Theory of Plan recognition. *PhD thesis*, University of Rochester, 87. Also TR215, University of Rochester, dept. of Computer Science, Rochester, N.Y.
[Kolodner, 1983] Kolodner, J., Reconstructive Memory: A Computer Model, *Cognitive Science*, 7, 281-328, 1983
[Kraus, 1994] Sarit Kraus, Interaction and Collaboration in Multi-agent Systems, *11th European Conference on Artificial Intelligence* (ECAI-94), Amsterdam, NL, 1994.
[Olson *et al.*, 1993] Olson, J., Card, S., Landauer, T., Olson, G., Malone, T., Leggett, J., *CSCW: reserch issues for the 90s. Behaviour & Information Technology*, vol12, n.2, pp 115-129, 1993.
[Retz-Schmidt, 1991] Retz-Schmidt G., Recognizing Intentions, Interactions, and Causes of Plan Failures, *User Modeling and User-Adapted Interaction* 1: 173-202, 1991.
[Stanfill and Waltz, 1986] Stanfill, C., Waltz, D., Toward Memory-Based Reasoning, *Communication ACM*, 29(12), 1213-1228, 1986.
[Stock *et al.*, 1989] Stock, O., Falcone, R., Insinnamo, P.. Bidirectional charts: A potential technique for parsing spoken natural language sentences. *Computer Speech and Language*, 3(3): 219-237, 1989.

[Vilain, 1990] Vilain, M., Getting Serious about Parsing Plans: A Grammatical Analysis of Plan recognition. In *Proc. of the IJCAI*, 190-197, Boston, 1990.

[Sycara, 1987] Sycara E., Resolving Adversial Conflicts: An Approach to Integrating Case-based and Analytic Methods, Ph.D. dissertation, *Technical Report* No. GIT-ICS-87/26, Sch. of Inf. and Com. Sc., Georgia Institute of Technology, Atlanta, Ga.; 1987.

Distributed Negotiation-Based Task Planning for a Flexible Manufacturing Environment

Stefan Hahndel[1] and Florian Fuchs[1] and Paul Levi[2]

[1] Department of computer science, Munich University of Technology, Orleansstr. 34, 81667 München, Germany
[2] Institute for Parallel and Distributed High-Performance Computers, University of Stuttgart, Breitwiesenstr. 20-22, 70565 Stuttgart, Germany

Abstract. In a flexible manufacturing environment a group of autonomous agents such as autonomous mobile robots and intelligent manufacturing units is supposed to cooperate and avoid bad interaction. Thus they must have the capability to build a common multi-agent plan through detailed adequate agreements and take into consideration the group goals as well as those of the individual agents.
We present an approach of a distributed planning method to solve dynamically some typical tasks of a production planning system at control level without using a fixed central component. To archieve this, a flexible manufacturing system has been modelled as a multi-agent system, while the planning method we present uses the structure of manufacturing plans to coordinate properly their activities through negotiation among the agents. The distributed planning method which was developed has been implemented and tested on a pool of workstations.

1 Introduction

Usually manufacturing planning is done by a central production planning system (PPS) [15, 12, 7]. A typical production planning system in a flexible manufacturing environment manages a large set of manufacturing plans in a representation which is independent of the exact structure of the manufacturing environment. These plans do not contain information about which individual machine to use, when several machines with overlapping capabilities are available. Also the operations for loading and unloading the machines and transport actions are missing in these plans. In general, engineers use so-called "net plans" for this purpose.

When the manufacturing system receives an order to produce n parts of an individual product P until a given time t, the production planning system passes the manufacturing plan over to a central manufacturing control system. This system expands the plan with the manipulation and transportation actions needed and generates a schedule of these activities, based on its current knowledge of the state of the manufacturing environment.

Such a system also controls the environment and gives the sub-orders to the individual agents just at the right time. Because of the high complexity of present-day manufacturing systems a central planning system is unable to react adequately on unavoidable production failures (e.g. broken tools, machine failures etc.). This strongly centralized and hierarchical built system represents a bottleneck, which makes it difficult to react with the desired flexibility to several differing failures at the same time under real-time conditions.

Most planning subproblems, e.g. job shop scheduling, are NP complete. For this reason most of the time it is not possible to build an optimal plan under real-time conditions. Therefore, most central systems use good heuristics to build suboptimal solutions. But from the DAI's (Distributed Artificial Intelligence) point of view that is also possible in a decentralized manner with the additional advantage of greater performance.

Over the last few years the interest in decentralized control and process planning has increased in this area as well as in many other domains of computer science. Examples for the usage of DAI for manufacturing planning and control systems are the system YAMS from Parunak [9], the works of Ayel [1], the system of Raulefs [11] and the works of Dilger [2]. Another important domain that is related to our work is the domain of dynamic and distributed scheduling, e.g. [3], [10], [14].

Some of the main problems of building such systems concern the distribution of the actions to the agents, the cooperation of these agents, the planning of the synchronization of actions, the building of proper agent groups and decentralized methods for conflict resolution. These problems are mostly derived from the local point of view of the agents.

We present an approach where no fixed component of central decision or a fixed hierarchical structure is needed. Further, planning and execution of actions is performed in a (temporal) overlapping manner. When we speak about planning in this context, we regard both (action) planning (generating local action plans) and scheduling of all actions.

The distributed planning method described in this article has been implemented and tested on a pool of workstations.

2 The Model

First, we describe a proper model for our production planning system. The model consists of an agent model and a model for manufacturing and action plans.

Each autonomous component of the flexible manufacturing environment (i.e. manufacturing cells, autonomous mobile robots) is modelled as an agent of our multi-agent system. Figure 1 shows the architecture of such an agent.

The multi-agent system consists of a set of autonomous agents. Each of these agents has a set of capabilities, its own knowledge base and a combined local planning and communication module for proper coordination and negotiation with other agents.

Knowledge base The knowledge base can be divided in a static and a dynamic part. The static part contains knowledge about the capabilities of its own and the capabilities of other agents, how to perform an action, and knowledge about negotiation and local planning. The dynamic part contains different types of

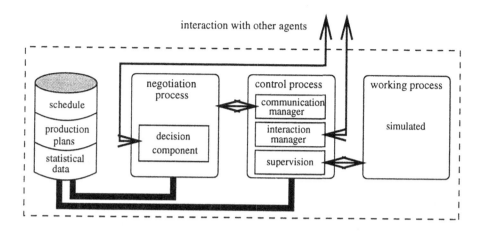

Fig. 1. agent architecture (simplified)

plans, that means the manufacturing plans and local action plans in which the agent is involved and a schedule of its own actions. Additionally, it contains statistical data about the reliability of the other agents and about the duration of past actions.

Planning and Communication Module The local planning and communication module has the following tasks:

- Expanding manufacturing actions to a local action plan which contains all additionally needed auxiliary actions (i.e. add actions for loading/unloading or transportation tasks, depending on the actual state)
- Distribution of all auxiliary actions which the agent cannot perform by itself to other agents through proper negotiation.
  - This includes formulating requests for offers, evaluating all offers received and selecting the best, in case an agent requests actions from other agents.
  - If the agent is the offender, it tests if and when it can perform the requested action, in order to generate a proper offer.
- Another task of the planning module is the local optimization of the agent's schedule.

Plan Structures A manufacturing plan $\mathcal{P}$ is a kind of skeleton plan which contains only manufacturing steps on the highest abstraction level together with the causal dependencies without the auxiliary actions needed. Formally, such a manufacturing plan can be seen as a semi-ordered set of actions $(A_\mathcal{P}, <_\mathcal{P})$. We restrict our manufacturing plans to only one starting action $a_\mathcal{P}^{\text{start}} \in A_\mathcal{P}$ and one ending action $a_\mathcal{P}^{\text{end}} \in A_\mathcal{P}$, that means, $\exists a_\mathcal{P}^{\text{start}} \in A_\mathcal{P} : \forall a_\mathcal{P} \in A_\mathcal{P} \setminus a_\mathcal{P}^{\text{start}} : a_\mathcal{P}^{\text{start}} <_\mathcal{P} a_\mathcal{P}$

and $\exists a_{\mathcal{P}}^{\text{end}} \in A_{\mathcal{P}} : \forall a_{\mathcal{P}} \in A_{\mathcal{P}} \setminus a_{\mathcal{P}}^{\text{end}} : a_{\mathcal{P}} <_{\mathcal{P}} a_{\mathcal{P}}^{\text{end}}$. To have only one starting action is not a real restriction, because a manufacturing plan can always be enriched by a dummy action performed by any agent.

A local (action) plan $\mathcal{A}$ consists of a set of auxiliary actions, supporting an higher level action $a_{\mathcal{P}} \in A_{\mathcal{P}}$. Additionally, the local plan contains this high level action $a_{\mathcal{P}}$ as final step. Again, we have a semi-ordered set $(A_{\mathcal{A}} \cup \{a_{\mathcal{P}}\}, <_{\mathcal{A}})$, together with the condition $\forall a \in A_{\mathcal{A}} : a <_{\mathcal{A}} a_{\mathcal{P}}$.

Of course, these structures can be expanded to more than two hierarchical levels, where the action plan of one level builds the manufacturing plan of the next deeper level.

3   A decentralized distributed planning method

This section describes an entirely distributed planning method which is simple to realize and which can be used in manufacturing systems and domains with similar structures.

If there is an order to produce a number n of a product P, the production planning system tests, whether it is possible to manufacture this product. First, the system verifies the existence of a proper manufacturing plan for it. Then it checks every action in this plan to find an agent able to perform that action.

If this (pre-)evaluation proves positive, the order for planning and execution is released. In a first step the PPS agent looks for an agent able to perform the first action of the manufacturing plan. That can be done by a protocol similar to the Contract Net Protocol [13]. The PPS agent then inserts the agent identification into the structure of the manufacturing plan and sends a copy to this agent, thus giving it the planning and execution control for the first action of the manufacturing plan. The agent takes over the responsibility for performing the action and for finding other agents for the successor actions through negotiation. We call such an agent a planning agent, by which we mean the temporary role of an agent and not a certain agent whose task is to make plans for one or more further agents !

The planning agent has to do several tasks:

- It looks for an agent for every action currently to be performed, through a proper negotiation (similar to the Contract Net Protocol).
- After doing these tasks, it inserts the instantiations and local decisions in the data structure representing the manufacturing plan. Then it passes on the plan control to the next agent or agents by sending the modified plan (without local expansions). If there is more than one successor action which can be done in parallel, it must determine a *"synchronization agent"*. We will explain this necessity in more detail in the next section. This synchronization agent is also inserted in the current plan structure.

3.1 The Planning Wave

To get good planning results, it is not enough just to react on situations, because resource conflicts would be unavoidable. For this purpose we do some lookahead in the distributed planning denoted as *planning wave*.

Lookahead The main idea of the planning wave is to pass on the manufacturing plan from agent to agent, until the given lookahead value is attained. The planning wave organizes itself using the structure of the manufacturing plan. An agent which receives a manufacturing plan, and thus the planning control, starts negotiations to engage agents for the successor actions, if the lookahead is not reached yet. Then it passes on the manufacturing plan to them.

Expansion lookahead The local plan expansion also is orientated on the planning wave. For that, we have a second lookahead value denoted as "expansion lookahead", which is less than or equal to the lookahead value. A manufacturing action is not expanded until the given value of the expansion lookahead is attained. This ensures that a fine graded planning of the next hierarchical level is not done as long as the planning state is still very uncertain.

3.2 Dependence on Plan Structures

Since our distributed planning technique is founded on the basic manufacturing plan structure, there must also be a proper treatment of the different types of plan sections.

Sequential Section Because there is only one successor, no special discussion is necessary.

Backward branching parts of manufacturing plans The difficulty in our kind of manufacturing planning arises from the fact that typical manufacturing plans are not only sequential but also have branches. If parts of a manufacturing plan are joined in one action, e.g. assembling, they must be synchronized to ensure that the predecessor agents of such a synchronization action agree on a common successor agent. This task is performed by a single *synchronization agent*, which must be determined at an early enough stage on one of the corresponding forward branches of the plan.

Forward branching parts of manufacturing plans In the last section we showed the necessity for determining a synchronization agent early enough and entering this decision in the manufacturing plan at the right time. Each time an agent receives planning control over a forward branching action, it calculates the set of all corresponding synchronization actions A_S. Then, it checks for each synchronization action $a_S \in A_S$, whether it has already been marked by a synchronization agent and marks it with its own identification, when necessary.

184

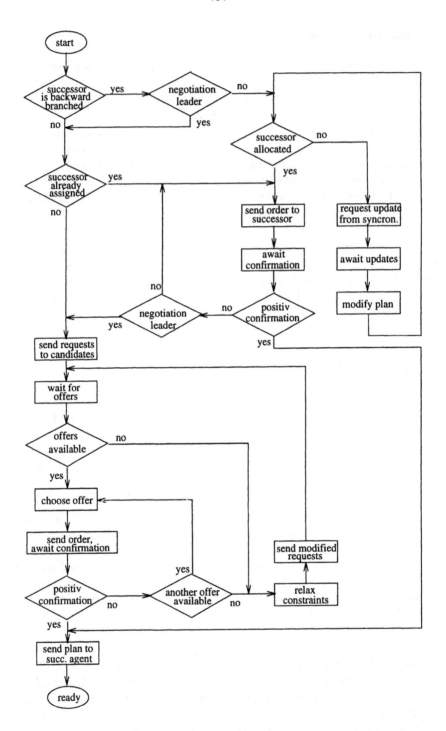

Fig. 2. negotiation process (simplified)

185

3.3 Negotiation Scheme

As stated earlier, the successor actions within a planning wave are distributed to other agents through negotiation. In a planning wave two phases should be distinguished (see figure 3).

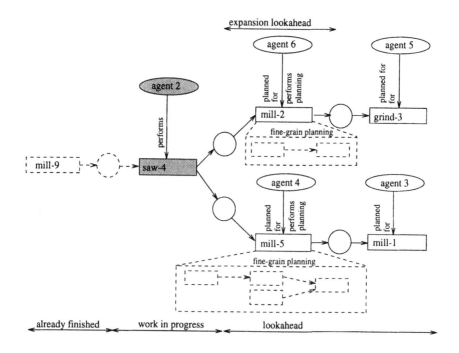

Fig. 3. Simple example for a planning wave with lookahead 2

The complete negotiation, including requests and offers, is only needed at the head of a planning wave. In the areas of the planning wave where the actions have been already assigned to agents, the decisions made earlier have only to be verified and the schedules adapted. Moreover, there is no necessity to send the complete manufacturing plans to the successor agents in this part of the planning wave. These requirements are respected by our negotiation scheme sketched in figure 2.

The planning and communication module generates its own negotiation process for each action which the agent cannot perform by itself. Thus, each agent can contribute to several negotiations at the same time.

3.4 Scheduling

Each agent has its own schedule containing all actions it must perform itself. The planned time intervals are not fixed and can be rearranged dynamically. An action a_{n+1} with starting time s_{n+1} and ending time e_{n+1} can only be inserted into the time plan when the following constraint holds:

$$\underset{t_1 > t_0}{\forall} \int_{t_0}^{t_1} \sum_{i=0}^{n+1} I_i(t)dt < t_1,$$

where

$$I_i(t) := \begin{cases} 1 \text{ if } s_i \leq t \leq e_i \\ 0 \text{ else} \end{cases}$$

and t_0 is the point of time, when the interval is to be inserted into the schedule.

Respecting the above constraint allows us to insert time intervalls in an overlapping way. At first sight this seems to produce conflicts, but in the early stages of the planning most actions are likely to be displaced several times anyway. Experiments have proved this overlapping method to be a good way of handling flexible time intervals. Of course overlapping is eliminated step by step by succeeding planning waves. This can be seen as a distributed iterative process which increases the certainty of the planning state with every planning wave.

4   Implementation

It is very difficult to verify such a complex distributed planning system by formal methods. Verification with reasonable expense is possible only by implementing this method and testing it by appropriate realistic experiments.

For this reason, we implemented a multi-agent system which runs on a pool of workstations connected by Ethernet. Each agent consists of several processes. One process (the central process of an agent) manages the local plans of the agent and decides when and how an action should be planned and for which actions other agents are needed. Another important task of this process is to start child processes to carry out negotiation with other agents. Because a new negotiating process is started for each action to be delegated, an agent can have several negotiating processes running at the same time. A second type of process started by an agent is the executing process, which handles the execution and monitoring of actions already planned. In our implementation, execution of planned actions is only simulated by the executing process. That means, if an action is started, this process determines randomly the result and the duration of the action. It is thus possible to test how the planning system works in uncertain and disturbed environments. The average duration of actions in this simulation is several seconds.

This time limit is acceptable when deciding the suitability of such a planning method for real-world applications. The typical duration times in real-world factory environments lies between several minutes and several hours.

187

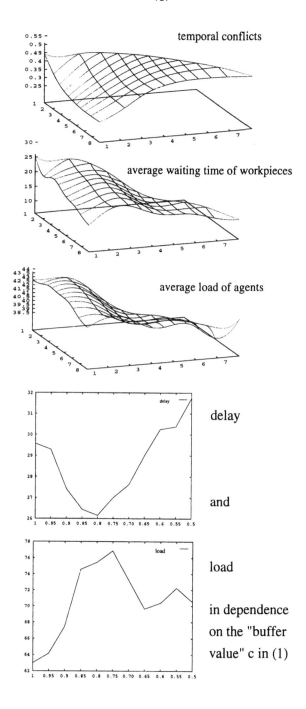

Fig. 4. Some Results

The test implementation for the processes and its communication is done by using the public domain tool PVM 3.2 (Parallel Virtual Machine). Currently we are running that multi-agent system in a net consisting of 80 HP9000/720 workstations. When the computers have no other load, it is possible to run up to 10 agents on each workstation. For our experiments we choose a set of typical manufacturing plans generated randomly by a grammar describing the main structure of these plans. The grammer consists of about two kinds of rules only. One describes forward branches and the other backward branches of production plans. A sequential part can be expressed by a forward branch of degree one. The basic plan structure is given by the derivation graph.

In a similar way we generate capabilities and orders for our multi-agent system. We use fixed starting states for our experiments in order to ensure that we can rerun each experiment several times under similar conditions. For the same reason, we can exclude any randomly generated results when simulating the executing process. Because the system is strongly non-deterministic, it is necessary to obtain average values. Figure 4 shows typical results from these experiments. The original (discrete) measurements were post-processed with bsplines in order to archieve better visualization of the tendencies. The conflicts shown in this figure are a measure for the overlapping of the requested and the finally offered time intervals.

In order to get satisfactory planning results, it is important to choose appropriate values for both the lookahead and the expansion lookahead. For most manufacturing environments the system shows the following behavior: if simple reactive planning is done with lookahead 1, good values for machine load are obtained, but the time a single product remains within the manufacturing process turns out to be very high. The obvious reason is that the planning process is not able to keep the manufacturing steps of a given product together within a certain time interval, because in a planning wave only one step at a time, and not an amount of several steps, is planned. While the lookahead value increases and the load becomes slightly lower, the manufacturing time for a product decreases due to the antagonism of the two values. Increasing the lookahead further leads to a point where the meassured values get worse because the overhead for the planning becomes too big. Another reason is the growing discrepancy between the planned and the real-world state. Unfortunately, the optimal values for lookahead and expansion lookahead are not the same for all manufacturing environments.

5 Conclusion

We have presented a new distributed planning approach that needs no fixed central component, which often builds a bottleneck in other systems. The multi-agent system can easily be extended with further agents without changing the existing structure. Planning and execution of actions is performed in an overlapping manner. This allows dynamic reaction to changes in the system in case conflicts or failures arise. With this planning approach it is possible to distribute the enormous complexity of manufacturing planning and scheduling on control level to an arbitrary number of agents.

In future work, we will carry out more experiments with different parameters for further optimization of the evaluation functions.

Remark This work was supported by the German research community within the project SFB 331, subproject Q4 ("Distributed cooperative planning between autonomous robots and vehicles on a tactical level")

References

1. Jacqueline Ayel. Decision coordination in production management. In *Proc. of the 5 th MAAMAW*, Pre-Proceedings of the 4th European Workshop "Modeling Autonomous Agents in a Multi-Agent World, 1992.
2. Werner Dilger and Stephan Kassel. Sich selbst organisierende Produktionsprozesse als Möglichkeit zur flexiblen Fertigungssteuerung. In Jürgen Müller, editor, *Verteilte KI*. BI Verlag, 1993.
3. K. Hadavi, W.-L. Hsu, T. Chen, and C.-N. Lee. An architecture for real time distributed scheduling. In A. F. Famili, D. S. Nau, and S. H. Kim, editors, *Artificial Intelligence Applications in Manufacturing*, pages 215–234. AAAI Press, Menlo Park, CA, 1992.
4. S. Hahndel, P. Levi, H. Schweiger, H.-J. Siegert, and M. Wirth. Eine verteilte Wissensbasis zur dynamischen Teambildung in Fertigungsumgebungen. In *9. Proc of the Fachgespräche Autonome Mobile Systeme*, pages 53–66, München, 1993.
5. Stefan Hahndel and Paul Levi. A distributed task planning method for autonomous agents in a fms. In *Proc. of Intelligent Robots and Systems (IROS) '94*, volume 2, pages 1285–1292, München, September 1994.
6. Stefan Hahndel and Paul Levi. Optimizing distributed production planning. In *Proc. of 2 nd International Conference on Intelligent Systems Engineering '94*, pages 419–424, Hamburg, september 1994.
7. C. A. R. Hoare. *CSP – Communicating Sequential Processes*. International Series in Computer Science. Prentice-Hall, Englewood Cliffs, Nj, 1985.
8. Paul Levi and Stefan Hahndel. Kooperative Systeme in der Fertigung. In Jürgen Müller, editor, *Verteilte KI*, pages 322–346. BI Verlag, 1993.
9. H. Van Dyke Parunak. Distributed ai and manufacturing control: Some issues and insights. In *Proc. of the 1 th MAAMAW*, pages 81–101, Cambridge, England, 1989.
10. P. Prosser. A reactive scheduling agent. In *Proc. of the 11 th IJCAI*, pages 1004–1009, Detroit, MI, 1989.
11. Peter Raulefs. Cooperating agent architecture to manage manufacturing processes. In W. Brauer and D. Hernández, editors, *4. Internationaler GI-Kongreß*, pages 6–17, München, 1991.
12. August-Wilhelm Scheer, editor. *Fertigungssteuerung – Expertenwissen für die Praxis*. Oldenbourg Verlag, München, 1991.
13. R. G. Smith. The contract net protocol: High-level communication and control in a distributed problem solver. In A. H. Bond and L. Gasser, editors, *Readings in Distributed Artificial Intelligence*, pages 357–366. Kaufmann, San Mateo, CA, 1988.

14. K. Sycara, S. Roth, N. Sadeh, and M. Fox. An investigation into distributed constraint-directed factory scheduling. In *Proc. of the Sixth Conference on Artificial Intelligence Applications CAIA-90 (Volume I: Papers)*, pages 94–100, Santa Barbara, CA, 1990.
15. Thomas E. Vollmann, William L. Berry, and D. Clay Whyback. *Manufacturing Planning and Control Systems*. IRWIN, Homewood, Boston, third edition, 1992.

A Multi-Agent Approach to
Dynamic, Adaptive Scheduling of Material Flow

Stefan Bussmann

Daimler-Benz AG, Research and Technology
Alt-Moabit 96a, D-10559 Berlin
email: bussmann@DBresearch-berlin.de

Abstract. Advanced manufacturing control still remains an important topic in current research. Especially aspects of dynamics and failures in the production process are insufficiently taken into account by systems in use. This paper presents a multi-agent approach to scheduling material flow that shows dynamic and adaptive behaviour. Even though machine scheduling has found a thorough treatment in AI literature, there are only few investigations on the material flow problem. In this paper, it is argued that a decentralized architecture with centralized control fits well with the local and global aspects of the scheduling problem. The top-level algorithms of the scheduling process are outlined and further improvements required are sketched out.

1 Introduction

Advanced manufacturing control has long been an important topic in Artificial Intelligence research and has recently also attracted interest of researchers in the field of Multi-Agent Systems because practical experience with existing approaches remains unsatisfactory. Classical scheduling methods typically aim at optimising the solution with respect to a global goal function while assuming a static environment, i.e., all necessary information is known beforehand. Real manufacturing control, however, is much more dynamic due to the continual arrival of orders and various perturbations of the manufacturing process, such as breakdowns. The dynamic character of most manufacturing problems renders the long-term optimisation of schedules pointless and demands a more adaptive scheduling strategy.

This paper presents a dynamic and adaptive approach to material flow scheduling that is based on multi-agent techniques. The material flow problem has been scarcely treated in the multi-agent literature. Known to us is only the work in [PLJ+86] that implements a Kanban-like strategy. Concerning dynamic scheduling, some work (e.g. [BO92], [OSH88], or [DK93]) has been done to tackle machine scheduling using the contract net protocol [Smi80]. The basic idea is to use bargaining between autonomous agents in order to find an optimal order assignment, much in the spirit of supply and demand in economics. In all cases the principle is as follows: a broker announces an order to be scheduled; the transporting units make bids; and the broker awards the order to the best bidder. However, for global problems such as scheduling in the manufacturing domain (which, in general, is NP-hard) the idea of bargaining is inappropriate. To arrive at an optimal solution to the overall (global) assignment process, it may be necessary to assign orders to a transporter even though the assignment is locally suboptimal. Therefore, the process of bidding, which is basically a local decision making, cannot guarantee a globally optimal solution (cf. [DS88]). As we will argue in later sections, it is necessary to introduce more centralized control.

Our design of the scheduling process is along the principle of "as decentralized as possible, as centralized as necessary". During the discussion of the material flow problem, we will outline which decisions can be made locally and which must be taken with a global perspective. Following these considerations, we will present an architecture that distributes all local computations to the transport units and leaves the responsibility for the global aspects to a coordinator. Additionally, we will analyse how the multi-agent techniques contributed to our solution of the material flow problem.

The remainder of the paper is organised as follows: the next section defines the scenario and the problem to be solved; section 3 highlights important aspects of the problem; section 4 describes the overall architecture and the main algorithm for the scheduling process; section 5 gives some more details on the implementation; and the last section evaluates the multi-agent approach to the material flow problem and outlines aspects that should be improved upon in future work.

2 Problem Definition

This section presents a *model of material flow* in a factory and defines the *transportation problem* to be solved.

Basically, the factory consists of a set of machines and a set of transporters. Machine orders specify *which machine* has to produce *which product* out of *which material* in *which time interval*. Implicitly, these orders define a material flow by listing produced material as consumed material in a later order. For transportation, the factory is equipped with transport units, such as forklifts or conveyer belts. The basic task of the material flow system is to compute a schedule for the transport units such that every piece of material reaches its next destination in time.

In the context of this paper, we assume machine orders to be created externally. They are inserted *dynamically* into the scenario while previous machine orders are in execution. Furthermore, the execution of the schedule suffers from *perturbations*. On one hand, orders may change with respect to their specification after being introduced to the system (for instance, production steps are delayed or become more urgent); on the other hand, failures, such as sudden breakdowns of transporters, may occur. Due to these imposed characteristics of the manufacturing environment, the material flow problem is *dynamic* and *perturbed.*

2.1 The Model of Material Flow

We will now describe the model of material flow. It consists of a set **S** of storage spaces $S_1, .., S_m$, a set M of machines $M_1, .., M_n$, a set T of transporters $T_1, .., T_q$, a set N of material, an environment E, and a time model $\mathcal{T}$. We assume the environment to contain a (planar) graph in which machines and storage spaces are placed at the vertices, whereas transporters can freely move along the arcs of the graph. Figure 1 gives an example of such a graph for a small factory.

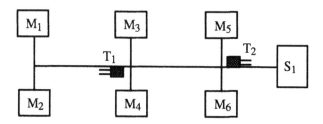

Fig. 1. Factory Example

Raw material flows through the production process and is transformed into intermediate or final products. For reasons of simplicity, we will refer to raw material, intermediate and final products simply as *material*. An instance of the set N of materials is of the form *(id, volume)* where id is the identification number of the specific material and volume is a positive, non-zero real number. Material can either be stored in a storage space, at a machine site, or on a transporter, all having limited storage capacity. This is expressed by the following functions ($\mathcal{P}(N)$ denotes the power set of N):

> capacity: $S \cup M \cup T \rightarrow \mathbb{R}_+$
> content: $(S \cup M \cup T) \times \mathcal{T} \rightarrow \mathcal{P}(N)$

The content of a storage space, of a machine storage space, or of the loading space of a transporter may never exceed the storage capacity, i.e. the following global constraint must hold:

$$\forall t \in \mathcal{T}, M_i \in (S \cup M \cup T): \Sigma_{\forall n \in \text{ content }(M_i,t)} \text{volume}(n) \leq \text{capacity}(M_i) \quad (2.1)$$

Any storage attempts that would exceed the storage capacity are declined.

Machine Orders and Their Generation

A *machine order* specifies that a machine M_i or a stock room S_i is supposed to produce the material $n_p \in N$ out of the material $n_c \subset N$ beginning from the starting time t_s up to the finish time t_f ($t_s < t_f$). In the case of a storage space, it either consumes or produces material in order to model the material import and export of the factory.

A machine order *is executed* iff $n_c \subset \text{content}(M_i, t_s)$. Then it is true that $n_p \in \text{content}(M_i, t_f)$. This definition implies that all consumed material must reach the machine in time, otherwise the order cannot be executed and the product will not be produced.

Machine orders are entered dynamically into the scenario, i.e. there exists a sequence $(t_i)_{i \in N}$ in $\mathcal{T}$, such that at time t_i a set MO_i of machine orders is generated. The generation is random from the point of view of the model (it may be deterministic for an outsider). It may also alter already announced orders by introducing new versions of previously generated orders (which models changes in the specification of orders). A set MO_i obeys a global consistency constraint which states that every product is consumed by a machine order scheduled later on:

$$\forall\, i \in N, o_2 \in MO_i: n_c \in \text{consumed}(o_2) \Rightarrow \exists\, o_1 \in MO_i: n_c = \text{product}(o_1)$$
$$\wedge\ \text{finish-time}(o_1) < \text{start-time}(o_2)$$

This constraint enables us to derive a set of *transport orders* for every material that is consumed, i.e. an order to transport *material n_c* from the site of *machine(o_1)* to the site of *machine(o_2)* between *finish-time(o_1)* and *start-time(o_2)*. Consequently, for each element t_i of the sequence $(t_i)_{i \in N}$ there is a set of transport orders TO_i which describes the material flow for the set of machine orders MO_i. A formal definition of a transport order is omitted, since it can be derived straight forward from what has been said above.

Transporter Actions

In order to achieve the material flow defined by the transport orders, the transporters execute a sequence consisting of *move*, *load*, and *unload* actions. A *move* defines the movement of the transporter, beginning at a specified start time, from one position on the routing graph to a second. Any acceleration or deceleration phases are omitted and a constant velocity is assumed (possibly different for each transporter). A *load* action describes that the transporter transfers the material from a machine or a storage space into its loading space. An *unload* is defined correspondingly. Of course, constraints concerning the consistency of the action sequence, the capacity limits of a stock, the existence of material for loads or unloads etc. apply. They are omitted here to avoid deviation from the main topic discussed.

2.2 The Material Flow Problem(s)

The basic task is to compute a transportation schedule which assigns an action sequence to every transporter such that every piece of material reaches its destination in time. This task is called the *fulfillment problem.*

Since the machine schedule is dynamic, the scheduling of transport orders must be done incrementally. At every t_i of the generation sequence (t_i), new orders must be incorporated into the existing schedule. Additionally, already existing schedules must be adapted because every generation step may change previously announced orders. Thus, the scheduling mechanism must be *dynamic* and *adaptive.*

For a specific generation sequence, it may be impossible to find a correct transportation schedule such that *all* orders are executed in time. This may happen, for example, because the time to schedule an order is too short or because concurrent orders exceed the total transport capacity. In such cases, we want the system to fill as many orders as possible, i.e. the percentage of transport orders that are executed should be maximized.

An extension of the basic transportation problem includes the possibility of transporter breakdowns. Whenever a transporter breaks down, all orders assigned to it must be re-scheduled. Furthermore, any material stored in a transporter that broke down must be picked up immediately and moved to its destination. The possibility of breakdowns stresses the need for adaptiveness in the scheduling process.

This problem extension is called the *failure-including fulfillment problem.* Formally, the problem is defined by a sequence in $\mathcal{T}$ such that at each time step certain transporters break down. The system receives the information about the breakdown immediately.[1]

3 Analysis of the Problem

This section discusses some aspects of the scenario that will be referred to in later sections. This concerns especially the computations necessary to schedule a transport order and the relation of a transportation schedule to the storage schedule at the machines.

3.1 Evaluation and Scheduling of a Transport Order

The execution of a transport order is depicted in figure 2. In this figure the actions of the transporter (shown on the upper axis) are related to the time constraints of the corresponding transport order (lower axis). In order to carry out an order, the transporter first drives

---

1. A delayed notice would be more realistic.

to the source (*arrival phase*), loads the material (*loading phase*), moves to the destination (*transport phase*), and unloads the material (*unloading phase*). The last three phases must fall into the interval between start and finish time of the transport order. Furthermore, whenever the transporter picks up the material later than the start time, then it must be temporarily stored at the source. This interval is called *lay time*. Analogously, there is a lay time at the destination.

An important aspect of the transport execution is that the *active transport* (loading, transport, and unloading phase) has a fixed time length, given a specific transport order and a specific transporter. The time length of the active transport does not depend on the start of the execution, whereas the length of the arrival phase changes whenever the transporter's position at the beginning of the execution changes. This position is normally the destination of the last executed order. Consequently, a permutation of orders in the schedule changes the time it takes to arrive at the next source.

Many computations for scheduling orders are *local* to a transporter. First of all, the computation of the arrival phase is different for every permutation of orders. Second, every transporter has a different schedule for its already assigned orders, and because of that the arrival phase for a new order is different for every transporter (even if scheduled at the same time). And third, if the scenario consists of heterogeneous transporters, i.e. transporters have different characteristics regarding average velocity, transport capacity, or even possible routes, then also the active transport has different lengths for every transporter. Due to these reasons, the question of whether and how an order can be incorporated into the schedule of a transporter is a computation that involves information only concerning the specific transporter, i.e. it is "*local*" *to the transporter*.

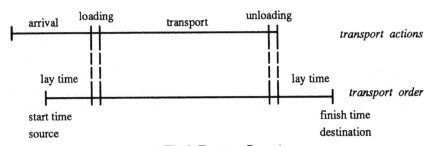

Fig. 2. Transport Execution

A second aspect of the transport execution is its dependence on the *storage profiles* of the machines. Even though the active transport may be scheduled any time between the start and finish time of the transport order, different loading and unloading time points cause different lay times. This affects the transportation schedule because machines have limited storage capacity (cf. (2.1)). For instance, a machine runs out of storage space if a transporter unloads material for a machine order o_2 before the machine order o_1 has been started (o_1 is executed on the machine before o_2) and the total consumed material of o_1 and o_2 exceeds the storage capacity. As a consequence, the unloading of material for order o_2 is denied. These situations cause additional perturbations.

Furthermore, the dependency between the transportation schedule and the storage schedule is strong because any changes in the transportation schedule alter the storage profile on at least two machines. This effect also arises if the execution time of a transport order is changed only slightly.

3.2 Multiple Trips and Combination of Orders

A transporter is unable to execute an order if the volume of the material exceeds its loading space. If this is the case for all transporters, then the material has to be divided into packages and each package must be transported separately. The new set of transport orders is in most cases assigned to several transporters because a single transporter has to shuttle between source and destination and therefore would travel a longer distance. Such multiple trips increase the size of the assignment problem because the number of transport orders increases.

On the other hand, a transporter may have enough free loading space to take along additional material while executing an order. Figure 3 gives an example of how to combine two orders by first picking up material at *source1*, then at *source2*, and finally dropping off the material at their destinations. Formally, the combination of transport orders is done by computing an action sequence that combines the action sequences necessary to carry out each single order. In contrast to multiple trips, the decision of whether to combine orders is local to a given transporter.

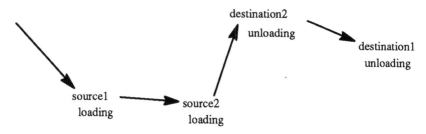

Fig. 3. Combination of Orders

4 An Architecture for Material Flow

Centralized approaches to scheduling problems suffer from the combinatorical explosion of the search space. Already fairly simple scheduling problems may be NP-hard. For real world scheduling applications, the search space tends to be even larger because they include more choices and dependencies (cf. section 3.1 on the relation between the transportation and the storage schedule). Multi-agent systems offer two advantages here: (i) as distributed systems they allow to utilize concurrency; (ii) by encapsulating declarative and procedural knowledge the overall system becomes easier to handle. Both of these advantages apply in the case of the fulfillment problem as it was described above. The computations that are local to a transporter, i.e., to decide whether it is able to execute an order, can be done concurrently. Furthermore, any details about the characteristics of a transporter (for example, its current schedule, the route chosen etc.) can be encapsulated in the transporter and hidden from the overall assignment process.

However, a *totally decentralized* approach is not appropriate. The task of assigning orders to transporters is a global process because an order may only be assigned to *exactly one* transporter. Consequently, to globally optimize the scheduling process, fully autonomous agents would need a large amount of coordination. Especially in the material flow scenario, every transporter needs to be coordinated with (potentially) every other transporter. The high communication costs that would originate from such a design will outweigh the advantage of distributed computing. Consequently, it is reasonable to introduce a central component that is responsible for global aspects and coordinates the assignment process. In particular, the evaluation should be done locally by the transporters and the following assignment globally by a coordinator, so that the schedule satisfies global optimality criteria. This has led to the architecture that will be described next.

4.1 The Principal Design

The architecture consists of an agent for every transporter and a *coordinator* that controls the overall scheduling process (see figure 4). The coordinator receives the new transport orders and keeps track of the order assignment; it announces, assigns, and retracts orders if necessary. On the other hand, each transporter has a (local) schedule for its assigned orders that contains the corresponding action sequence (cf section 2.1). On the basis of this schedule, it performs an analysis of new orders.

The top-level scheduling algorithm is shown in figure 5. The system is in a constant cycle of analyzing and assigning orders. Each cycle goes through four phases. Given a pool of new orders, the coordinator heuristically selects a subset and broadcasts it to the transporters. A good strategy is to announce only those with deadlines in the near future. In the second step, every transporter analyzes the orders with respect to its current situation and its specific abilities (for more details see section 4.2). The results are sent to the coordinator who evaluates them with respect to global criteria. In particular, the coordinator searches for an assignment that covers a maximum number of orders. Then the transporters are informed of the assignment and all orders not yet assigned are either declared as *impossible* or must be splitted to fit the transport capacity of the transporters (for more details see section 4.3).

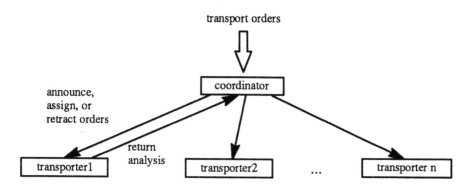

Fig. 4. Interactions during the Scheduling Process

The principal structure of the scheduling algorithm is similar to the contract net protocol as it was first proposed by Smith [Smi80]. In his proposal, a manager announces tasks to contractors; these bid for suitable tasks; and finally the manager assigns the tasks to the best bidders. The main difference is that the contract net protocol is based on *bargaining* between manager and contractors, whereas in our approach transporters only perform local computations and leave the decision making to the coordinator. In particular, the agents return the result of the evaluation to the coordinator instead of making bids, i.e. they do not bargain with the coordinator.

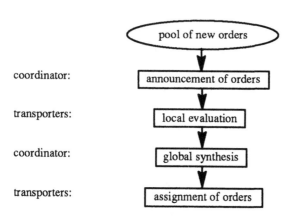

Fig. 5. Phases of the Scheduling Algorithm

4.2 Local Evaluation by Transporters

The local analysis of new orders is done on the basis of the transport abilities of the transporter and its current transport schedule. The transport abilities concern, for instance, the average speed, the loading space capacity, and any other special constraints on the transportation process (e.g. routing restrictions).

The analysis is divided into two steps. In the first step, the transporter considers each transport order separately and evaluates it according to the following criteria:

1. Is it possible to execute the order?
    a. Can the active transport be done between start and finish time?
    b. Is the loading space capacity sufficient?
2. Is there a free interval large enough to execute the order?

In the second step, the transporter checks whether combinations of the announced orders can be incorporated into its current schedule since a combination of orders introduces additional constraints. But considering every combination of orders would result in an exponential algorithm (exponential w.r.t. the number of announced orders). Furthermore, even if enough computational power were available, such an effort would be in vain due to the frequent perturbations in the manufacturing process. Therefore, the transporter only estimates the possibility of a conflict by computing a conflict probability between two orders:

For every two orders compute the percentage of scheduling possibilities that result in a conflict.[2]

The result of the order evaluation is returned to the coordinator in a condensed form, mainly stating only the qualitative result of the analysis. This result is incomplete (w.r.t. all possibilities of scheduling the set of orders) because it contains only a conflict probability for combinations.

The consequence of this incompleteness is that the coordinator may assume assignments to be feasible that cannot be scheduled. In such a case, the coordinator is informed about the failure and puts the orders that were not scheduled back into the pool of transport orders. Note that a transporter can always schedule at least one order since the evaluation of a single order is correct.

4.3 Global Synthesis by the Coordinator

The coordinator combines the results of the local analyses of all transporters and searches for an assignment covering a maximal number of orders. If several maximal assignments

---

2. An order can be scheduled at any (discrete) point of time between start and finish time. A conflict arises if the specific transportation intervals (including the arrival phase) overlap. The total set of possibilities for two orders is their cross product.

exist, it minimizes the (average) conflict probability per transporter. For every order that has not yet been assigned, it analyzes the reasons and takes appropriate actions:

> IF for every transporter it is impossible to execute the order
> THEN it cannot be executed by the system.
> ELSE
> IF for every transporter the loading capacity is exceeded
> THEN divide the order into smaller orders and re-announce them.

Afterwards, the coordinator continues with a new cycle of the top-level algorithm (cf. 4.1).

4.4 Evaluation of the Design and the Algorithm

The architecture proposed exhibits the structure that was demanded at the beginning of this section. Local computations, such as the evaluation and the scheduling of new orders, as well as transportation characteristics are encapsulated in the transporter agents. The agentification additionally allows concurrent processing. On the other hand, the coordinator has a global view on the scheduling process. It keeps track of the order assignment and receives an abstract analysis from every transporter. On the basis of this view, it computes a (maximal) assignment that meets global criteria.

The scheduling algorithm is *dynamic and adaptive by design*. The system incrementally adds new orders to the existing schedule(s). By the same mechanism, changed orders are *re*-scheduled. The coordinator first retracts the old version from the corresponding transporter and then announces the new version. In total, the system designed solves the *fulfillment problem*.

The architecture also solves the *failure-including fulfillment problem* provided that breakdowns only occur at empty transporters.[3] In this case, assigned orders are retracted and put back into the pool of new orders, just the same way changed orders are treated. Nevertheless, such events demand more timely rescheduling.

The demand for real-time behaviour has not yet been adequately met. In principle, real-time behaviour can be achieved by managing the computational resources of the agents appropriately. The computational time for a scheduling cycle mainly depends on the time for a single analysis, on the total time until all analyses are returned, and on the local scheduling. The time to find an assignment and any communication costs can be neglected. To speed up this process, the number of orders announced must be reduced to the most urgent ones (this reduces the number of combinations). Furthermore, the coordinator must assign urgent orders as soon as it receives a positive analysis if the system runs

---

3. For transporters carrying material, additional orders that recover the lost material must be generated.

out of time to schedule these orders. Note that the transporters must analyze the orders in order to be able to guarantee their execution.

5 Implementation

In this section we will describe the implementation tool, the system performance, as well as the experience gained during the implementation phase.

5.1 The Multi-Agent Testbed DASEDIS

The scenario depicted in section 2 and the architecture described in the previous section have been implemented in the DASEDIS testbed for multi-agent systems [BS92]. The main advantage of this testbed is the built-in agent architecture. This architecture represents the actoric, sensoric, communicative, intentional and cognitive aspects of an agent in separate modules. Except for the module COGNITION, representing the cognitive aspects, all other modules are simulated according to the application in question. COGNITION itself is implemented as a knowledge-based system whose problem solving is based on scripts and cooperation protocols. A script encodes a stereotypical course of actions which an agent may take in order to respond to its surrounding or to achieve a goal. A cooperation protocol represents the possible flow of messages between two agents, abstracting from the low-level communication details. The structure and algorithms for scripts and protocols are generic. For the application programmer it remains to implement the knowledge of the agents in terms of scripts, resources necessary to execute a script, means to acquire the resources (possibly via protocols), and the relation of scripts to goals.

In the prototype implemented for the material flow scenario, the user creates agents for machines, storage spaces, and transporters, after having defined an environment including a graph and a production program; the coordinator is created automatically. All agents can be configured according to their characteristics, i.e., for example, the machine type, the storage capacity, or the average velocity. Once the scenario is started, the coordinator randomly computes new machine orders for a given time horizon. The structure of these orders is taken from the production program that prescribes possible order sequences for machine types. Machine orders are executed while new orders are scheduled. From the machine orders the coordinator derives the corresponding transport orders and announces them to the transporters. Then the assignment process evolves as described in the previous section.

An example test run with five machines and five transporters produced the following results: A total number of 2406 transport orders was introduced to the system in 50 steps.

780 of these were revised later on. Of the remaining 1626 orders the system was able to schedule 89 %. 9 % of orders were impossible to schedule (not enough transport capacity) and with the remaining 2 %, the system ran out of time.

5.2 Experience with the Multi-Agent Testbed

The multi-agent part of the scheduling system was readily implemented in the DASEDIS testbed. As mentioned above, DASEDIS supplies a complete agent model and high-level interaction protocols onto which the agents and the interactions of the scheduling system was easily mapped. In particular, it was only necessary to program the knowledge base, i.e. scripts, resources, and execution conditions of scripts. Services like communication (even protocols), concurrency, and execution were provided by DASEDIS.

On the other hand, multi-agent techniques did not cover all aspects of the scheduling problem. Agents perform complex (cognitive) computations, such as analysing, scheduling (both done by the transporter), or assigning orders (done by the coordinator). These were implemented by conventional algorithms for which the programming consumed a considerable amount of time. For these subproblems, it is reasonable to employ other techniques, such as constraint-based reasoning or even Operations Research methods. The order assignment, for example, can be formulated as a static mathematical problem (with a clear optimum).

Thus with the help of multi-agent techniques the scheduling problem was decomposed into smaller problems which were solved with other techniques.

6 Conclusion

This paper presented a multi-agent approach to material flow scheduling. In the first part, the material flow was described by a formal model. The scheduling problem to be solved was identified as being *dynamic* and *perturbed*. It turned out that many computations are local to a single transporter. On the other hand, global optimality criteria must be met. This led us to a mixed architecture, i.e., a distributed system with centralized control.

The main idea was to leave the evaluation and the scheduling of new orders to each transporter, whereas the assignment remains in the responsibility of the coordinator. The coordinator receives a global view of the scheduling process with the help of a condensed result of the transporters' analyses.

The design process and the implementation were based on multi-agent techniques and tools. After identifying the need to distribute computation, a multi-agent approach provides an agent and a cooperation model that allowed the system to be designed at a *more abstract and conceptual level.* Terms such as *announce* or *assign* fit perfectly well into these models. Furthermore, multi-agent techniques supplied methods to *coordinate* the scheduling process. On the implementational level many mechanisms, such as concurrency or interaction protocols, were provided by the existing multi-agent environment DASEDIS. Thus, our experience with applying multi-agent techniques to the material flow problem can be summarized as follows: multi-agent techniques support the design process and available tools facilitate rapid prototyping and experimentation.

The implemented system has shown that dynamic and adaptive scheduling of transportation demands a more 'reactive' system, in the sense that schedules are computed more rapidly. In many circumstances, for instance, new changes render the high communication effort put into the analysis obsolete. In this case, it seems more reasonable to quickly compute a preliminary schedule (for example, schedule one order at a time) and, if the situation allows, improve the schedule afterwards.

Furthermore, it seems promising to combine machine and transportation scheduling. First of all, the transportation problem cannot be isolated, since it is heavily dependent on machine scheduling. Secondly, a feasible machine schedule should in principle guarantee a feasible transportation schedule. Consequently, coordination of both schedules will result in better performance in comparison to the sequential scheduling of machine jobs and transportation, as is the case in current manufacturing control. Although the overall system becomes more complex, an extension of the approach presented in this paper would keep the complexity of the interrelations at a minimum.

Acknowledgement

I am indebted to Kurt Sundermeyer and Afsaneh Haddadi for their valuable comments and discussions on the contents of this paper. I do really appreciate their efforts.

Bibliography

[BS92] B. Burmeister, K. Sundermeyer: "Cooperative Problem-Solving Guided by Intentions and Perception", in: E. Werner, Y. Demazeau (eds.), Decentralized A.I. 3, North-Holland, 1992, pp. 77-82

[BHS93] B. Burmeister, A. Haddadi, K. Sundermeyer: "Generic Configurable Cooperation Protocols for Multi-Agent Systems", Pre-Proc. MAAMAW-93, Neuchâtel, 1993

[BO92] J. Butler, H. Ohtsubo: "ADDYMS: Architecture for Distributed Dynamic Manufacturing Scheduling", in: A. Famili, D.S. Nau, S.H. Kim (eds.), *Artificial Intelligence Applications in Manufacturing*, AAAI Press/MIT Press, 1992, pp. 199-213

[DS88] R. Davis, R.G. Smith: "Negotiation as a Metaphor for Distributed Problem Solving", in A.H. Bond, L. Gasser (eds.): "Readings in Distributed Artificial Intelligence", Morgan Kaufmann Publ., Ca., 1988, pp. 333-356

[DK93] W. Dilger, S. Kassel: "Sich selbst organisierende Produktionsprozesse als Möglichkeit zur flexiblen Fertigungssteuerung", in J. Müller (ed.): "Beiträge zum Gründungsworkshop der Fachgruppe Verteilte Künstliche Intelligenz", DFKI Document D-91-06, Saarbrücken, 1993

[OSH88] P.S. Ow, S.F. Smith, R. Howie: "A Cooperative Scheduling System", in M.D. Oliff (Ed.): *Expert System and Intelligent Manufacturing*, 1988, pp. 43-56

[PLJ+86] H. Van Dyke Parunak, P.W. Lozo, R. Judd, B.W. Irish, J. Kindrick: "A Distributed Heuristic Strategy for Material Transportation", Proc. of the Conference on Intelligent Systems and Machines, Rochester, MI, pp. 305-310

[Smi80] R. Smith: "The Contract Net Protocol: High-Level Communication and Control in a Distributed Problem Solver", IEEE Transactions on Computers, C-29(12), December 1980, pp. 1104-1113

Motion Planning for an Articulated Robot: A Multi-Agent Approach

Lars Overgaard*, Henrik G. Petersen, John W. Perram **

Lindø Center for Applied Mathematics, Odense University,
Forskerparken 10, DK-5230 Odense M, Denmark

Abstract. Traditional motion planning techniques consider the problem of collision-free motion of an articulated robot as a global high level planning problem for one agent with internal degrees of freedom. The consequence is centralized explicit control of all joints. We suggest a simple multi-agent approach to motion planning with local low level collision avoidance. The control is distributed and there is no explicit control of the joints. Each individual link of a robot is a self-contained agent and the motion planning problem is formulated as a constraint satisfaction problem. Equations of motion for the multi-agent system incorporate satisfaction of the equality constraints between joined agents, while artificial forces ensure the satisfaction of inequality constraints preventing collisions. The artificial forces are local to each individual agent and solution of the equations of motion gives an emergent behaviour of the multi-agent system. The presented method has been successfully applied to various problems, including the simulation of a multi-tool robot and a 19-link snakelike robot moving through a maze. Finally, the method is used in an actual application: an industrial robot welding ship sections.

1   Introduction

The work described in this paper is part of the Autonomous Multiple Robot Operation in Structured Environments (AMROSE) project, a joint research project between Odense University and Odense Steel Shipyard Ltd. The purpose of this project is to make a system able to control multi-link robots of different types working together in a complex environment. A more detailed description of AMROSE is found in [1, 2]. In the framework of AMROSE the problem of collision-free motion planning for a single articulated robot has been considered.

When planning the collision-free motion of an articulated robot, it is required that the robot does not collide with objects in the environment, that the robot does not collide with itself, and that the robot's joints stay inside their legal range. These requirements are expressed by the following collision avoidance *inequality constraints*

---

* Lars Overgaard wishes to thank the Danish Research Academy and Odense Steel Shipyard Ltd. for their financial support.

** The authors wish to thank all members of the AMROSE research team.

- the minimum distance between any link of the robot and any object in the environment must always be greater than zero
- the minimum distance between any two non-neighbour links of the robot must always be greater than zero
- the value of any joint coordinate must always be greater than its lower limit and less than its upper limit

The latter constraint ensures that neighbouring links do not collide.

Classical motion planning techniques represent the robot's configuration in *configuration space* C where each dimension represents a joint coordinate. The robot tasks and objects in the environment are represented in *Cartesian space* and this discrepancy calls for transformations between the two spaces.

Direct kinematics is the transformation of the robot's configuration from joint coordinates into Cartesian coordinates. An introduction can be found in [3, p.195–201].

Inverse kinematics is the reverse operation. For a required path of the end-effector, the set of direct kinematics equations can be solved for the joint coordinates [3, p.201–207]. Plain inverse kinematics requires the number of joints to be equal to the number of controlled end-effector coordinates. Then there is no freedom left for collision avoidance. Having a *kinematically redundant* robot with more joints than controlled end-effector coordinates the space spanned by the extra joints can be searched for collision-free inverse kinematics solutions [4]. An alternative is to expand the set of equations, to have as many equations as unknowns (joint values). The additional equations may be optimization criteria meeting various demands, e.g. the collision avoidance constraints [5, 6]. Solving the set of equations for the joint coordinates is intrinsically a centralized control.

A collision-free path between any two configurations of a robot can be found by *path planning in configuration space*. This is done by planning the path of a point in C_{free}, the space volumes of C which represent collision-free configurations. The major difficulty is that the mapping of obstacles from Cartesian space to volumes in C is computationally very expensive. For robots with many joints, C has a high dimension, and the complexity of the path planning problem increases non-polynomially with the dimension of C. For robots with fewer joints, say 6, the computational cost is still very high, but quantization of C and projection of C on to lower-dimensional slices somewhat simplifies the problem [7, 8, 9]. Also path planning in configuration space centralizes the control.

In this paper an articulated robot is considered to be a Multi-Agent System (MAS): each individual link is a self-contained agent. The configuration of an agent is represented in Cartesian space. This choice of coordinates removes the need the transformations to and from configuration space. The system contains *passive link agents* and one *active tool agent*. There is no problem in having several tool agents. The active agent must perform tasks and transfer-movements from the end of one task to the start of the next. All agents must satisfy the collision avoidance constraints. Furthermore neighbouring agents must satisfy the constraints of being attached by a joint. We implement a joint by imposing a set of 5 independent geometric *equality constraints* (holonomic), relating the coordinates of the two agents. Thus, the described multi-agent system must satisfy both inequality constraints and equality constraints.

This formulation of the problem enables us to replace the traditional high level planning approach by a method with local scope and distributed control. A local method alone will not solve maze-like path finding problems of global character. We will rely on assistance from a simple method described in [10]. The method makes a kind of rough path finding and decomposes the problem into a sequence of smaller motion planning problems of local character. A suggested "path" is constructed by identifying key points on the way to the goal. Our local method produces a collision-free motion from one key point to the next.

Distributed Artificial Intelligence (DAI) provides useful techniques for solving many problems in multi-agent systems. Examples of DAI/MAS approaches to constraint-satisfaction in planning problems are given in [11, 12]. For some simple problems, however, simpler non-AI approaches give good results.

We will use a method based on the *artificial force* idea. This class of methods use artificial forces to produce the motion of a dynamic model of a robot. The forces are chosen such that they encourage the robot to do what it is supposed to do and discourages it from doing what it should not do. The motion obtained from artificial force methods is not planned, but *emerges* because of the forces. The local character of these methods makes them interesting in the context of on-line systems with sensory input. Some of the seminal papers in the field of artificial forces are [13, 14, 15, 16].

The dynamic model we use incorporates the automatic satisfaction of holonomic constraints. The agents have a strategy for choosing artificial forces acting on them, and the forces govern the motion of the system. Artificial forces ensure satisfaction of the collision avoidance constraints and they are responsible for the tool agent's active behaviour. All agents are repelled by possible obstacles in the environment and by each other, and joint coordinates are repelled from their limits. The tool agent is attracted by its goal, and dissipating forces limit the speed of the agents in various situations. This distributed control gives an emergent behaviour of the multi-agent system satisfying all constraints and leading towards the goal of the tool agent. When the tool agent's task requires highly accurate motion, which cannot be obtained by artificial forces, the tool is constrained to an *artificial task agent* that moves according to the task.

The major advantages of the presented method are

- *Flexibility.* The only non-trivial operation in the derivation of equations of motion for an arbitrary robot is the identification of constraints. A computer program does not need to be compiled specifically for one type of robot. It may take the kinematic and geometric description of any robot as input. There is no fundamental limit on the number of joints in the robot, in contrast to inverse kinematics methods. The agent's force strategy is widely applicable from one robot to another.

- *Efficiency.* The presented forward dynamics method is computationally rather cheap and may be used in off-line robot programming as well as in on-line control of real time robotic systems. The efficiency is seen very clearly for robots with many joints, since the computational complexity is between $O(j)$ and $O(j^3)$, where j is the number of joints. This is to be compared with the non-polynomial complexity of configuration space techniques.

- *Elegance.* The distributed control gives rise to a very smooth and elegant movement of the articulated robot. All joints move simultaneously, and due to the dynamic model of the robot, there are no sudden accelerations or other discontinuities in the movement. This quality has an aesthetic value, and also a practical one in the motion planning for high speed robots.

In Sect. 2 we show how to derive the constraint dynamic equations of motion for a system with holonomic constraints. The multi-agent properties of our method are seen very clearly when the agents move independently; we consider a system of free agents that are not restrained by joints in Sect. 3. In Sect. 4 we discuss holonomic constraints implementing revolute and prismatic joints between neighbouring pairs of agents. Section 5 reports some results of applying our method to various problems.

2 Constraint Dynamics

We will now show how to derive equations of motion for a system with holonomic constraints. In the following boldface uppercase letters denote matrices and boldface lowercase letters denote vectors. A vector $\mathbf{q} = (q_1, q_2, \ldots, q_N)$ represents the configuration of the system. The N coordinates must satisfy M geometric constraints on the form

$$c_m (q_1, q_2, \ldots, q_N) = 0 \ . \tag{1}$$

The set of all possible configurations that satisfy the constraints (1) form an $N - M$ dimensional *constraint surface* in an N dimensional space. Only points on this surface represent legal configurations of the system. External forces on the system may have any size and direction, but *constraint forces* act in the direction of the constraints, i.e. orthogonal to the constraint surface. Constraint forces always have exactly the size needed to make the total force parallel to the surface, and thus they keep the evolving system on the constraint surface.

A classic example is the pendulum. The constraint is constant length of the string, the surface of legal configurations is a sphere, and the constraint force is the string force. The constraint force acts along the string and it always has exactly the size necessary to keep the pendulum on the sphere.

For a system subject to M independent constraints, the direction of the m'th constraint is the m'th column of the $N \times M$ matrix $\mathbf{D}$ with elements

$$D_{nm} = \frac{\partial c_m}{\partial q_n} \ ,$$

and the vector of constraint forces $\mathbf{f}^c$ directed along the constraints can be written as

$$\mathbf{f}^c = \mathbf{D}\boldsymbol{\mu} \ ,$$

where μ is a vector of scalar multiplicators giving the size of the individual constraint forces. We write the total force on the system, $\mathbf{f}$, as the sum of the external forces $\mathbf{f}^e$ and the constraint forces $\mathbf{f}^c$. According to Newton's 2.nd law we have that

$$\mathbf{f} = \mathbf{f}^e + \mathbf{f}^c = \mathbf{I}\ddot{\mathbf{q}} \ ,$$

where $\mathbf{I}$ is the diagonal mass matrix. A dot denotes the time derivative, and $\ddot{\mathbf{q}}$ is the acceleration vector. By rearranging the above equation we finally have an expression for the Newtonian equations of motion for the constrained system

$$\ddot{\mathbf{q}} = \mathbf{I}^{-1}(\mathbf{f}^e + \mathbf{D}\mu) \ . \tag{2}$$

The vector of multiplicators μ is found by solving a system of linear equations, which is obtained by substituting $\ddot{\mathbf{q}}$ from (2) into the double time derivative of (1), see [17]. Numerical methods for solving equation systems are discussed in [19]. The computational complexity for robots with j joints varies between $O(j)$ for a robot with a single chain of bodies (the equation matrix is block tridiagonal) and $O(j^3)$ for a very complex robot with many branches and closed loops (the matrix is un-regular but, however, sparse).

The general procedure for obtaining the equations of motion for a specific system is to choose coordinates for the representation of the system, identify the constraints relating these coordinates, and evaluate (2).

In this paper we represent the configuration of the i'th agent A_i in Cartesian space by the vector $\mathbf{r}_i$ giving the position of the centre of mass and the three principal axis vectors $\mathbf{u}_{i1}, \mathbf{u}_{i2}, \mathbf{u}_{i3}$. Thus, for a system of N agents,

$$\mathbf{q} = (\mathbf{r}_1, \ldots, \mathbf{r}_N, \mathbf{u}_{11}, \ldots, \mathbf{u}_{N3}) \ .$$

In the following two sections we will identify the constraints on $\mathbf{q}$ for two types of multi-agent systems.

3 A System of Free Agents

We want to show the multi-agent properties of our method as clearly as possible. This is most striking when the agents move freely. Then the system's behaviour is governed purely by the agents' selfish utility optimization. In this section we consider a system of n independently moving rigid bodies, of which each is an autonomous agent. We choose to describe the configuration of the system by a redundant set of Cartesian coordinates. We identify a set of constraints, as in (1), needed for the derivation of the equations of motion corresponding to (2). Each agent subjects itself to various artificial forces. Numerical integration of the equations of motion for a specific test case will give us the motion of the multi-agent system.

A rigid body has three translational and three rotational degrees of freedom (DOF). The 4 vectors defining the agent have twelve coordinates, so they form a redundant representation. But the $\mathbf{u}_e$'s must form an orthonormal basis, and the redundancy is removed by the 6 constraints of orthonormality presented in [18]

$$\mathbf{u}_{ie} \cdot \mathbf{u}_{if} - \delta_{ef} = 0 \ , \quad 1 \le e \le f \le 3 \ ,$$

where δ_{ef} is the Kronecker delta-function. The $12n$ coordinates must satisfy these $6n$ independent equations, leaving $12n - 6n = 6n$ DOF. These are exactly the 6 DOF of each agent.

Having an initial configuration $\{\mathbf{r}_i(0), \mathbf{u}_{ie}(0), \dot{\mathbf{r}}_i(0), \dot{\mathbf{u}}_{ie}(0)\}$ and a strategy for choosing the external artificial forces $\mathbf{f}^e$, the equations of motion (2) can be numerically integrated through time t to yield the motion of each agent A_i given by $\{\mathbf{r}_i(t), \mathbf{u}_{ie}(t), \dot{\mathbf{r}}_i(t), \dot{\mathbf{u}}_{ie}(t)\}$. Standard methods for numerical integration of differential equations can be found in [19].

We consider a simple test case, where a gantry-mounted 5-DOF Hirobo WR–L80 robot welds two seams in a ship section. The real gantry on Odense Steel Shipyard can translate freely in three dimensions, but it cannot rotate at all. This is easily modelled by taking the corresponding elements of the matrix of generalized masses $\mathbf{I}$ to infinity. The task of welding requires high precision, more than can be achieved by using artificial forces. We obtain the precision by constraining the tool agent to an imaginary task agent that moves according to the specifications of the task. When the task agent moves along a seam to be welded, the constraints force the tool agent to come along. Only the necessary constraints between the two agents are imposed, the remaining freedom is left for the tool agent. The process of welding normally requires control of only 5 out of the tool's 6 DOF – there is rotational symmetry about the torch. Therefore, we join the tool agent and the task agent with a revolute joint about the torch. How to do this is described in the next section.

Artificial forces $\mathbf{f}^e$ are found according to the following ideas. We introduce gravity, so that all agents tend to fall down towards the steel plates of the ship section. The parts (agents) of the robot must not collide with the steel plates or with each other. This is obtained by letting each agent set up suitable repulsive forces pushing it away from plates and other agents. Neighbouring agents are not linked together here, so they also repel each other. The welding torch must move to a position in one corner, weld a short vertical seam, move to another corner, and weld a horizontal seam there. The tool agent lets an attractive force pull it towards the task and this makes the agent move towards obstacles, as well. Repulsion still acts, though, and the sum of attractive and repulsive forces gives the tool agent a collision-free path towards its goal. To make the motion as smooth as possible, all agents use frictional forces to damp high velocities and take away some kinetic energy. Ideas on how to find well-related functions for the artificial forces in a systematic way is found in [20], but basically the applied forces have been found heuristically.

Figure 1 shows snapshots from the result of a numerical simulation of the multi-agent system. The pictures show various stages of the scenery:

1. The robot is in its initial configuration and all velocities are zero.

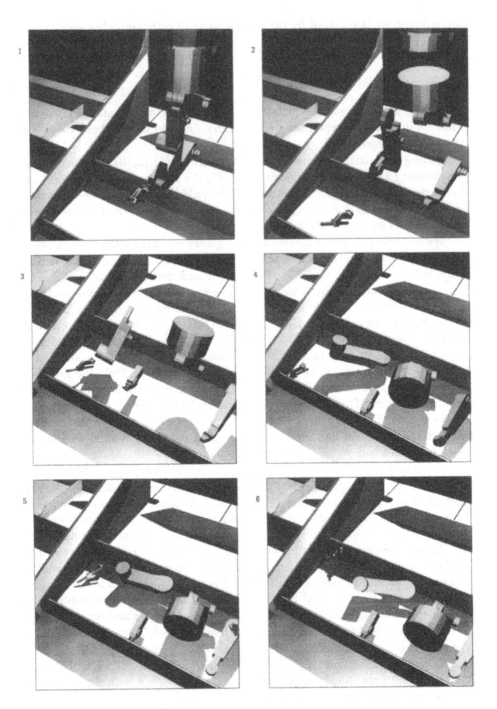

Fig. 1. A system of free agents

2. The robot disintegrates because of the agents mutual repulsion. Gravity makes the agents fall down towards the steel construction. The tool falls faster than the other agents because of the attraction towards the corner.

3. The tool is close to the start of the first seam. At the same time the link agents stop falling because of repulsion from the steel plates.

4. Now the tool is attached to the task agent and it has started to weld. The various repulsions make the agents float at safe distances from steel plates and each other.

5. Next, the tool released from the task agent and is attracted towards the other corner. One link agent is in the way, but repulsion makes it move away. Some other link agents are pushed away to make room for the unlucky link agent.

6. Finally, the tool starts welding the second seam while being joined to the task agent. The link agents are repelled further away to make more room for the tool agent.

It is obvious that the simple force strategy may fail in more complex cases, where more advanced techniques to find the forces may be necessary. But in simple cases like this one the simple force strategy works very well.

4   A System of Constrained Agents

In this section we do exactly as in the previous section, with one extension. We introduce the joints between neighbouring agents.

One rigid body has 6 DOF relative to another rigid body. This freedom can be limited to the one DOF of a revolute or prismatic joint by imposing 5 geometric constraints between $\{r_i, u_{ie}\}$ and $\{r_j, u_{je}\}$, the coordinates of the two joined agents. Then our Cartesian coordinates become a non-redundant description of an articulated robot.

The geometric constraints we use to obtain a revolute joint are demands for constant distances between pairs of points fixed in the two agents. If the points are chosen as showed in Fig.2, the only remaining freedom is rotation about the axis through the points $s_{ij,0}$ and $s_{ji,0}$. Let $d_{ij,m}$ be the distance between the two points $s_{ij,m}$ and $s_{ji,0}$. Then the 5 constraints can be expressed as

$$d_{ij,m} - l_{ij,m} = 0 , \quad m = 0, 1, 2 ,$$
$$d_{ji,m} - l_{ji,m} = 0 , \quad m = 1, 2 ,$$

where the $l_{ij,m}$'s are constants. This description of revolute joints has been given in [21].

We do something similar to obtain a prismatic joint. Now the 5 distances between the points must not be constant, instead we demand them to be equal. These 4 constraints leave one rotational and one translational DOF. We prevent the rotation by demanding two vectors fixed in each agent to be orthogonal, as can be seen in Fig.3,

$$d_{ij,m} - d_{ij,0} = 0 , \quad m = 1, 2 ,$$

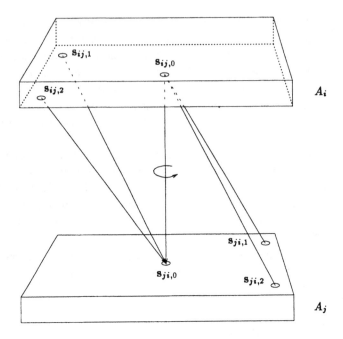

Fig. 2. A revolute joint obtained by 5 distance constraints

$$d_{ji,m} - d_{ij,0} = 0 \ , \quad m = 1,2 \ ,$$
$$\mathbf{v}_{ij} \cdot \mathbf{v}_{ji} = 0 \ .$$

Note that $d_{ij,0}$ is not constant. The above implementation of prismatic joints was originally proposed in [20].

We will now show the result of a simulation of the gantry-robot system described in Sect. 3 including the above joint constraints between neighbouring agents. Now the constraint forces acting between pairs of joined agents convey a flow of information through the multi-agent system. This communication was absent in the system of free agents in Sect. 3.

As before, the tool must weld the two seams starting in the corners. The gantry has 3 DOF and the robot has 5, so the gantry-robot system is in fact an 8-DOF device. We control 5 of the tool's DOF, so the system is kinematically redundant. Thus it has the freedom to avoid collisions, not only during the transfer-movement between tasks but also when welding.

This time also joint limits must be respected. This is achieved by introducing joint forces (or torques) along (or about) joint axes, i.e., pairs of joined agents use joint limit repulsion to avoid hitting the joint limits. Joined agents exert a weak attraction towards a safe joint goal, to optimize the joint position. Like all other control forces in the system, the joint forces are found heuristically.

Snapshots from this simulation clearly show the effect of the joint constraints on the multi-agent system, see Fig.4:

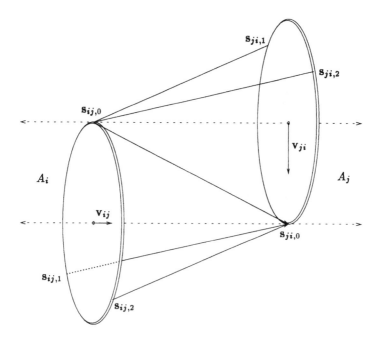

Fig. 3. A prismatic joint obtained by 5 geometric constraints

1. The robot is in the same initial configuration as previously.

2. The tool is attracted towards the corner and all the other agents have to follow it because of the joint constraints. The effect of gravity is smaller than before because of the support force from the gantry.

3. Now the tool has pulled the robot closer to the corner with the vertical seam. The compromise between attraction and repulsion gives a collision-free path.

4. Here the tool has been constrained to the task agent and is started to weld. The collision-free path to this configuration has never been planned, but has simply emerged.

5. After finishing the first task, the tool is released and attracted towards the start of the next task in the other corner. Repulsion pushes the tool, and thus the other agents, too, away from the steel plates on the way to the other corner.

6. The tool has started to weld the horizontal seam. The task agent controls the process but not the tool's rotation about the torch.

The apparently intelligent behaviour of the robot was achieved purely by the simple force strategy. This approach gives good performance for local problems like this example. Problems of global character must be decomposed into smaller local problems before using an artificial force method.

Fig. 4. A system of joined agents

5 Applications

The presented artificial force method is a local method to produce collision-free motion in "near-convex" environments, it does not solve very complicated path-finding problems. In all applications we place a level of centralized control on top of the described method, we combine it with the simple global path finder described in Sect. 1. This level of control may be seen as a *controller* giving input to the multi-agent system. The controller assigns new tasks to tool agents when they are ready for it.

This approach has showed to work well in several different cases. We have simulated a 19-link snakelike robot moving through a simple maze. The snake's nose was the active agent while the other (passive) agents were pulled through the maze without collisions.

Our approach has two main consumers of computing time. One is the agent's computation for finding the closest obstacle. This cost is proportional to the number of agents in the robot. The other consumer is the solution of linear equations for the constraint force multiplicators μ in (2). Solving sets of n linear equations in general has the computational complexity $O(n^3)$. But the equation matrix for robots with a single chain of bodies is block tridiagonal, so the computational complexity for a linear robot with j joints reduces from $O(j^3)$ to $O(j)$. It would have been computationally much more expensive to transform the maze into the snake's 19-dimensional configuration space and subsequently search C_{free} for a feasible path.

A branched 19-link robot with two tools has also been simulated. Our method was immediately applicable. The only change was that the controller now had to coordinate the actions of the two tool agents.

The AMROSE project is currently maturing an off-line robot programming system for welding robots. The first large-scale tests with Hirobo WR–L80 robots have turned out successfully. By the end of this year (1994), the system will be used to program Motoman K–3 S robots in actual production. The backbone of the system is the motion planning technique described in this paper.

6 Conclusion

We have proposed a multi-agent approach to spatial planning, where the individual links of a robot are constrained autonomous agents. Our approach is an artificial force method based on a constraint dynamics model of the multi-agent system.

The distributed reactive method gives an emergent behaviour of the system. This is very efficient in non-static environments, like e.g. on-line systems with sensor input, systems with moving obstacles, or multi-robot systems. It should be mentioned that our method has several advantages compared to other methods for collision-avoidance, especially for highly redundant robots.

We have successfully applied the method to off-line control of standard robots at Odense Steel Shipyard Ltd. In future applications we will exploit the method's

218

obvious advantages in on-line control of multi-link robots and multi-robot systems.

References

1. Jacobsen, N., Overgaard, L., and Perram, J. W.: Autonomous Multiple Robots Operation in Structured Environments. 2nd Workshop Proc., Esprit Parallel Computing Action (1990)
2. Larsen, R., Overgaard, L., Jacobsen, N., Truelsen, B., Leonard, M., and Immerkaer, J.: Autonomous Multiple Robots Operation in Structured Environments. 3rd Workshop Proc., Esprit Parallel Computing Action (1991)
3. McKerrow, P. J.: Introduction to Robotics. Addison-Wesley (1991)
4. Reynier, F., Chedmail, P., and Wenger, P.: Automatic Positioning of Robots for Following Continuous Trajectories among Mobile Obstacles. Proc. 23rd Int. Symp. on Industrial Robots (1992) 737–742
5. Maciejewski, A. A. and Klein, C. A.: Obstacle Avoidance for Kinematically Redundant Manipulators in Dynamically Varying Environments. Int. J. Robotics Res., 2(3) (1985)
6. Höfer, A.: Configuration Control of Redundant Manipulators. Proc. 23rd Int. Symp. on Industrial Robots (1992) 91–96
7. Lozano-Pérez, T.: Automatic Planning of Manipulator Transfer Movements. IEEE Transactions on Sys. Man. Cyber. 11(10) (1981) 681–698
8. Lozano-Pérez, T.: Spatial Planning: A Configurational Space Approach. IEEE Transactions on Computers 32(2) (1983) 108–120
9. Lozano-Pérez, T.: A Simple Motion-Planning Algorithm for General Robot Manipulators. IEEE J. Robotics and Automation 3(3) (1987) 224–238
10. Jacobsen, N., Overgaard, L., and Perram, J. W.: Controlling an n-Axis Robot in Complex Environments. Proc. 23rd Int. Symp. on Industrial Robots (1992) 363–368
11. Nagao, K. and Hasida, K.: Emergent Planning: A Computational Architecture for Situated Behavior. Proc. 5th European Workshop on Modelling Autonomous Agents in a Multi-Agent World (1993)
12. Liu, J. S. and Sycara, K. P.: Emergent Constraint Satisfaction through Multi-Agent Coordinated Interaction. Proc. 5th European Workshop on Modelling Autonomous Agents in a Multi-Agent World (1993)
13. Renaud, M.: Contribution à l' Étude de la Modélisation des Systèmes Mécaniques Articulés. PhD thesis, Dept. of Engineering, University of Toulouse, France, (1976)
14. Khatib, O. and Maitre, J. F. Le.: Dynamic Control of Manipulators Operating in Complex Environments. Proc. 3rd CISM-IFToMM Symp. Theory and Practice of Robots and Manipulators (1978) 267–282
15. Krogh, B.: A Generalized Potential Field Approach to Obstacle Avoidance Control. World Conf. on Robotics Research, Bethlehem, Israel (1984)
16. Khatib, O.: Real-Time Obstacle Avoidance for Manipulators and Mobile Robots. Int. J. Robotics Res. 5(1) (1986) 90–98
17. de Leeuw, S. W., Perram, J. W., and Petersen, H. G.: Hamilton's Equations for Constrained Dynamical Systems. J. Stat. Phys. 61(5/6) (1990) 1203–1222
18. Perram, J. W. and Petersen, H. G.: New Rigid Body Equations of Motion for Molecular Dynamics. Molecular Simulation 1 (1988) 239–247

19. Press, W. H., Flannery, B. P., Teukolsky, S. A., and Vetterling, W. T.: Numerical Recipes in C. Cambridge University Press (1988)
20. Overgaard, L.: Pseudo-Force Methods for Generating Collision-Free Motion of Multiple Agent Systems in Unpredictable Environments. Master's thesis, Odense University, Denmark (1991)
21. Perram, J. W. and Petersen, H. G.: Algorithms for Computing the Dynamical Trajectories of Flexible Bodies. Molec. Phys. **65** (1988) 861–874

Springer-Verlag
and the Environment

We at Springer-Verlag firmly believe that an international science publisher has a special obligation to the environment, and our corporate policies consistently reflect this conviction.

We also expect our business partners – paper mills, printers, packaging manufacturers, etc. – to commit themselves to using environmentally friendly materials and production processes.

The paper in this book is made from low- or no-chlorine pulp and is acid free, in conformance with international standards for paper permanency.

Lecture Notes in Artificial Intelligence (LNAI)

Lecture Notes in Computer Science